Against the Few

Against the Few

Struggles of India's Rural Poor

Arun Sinha

Zed Books Ltd
London and New Jersey

Against the Few was first published by Zed Books Ltd,
57 Caledonian Road, London N1 9BU, UK and 165 First Avenue,
Atlantic Highlands, New Jersey 07716, USA, in 1991.

Copyright © Arun Sinha, 1991.

Cover designed by Andrew Corbett.
Cover photograph by Mark Edwards.
Typeset by Interpress Magazines Private, New Delhi.
Printed and bound in the United Kingdom
by Biddles Ltd, Guildford and King's Lynn.

British Library Cataloguing in Publication Data

Sinha, Arun
   Against the few : struggles of India's rural poor
   1. India. Social conditions
   I. Title
   954.05'2

   ISBN 0-86232-718-0
   ISBN 0-86232-719-9 pbk

Library of Congress Cataloging-in-Publication Data

Sinha, Arun
   Against the few : struggles of India's rural poor /
Arun Sinha.
     p.   cm.
   Includes index.
   ISBN 0-86232-718-0.—ISBN 0-86232-719-9 (pbk.)
   1. Rural poor—India—Bihar.   2. Bihar (India)—Rural
conditions.   I. Title.
HC437.B47S565   1989
362.5'0954'12—dc20   89-8869
               CIP

Contents

Foreword

Arun Sinha is one of India's finest journalists. The area which he patrols and which he knows intimately is his native state of Bihar, in eastern India. This book concerns Bihar.

Bihar is a state with a current population of more than 70 million. It is a state rich in raw materials (such as iron ore, coal, copper, bauxite and uranium), but poor in manufacturing industry; a state with a backward agriculture; a state disfigured by the deepest poverty; a state which is part of the heartland of Hindu orthodoxy; a state which, in Sinha's own words, is 'extremely violent, subversive, perilous, ungovernable, a place where human life is as cheap as in a spaghetti Western'. By some it is seen as the site of a deeply-rooted semi-feudalism. Certainly, we here have a paradigm of the extreme forms taken by contemporary economic backwardness; and of the distortions and barbarities wrought by the powerful intrusion of a capitalism which extracts but which fails to transform progressively. Arun Sinha casts a penetrating light upon it.

Sinha's signal contribution as a working journalist has been in reporting and analysing events in the countryside of Bihar. In particular, he has concentrated on the plight of the rural poor: on landless labourers, poor peasants and artisans. This has meant a preoccupation with sharecroppers and bonded labour, and with tribals as well as Hindus. Over the last decade, he has described and analysed the condition of the poor, the forms taken by their exploitation and the impact that change has had upon them. But, more than that, his concern has been with the struggle they have waged against their oppressors. This book is about that struggle.

The book has three parts. In the first, the context is established. Arun Sinha starts with a brief introduction on Bihar. Then, in a powerful essay, he describes a Lohar ironsmith who has become a successful gunsmith. Here is a single image to sum up contemporary Bihar: an artisan, whose traditional, productive skills have been rendered obsolete by the 'new technology' which has been introduced into Indian agriculture, and who survives by meeting the deadly needs of a society in which violence and conflict have become endemic. It is an image which remains with one throughout the book.

The final essay in Part One discusses caste. Caste is here rendered in all its stark reality. Stripped of its ideological props, it is revealed for what it is: a means of subjecting subordinate classes in an awesomely total fashion. He gives central emphasis to the rooting of caste in economic structure, and suggests the manner in which class formation proceeds in a society in which caste relationships are crucial. But caste does, indeed, need to be given independent treatment in any serious examination of rural Bihar. It cannot be simply reduced to class. Where there is the opposition of caste Hindus and untouchables (say landlords and sharecroppers, or rich peasants and landless labourers), it possesses a deeply-rooted force which can give to social conflict—if it arises—a violence which is startling in its savagery and intensity. That force exists independently of class relationships, but intensifies class contradictions. Caste, however, can have the opposite effect. Where subordinate classes (say landless labourers, or sharecroppers) are composed of both untouchables and caste Hindus, the existence of caste may prevent or stifle the emergence of class consciousness or class action. The manner of caste's operation, moreover, is complex—more complex than can be suggested in this Introduction. The tension between caste and class returns frequently in the rest of the book. Sinha gives caste the necessary, independent treatment: without, however, mystifying caste relationships by disconnecting them completely from class.

In Part Two Sinha sets the historical context of the major part of the book: the treatment of struggle which is provided in Part Three. In a series of five essays, he provides perspective on the colonial handling of the agrarian question by the British and the response it engendered. But he does more than that. With some skill, he shows how past and present commingle; how the legacy of the past is powerfully at work in present-day Bihar. He does this in three major respects.

Firstly, he traces the origins of contemporary agrarian structures, both in the plains and in the tribal areas, and enhances one's understanding of these structures. Here, the impact of the Permanent Settlement and the alienation of tribal land are central. Secondly, he sketches the nature of pre-1947 peasant and tribal movements and so illuminates the character of the struggle discussed in Part Three. He highlights the profound limitations inherent in tribal struggles, and the absence of any common class consciousness between tribals and non-tribals; he shows the formidable difficulties associated with a movement which seeks to represent the interests of both the landless and of peasants. In other words, he reveals a dangerous fragmentation of the interests of subordinate classes: a fragmentation which continues in the post-1947 era. Thirdly, he traces something, at least, of the practice of the Indian post-colonial state back to its fledgling origins in the inter-war years. At that time, Sinha tells us, Congress spokesmen dismissed any suggestion of serious action on behalf of the agrarian poor with the observation that it was not 'practical politics'. Here, indeed, was the language of reaction. 'Practical politics' has been the stuff of the Indian state ever since. In power, for the first time, in the Bihar Provincial Assembly in 1937, Congress behaved with respect to landlords and tenants 'in a fashion that would become its standard politics in the years following Independence—speaking for the poor and acting for the rich'. Whether, and to what extent, these politics could be successfully defied in the interests of the various strata of the poor would depend upon the nature of the struggle waged by the poor themselves. It is to that struggle that Sinha turns in Part Three.

Sinha proceeds in a novel way in his treatment of contemporary agrarian struggle. He covers, each in a separate chapter, seven quite distinct forms taken by that struggle in different parts of Bihar; he encompasses struggle by both non-tribals and tribals; and he examines the role in that struggle of a different political agency in each case.

The seven cases span a Christian (Catholic) organization, which sought change without direct conflict; the Communist Party of India; the Communist Party of India–Marxist; the Communist Party of India–Marxist-Leninist; a movement led by Jayaprakash Narayan, who eventually proposed 'peaceful class struggle'; a struggle of the Santhals, led by Shiboo Soren, in which an attempt to forge a 'worker-peasant alliance' was made; and a movement of a hill people, the Paharias. He provides, first, where appropriate, a careful, general statement of the overall line or strategy of the part/organisation in question. He then proceeds to consider the actual practice, in a concrete agrarian situation. From this he attempts, in a concluding chapter, to distil the relevant lessons and to take stock of the present situation.

The account of these different forms taken by struggle by, or on behalf of, the rural poor, is arresting throughout. The reader cannot fail to be engrossed by it. Arun Sinha writes with passion and with a fierce sense of the appalling injustice which is pervasive in rural Bihar. He writes vividly and with a striking ability to convey atmosphere and place. One learns an immense amount about the variety and the specificities of agrarian change in Bihar. There is, in this book, an immediacy, a sense of actuality, that is rarely present in academic writing. It leaves with the reader a whole series of haunting images and a feeling of having actually experienced something of the reality of the villages of Bihar. That is a significant achievement.

There is no sense, here, of a single pattern being imposed upon agrarian reality: of all being shaped on the Procrustean bed of one view of the processes at work. Sinha is too aware of and sensitive to the realities which he describes for that. That, too, is important. Certainly, however, the book is given coherence and shape by a passionate concern for the poor, and by an insistence that the relevant analysis must proceed in terms of class and class relationships.

What emerges with great clarity, and repeatedly, is the violence which pervades rural Bihar. That violence is, sickeningly, everywhere. Amid crushing poverty, it is used as a means of reproducing that poverty, to the advantage of dominant classes. It is employed, increasingly, as a response—by the state and by dominant classes—to efforts by the oppressed to mitigate that poverty: whether by trying to gain rights, which they have in law; or by action to secure what natural justice might suggest; or in final defiance of the indignities to which they are daily subject.

The reader must decide for himself/herself what conclusions to draw from Arun Sinha's case-studies, and what to make of Sinha's own assessment. Certainly, however, there is little support here for any romantic notion that India is ripe for revolution. Contradictions of an antagonistic nature there assuredly are. But fragmentation of subordinate class interests, an absence of highly developed class consciousness, and a lack of sustained organisation are only too obvious. Moreover, the Indian state, in its central and its regional manifestations, is seen to be powerful, ruthless and sophisticated in its handling of the relevant contradictions.

Sinha himself is abundantly aware of this. He is not, however, despondent. Of one of the case-studies, he concludes that it represents 'a minor satisfaction about "growth with justice"'. He finishes, however, on a note of hope. Change for the better, within the structures of attempted capitalist development, is possible. It has taken place, albeit to a relatively minor degree. It can take place in the future, but slowly, fitfully, and unevenly—and not without pain. If, in the end, one notes in Arun Sinha something of a triumph of 'optimism of the will' over 'pessimism of the intellect', then one must recall that it is a position which has not been taken lightly. It is the result of intimate knowledge of the objective circumstances and of an unromantic refusal to give up support for a struggle which continues, throughout India, against formidable odds.

Arun Sinha's book is fascinating and instructive. It represents a most valuable addition to the political economy of agrarian change.

T.J. Byres
School of Oriental and African Studies
London University

An Introduction: Bihar

Bihar is the 22nd state that, with the directly New Delhi-administered units called Union Territories, make up India—vast, and in theory, federal. In the newspapers and in academic studies, Bihar is sometimes included in northern India, sometimes in eastern. Geographically, it lies between the north and the east. Politically, too, for throughout the whole of the medieval period and even the modern, until 1912, Bihar was sometimes tagged on to the north, sometimes to the east, dominated either by Delhi or by the changing capital (most recently Calcutta) of neighbouring Bengal. In 1912, Bihar was, at the demand of the Bihari elite, detached from Bengal and made a separate province by the Raj, then being run from Delhi, or, more accurately, from London.

In more ways than one, Bihar, after becoming centred after 1912 on its own capital, Patna, began moving away from Calcutta, about 600 kilometres to the east, and began to identify itself with Delhi, nearly 1,000 kilometres to the north. By that time Delhi had become the established political centre of India, having started to acquire importance at the beginning of the medieval period as the seat of the Indian empire of the Muslim conquerors. Before the Muslim conquest, the capital of India had changed, depending on the destinies of local princes and the outcome of the endless expansionist wars that they fought among themselves. In the ancient period, for quite a long time, India—or large parts of it—was imperially ruled by kingdoms centred on what is now Bihar and Uttar Pradesh (this now being the state between Bihar and Delhi). Among these the most famous was the kingdom of Magadha which had its seat at Pataliputra, today's Patna.

Educated Biharis take a great pride in ancient Magadhan imperialism; the glories of the Magadhan past make up a good part of their social self-esteem. An outline of these glories never fails to take up the first few paragraphs of the welcome speeches made to all-India or international conferences held in Patna today. When the Bihari intelligentsia was demanding Bihar's separation as a province from Bengal, they argued that it could not be denied an autonomous existence since this was the place whence kings in olden times had marched to establish the political unity of India!

These days, in post-colonial India, there is much talk about the 'heartland' and the 'periphery'. It is said that Bihar and other Hindi-speaking states constitute the heartland of the country politically; and the rest of India the periphery. The heartland, according to this theory, is most patriotic, most close to New Delhi. Here arrogance goes to the extent of making a claim to dominate the different nationalities living in the states on the periphery—the nationalities, who spoke languages other than Hindi and who had never in history fully integrated themselves with any one Indian centre, not even Delhi. That may be true only in part; yet certain features of this 'heartland', like its total identification with Delhi as the political centre, have to be noted. And, besides, a people like the Biharis, who take pride in being the *founders* of India's political unity, cannot but be patriotic and volatile enough to consider almost as sedition even a distant or unintentional hint of a demand for greater autonomy from the states on the periphery.

The relationship between the heartland and New Delhi is, however, not one that admits of discord or clash of interests. Patriotic sentiment can subdue expressions of partisan aspirations only to a certain extent. Therefore, now and then, some Bihari intellectual or politician speaks of this Bihar as an 'internal colony of India'. Here the sense is invariably economic or fiscal. Bihar has been extraordinarily rich in minerals—coal, copper, iron ore, uranium, bauxite, mica, etc—but the mining of these minerals has remained under the direct control of the central government through the huge public sector. Bihar derives little from its mineral wealth, except trivial annual royalties and fees; and neither has there been a growth of ancillary industries or substantial employment as a result of heavy investment in the public sector in the state. New Delhi, says the Bihari, extracts income and resources, using the state as a colony.

These are not a politician's regionalist fulminations, but a view well backed by evidence. And educated Biharis are aware of it. Nevertheless, this awareness of being an 'internal colony' has never developed into a political issue. It has never agitated and united Biharis as, for instance, it did in Assam or Andhra Pradesh. There was never a mass struggle in Bihar for real autonomy. A possible explanation (and that takes us back to the heartland-centre identity at the political level) is that New Delhi, focus of their motherland, does not strike Biharis as an *imperialist* centre that exploits and oppresses them. So all that the awareness of being an internal colony excites is a feeble complaint about the rates of royalty. And New Delhi has never really bothered much, for patriotism always prevents the complaints from turning into a serious threat to its concentration of economic power.

There are some who, rather than describing Bihar as an internal colony of New Delhi, would give this name strictly to only that part of the state where the mines and industries actually are. Geographically, Bihar is made up of two regions, each with a distinct history, culture, speech and type of economy. One is the plains—the central-eastern region of the Ganga river-plains, alluvial, fertile, full of promise—which region is cut by the Ganga from end to end into the two sub-regions of the North Bihar plains and the South Bihar plains. The North Bihar plains depend for irrigation on the eastern Himalayan rivers that flow down from Nepal all the year round. The South, blessed mostly with monsoon-fed rivers that turn into channels of dry sand for the rest of the year, developed, in contrast, an indigenous irrigation system called *ahar-pyne* (reservoir-and-short distribution canals), operated at village level with water stored from the rains and side-openings cut in the banks of the short-lived streams. The other region of Bihar is the Chotanagpur plateau, populated by tribal people who remained unknown to the world until the early Mughals overran the region in the search for diamonds, gold and gems.

These tribals grew chiefly rice, in red soil watered by rains, though they too, like the South Bihar peasants, had out of agricultural necessity built up some skill in constructing small dams with rocks across hill streams. (That indigenous skill, like the reservoir-short canal technique of South Bihar, is dying without replacement for want of attention from engineers trained to consider only big dams and large long canals as the technology of irrigation.) It was in the Chotanagpur plateau, in the region of the tribal people, that all the minerals were found. For that reason primarily, the region saw an invasion by the British and other European, and even Indian, capitalists in the nineteenth century. They rushed in first for coal and iron ore. At one point some of these capitalists became wildly excited over the news that there was gold still left in the region; a number of companies were established overnight, to be ready to grab leases for gold mines; but after some frantic prospecting it was discovered that the news was no more than a rumour.

According to those who describe Chotanagpur as New Delhi's internal colony, the invasion has not ended. It continues to bring in associations of people, and individuals, whose aim is plainly to accumulate wealth and profits and 'black money', for the minerals have not been exhausted. In their train come people from the Bihar (and Uttar Pradesh) plains who have to look for jobs outside the rice fields in their village. It is, on the one hand, the accumulation made in Chotanagpur by New Delhi's state sector and by the private industries and the traders and contractors, and on the other the cultural domination, arrogance and cruelty with which these men of the plains, irrespective of class, treat the tribals, the natives of Chotanagpur, that have created the demand for Chotanagpur to be made a state separate from Bihar, as a first step towards the 'liberation' of this internal colony.

Part One
Myth and Reality

1. A Thriving Trade

Gyaneshwar Vishwakarma, Gyanu Mistry for short, lived in a back street of Bhagwanpur; a bazaar town south of the Ganga in Bihar. Bhagwanpur was the same as all Indian bazaar towns: pivoted on a single square on each of whose eight road-sides stood small shops, above open black gutters, interspersed with tea and sweet stalls with sackcloth awnings: a square by the edges of which vendors squatted with baskets of vegetables or oranges or boiled sweet potatoes; a square where buses urgently needing to go into a repair shop rattled up and down a few times a day, carrying their three storeys of load—inside a choked mass of humans, goods in bundles of all sizes on the roof and then humans again, perched on top of the bundles; buses which dragged whirls of dust that eventually came to rest in the vendors' baskets, grocers' flour and grains and the lidless fly-infested bowls of sweets being sold by paunchy confectioners in soiled dhotis, sitting on their haunches behind their small wooden cash boxes. In that unmetalled residential back street, some 50 paces off the westward road from the square, Gyanu Mistry's house bore no outward marks of distinction but, at the entrance to the lane, you only had to ask for his place once. Neighbours knew him.

Three or four houses in the lane were whitewashed or lightly painted or had two floors. Mistry's in the right-hand row was unplastered and single-storeyed, conforming to the general architecture in Bhagwanpur, the town that had long served as the market nucleus of the set of surrounding villages. It was a constricted row; there were no clearings between the houses. Gyanu, unlike most other dwellers, was a newcomer. Where he cleared space and raised his house was once a decaying tile-roofed hovel. The ironsmith's family who were living there, penniless because of little and low-paid custom, had blamed their luck on their caste-craft, sold the homestead and moved out of Bhagwanpur.

Gyanu, who himself was a Lohar *mistry* (ironsmith) got by where his predecessor in that place had failed. He was, at forty-six, acknowledged as one of the success stories in his part of the countryside, especially among the men of his Lohar caste. The fact that the departed hut-owner and Gyanu were both ironsmiths was no more than a coincidence. When the bankrupt ironsmith thought of putting his piece of backstreet land on sale he wasn't thinking only of finding a Lohar buyer. And neither was Gyanu, eager then, 13 or so years ago, to get away from his village for a potentially larger business in the bazaar town looking particularly for a caste-mate's plot to buy. It was a sale to the highest offer—though that still was excessively low for the seller. But, then, he lacked resources to delay his flight from Bhagwanpur.

That was how the rising village ironsmith had begun to establish himself in the town. The house that Gyanu built for himself was shaped like a rectangular box. The front room was set apart, by a faded flower-patterned cotton curtain in the doorway, from the inner portions of the house where Gyanu lived with his wife and two sons, the older of whom, 27 now, was married with three children. The ironsmith's two daughters had both been married off and lived away from Bhagwanpur with their Lohar husbands, paying their parents an occasional visit. That morning, when we arrived at his house, Gyanu in a sleeveless vest and dhoti, was playing with his toddling grandson by the entrance door: a dark man of average height, soldier-style hair, steadily greying, and cavernous gleaming eyes set in a long face adorned with a black-and-white moustache which he had shaved off abruptly above either corner of his upper lip.

His face showed surprise at our visit, but in a moment the suspicion was gone and he quickly recovered his ease. He assumed the confident air of a man who was accustomed to receiving strangers at odd times. Without asking us too many questions he led us into his front room; we sat down to talk. From time to time, absently, he caressed his grandson whom he sat on his lap, and reminisced. Looking back on his years in the village as a young man, early-married and (after the period of the customary ban on cohabitation was over) rapidly blessed with children, Gyanu now felt a kind of contentment.

Factory technology had come into agriculture and even into the household goods sector, and it was destroying his ancestral trade. And there he was, in the village, sitting all day in his forefathers' workshop, a tiny smoke-blackened room, working—when he had customers—behind his charcoal furnace, kept red-hot with blasts of air from a buried leather bellows which he worked by a cycle chain strung overhead. His father could no longer leave his sick bed and he, Gyanu, at 26 or so, no matter with how fine a skill he drudged, looked like fading out of the world of ironwork, just like the ex-owner of his house-plot in the town. And then, piercing the darkness of his life, there had gleamed a strange shaft of light. A maternal uncle, who lived in a village some ten miles away, had received Gyanu with his family on a visit, and had, once during the stay, whispered to him news of a fresh skill. Should Gyanu wish to learn it, said the old man, he had someone to train him. And in a few months, Gyanu, the failing ironsmith, had embarked on a completely new venture.

Not that Gyanu ran no danger in putting his newly acquired skill to use. In the village as well as in Bhagwanpur, there were people, including other Lohars, who would be eaten up with jealousy; and then there were the unpredictable selling agents of his new products, and there were the policemen. The police had contrived to get him in their net in his very first year at Bhagwanpur; he returned from prison on bail two long months later. But that happened only once, when he wasn't fully aware of the rules of the game; afterwards, the policemen joined the ranks of his well-wishers, and the solitary criminal case against him made no progress in court. He was free to get ahead and to make a fair income, if not a fortune. He was able to marry his daughters into stable families, and to provide his own family with far better living standards than ninety-seven per cent of the Lohars.

He also kept his older son free from family responsibilities and spent liberally for him to be educated, unlike himself or his father or grandfather. How Gyanu wished to make his son anything but a Lohar *mistry*! The son passed through school, and went on to a college, but halfway through his degree gave up his studies. Education, Gyanu said, analysing his son's failure, was not in the caste tradition of the Lohars. Yet he made his son look for a job, just in case, on the strength of his school certificate; Gyanu had also tapped connections with his own customers. Then both resigned themselves to the situation, and the son finally settled down to work at home to assist his father. Together father and son were now doing very well, for there was no dearth of custom in their new field. Already there was a classification among the Lohars stemming from the tools one used: there were 'Lathe Lohars' and *'bhathi* or Leather Bellows] Lohars' depending on your reliance on the lathe or the bellows. In his front room where we sat, a living-room-cum-bedroom-cum-workshop, Gyanu the lathe-Lohar retained his leather bellows and charcoal-fired furnace. A couple of stools and a wooden chair were placed against one wall, and against the other, beside the doorway to the inner room, a bare wooden bed upon which, in the daytime, a cotton-filled mattress and a bedspread would be put if a distinguished visitor or customer came in, but which otherwise was meant for Gyanu to sleep in at night. The remaining space was taken up by a lathe, a drilling machine, a grinding wheel and a motor which ran these machines; hammers and screwdrivers of all sizes, chisels, a wrench set, and other tools were on the deep wall racks.

Here, in this workshop, Gyanu used the skill his uncle had taught him, in order to produce all kinds of guns. The old uncle had himself learned to make guns by accident. In 1946, when the districts, chiefly of Southern Bihar, were witnessing large-scale riots between Hindus and Muslims, the Hindus of the province were clamouring for arms. (The Hindus even told Gandhi, who came to tour the riot-hit areas, that there was a belief that the 'Muslims are being secretly armed on a wide scale', and that there was 'a fear that the nationalists, unless they immediately started learning self-defence with firearms, may suffer and ultimately find themselves under the heel of the Muslim League').[1] A police camp was set up near the village of Gyanu's maternal uncle and some men from that all-Hindu police force lent him and one or two other Lohars' rifles as models: they were to examine the parts and make replicas in their home workshops. The policemen, his uncle had recalled to Gyanu, wanted to get firearms in the hands of as many of the Hindus as possible. Yet it was not only at policemen's prompting that ironsmiths everywhere in Southern Bihar had got started on the new venture of gun-making. In other villages, big people, especially landowners, would bring factory-made guns to the local ironsmith and force him to make copies. Gyanu, as long as he stayed in the village, was not put under such pressure, but he remembered, before the maternal uncle gave him the *guru-mantra*, having been casually told two or three times by a farmer that his future as an ironsmith lay in this new skill alone.

Today there was hardly a make of a gun that Gyanu could not turn out on his machines: Indian, English, German, American—all kinds of pistols, even revolvers, and occasionally a light rifle. For replication, you had just to show him a piece, for close inspection. Generally, Gyanu's workshop made guns to order. The materials he used were not very difficult to procure: steering-rods, wood, iron. Wood was for shaping out the grip and the butt, iron for the trigger and the cartridge chamber, while for the barrels he used the iron rods supporting the steering wheels of trucks and buses (those of cars and jeeps were unreliable, prone to burst when the gun was fired). A single steering-rod—freely available in the junkshops in Biharsharif, Gaya and other towns of Southern Bihar and in Patna—cost Rs. 100-200 and could be cut up into no fewer than nine six-inch pieces to fit as pistol barrels, to be rifled on the lathe.

With people like Gyanu Mistry diversifying into the home production of firearms, the tactics of conflict in rural as well as urban Bihar had undergone a change. Where in the past you relied on *pahalwan* or *khalife* (wrestlers) and *lathait* (club men) to frighten your enemies, today mere brute strength had become useless in inspiring fear. Now you only had to be strong enough to fire a gun. So, every man of worth seemed to be ordering a gun for himself: the farmers, the Muslims and Hindus in the riot-prone areas; gangs of robbers, purse-snatchers, politicians; bullies among students, gentlemen thinking of self-defence, police officials worried about their families and valuables—everyone; even those who kept guns under government licence. And once the use of the gun became common, once there was a leap from muscles to firearms, sophisticated arms produced by the ironsmiths were needed—longer range, more lethal, more dependable in action, more durable.

Though Gyanu did not, there were others who regularly produced rifles and even cartridges in their home factories. One had even produced what he called a 'chain gun'—gun perched on a stand whose cartridge chamber could be rotated by pulling a bicycle chain, so that it operated almost like a machine gun, a primitive Gatling. Little wonder that shooting someone down had become a routine event in the state of Bihar, particularly in certain areas in the south of the state—in several pockets of the districts of Patna, Nalanda, Gaya, Aurangabad, Nawada, Bhojpur, Rohtas, Munger. Bihar had consequently acquired almost the image of a Sicily among the states of India: extremely violent, subversive, perilous, ungovernable; a place where human life was as cheap as in a spaghetti Western.

Probably the Biharis *are* more militant than other people of India: abundance of firearms has only added to it. It has proved very difficult, though, to understand and explain this militancy. There cannot be any straightforward explanation. Yet there are certain explanations which may be plausible. First, the Southern Bihar plains, where the Magadha kingdom was located and which the Muslims invaded before they took over the whole of Bihar, had almost throughout known history been a region where wars were fought very frequently, and armies were raised on a regular basis for defence and conquests so that in a way the region was militarized. Secondly, the region came to have a high population which made the competition for agricultural land, alluvial and rich, very intense. Thirdly, the local chiefs maintained levies of soldiers for emperors, and the *zamindars* (or landlords) created by the Raj kept bodies of retainers too. Finally, the districts of the Southern Bihar plains were among the areas where the British from the outset recruited troops for their armies. (The establishment of a gun factory in Munger by the British also played no small role in disseminating the secrets of the craft across the region.)

Lohars like Gyanu could not be blamed for filling the Southern Bihar plains with gun manufactories. From their point of view, modern technology had torn them from their traditional roots, while simultaneously, as Gyanu found to his comfort, social conflicts and dangers had grown phenomenally to create a market for home-made illegal firearms and cartridges. How many died in shooting every day in the countryside did not matter to Gyanu. Yet Gyanu, personally, was always ready to give up this business should some institution help him to set up in other ventures, for instance, the small-scale manufacture of small agricultural machines.

Even now gun-making was not his whole business; his clients did not only want guns. Farmers or their servants brought agricultural machines for repair, owners of rice or flour mills their machines and motors. Tractor blades needed to be replaced, sugar presses, threshers, electric appliances, household items, buckets needed repairing; his day at his town workshop was half-filled with such assignments. Even in the village—except for the orders for guns—it was usually repair work that was demanded of *mistries*, not manufacture. A technologically advancing society could offer them only the minor and uncertain role of repairers, in which it was not possible to earn a living.

In the village Gyanu had the direct experience that after the landowners bought new machines for themselves they became indifferent to the permanent ties they had maintained hitherto with the local ironsmiths. Gyanu's father had been the only ironsmith serving 50 or more of the local agricultural families. He had made all their spades, ploughshares, blades, sickles, axes and other farming tools; he also supplied them with cooking utensils and water buckets, and lock-rings and lock-chains for the doors. As remuneration, they each gave him one *paseri* (four and a half kilos) of grain when their crop was in. At each harvest he was also allowed by custom to take home as big a single load of grains as he could carry from the fields on his head (which Gyanu remembered as coming roughly to six *paseri* (27 kilos) from each employer). When a landowner's buffalo calved he would call the ironsmith to collect a *pao* (200 grams) of the first milk. On religious occasions, the ironsmith received a few hundred grams of beaten rice. Then, at the time of a marriage in the ironsmith's family, he would go to every client to receive the customary donations of grain, lentils, curd, milk, molasses for the wedding dinner, and straw and bamboo to give his hut a new thatching. For so slender a reward the ironsmith worked constantly. He made, and then repaired, the farming tools and domestic utensils for his clients. He had no way to commercialize his skills. But then neither did his clients have an organized market to turn to. Therefore, the ties continued without strain from generation to generation, and the customs were never breached by either side, until new agricultural machines started arriving in the village.

In the years after the coming of Independence, particularly since the middle of the 1960s—the beginning of the Green Revolution—an ever-growing number of landowners became interested in the new machines. Thus the Green Revolution carried within it the seeds that were to destroy the blacksmith's trade. Even one of the richest and most powerful industrial groups in the country, the Tatas, diversified into ironsmiths' products such as spades and axes. Sugar presses, threshers and fodder machines began to be produced in small factories; water buckets and kitchen utensils were now manufactured everywhere from a variety of materials. The village ironsmith's patrons came increasingly to depend upon items from outside; the bonds were eroded; old customs lapsed. Under the pressure of the times the *mistry* had to diversify—or perish. A good number of them threw themselves into the ranks of the agricultural labourers; the majority continued eking out livings as 'leather-bellows Lohars'; while a few, like Gyanu, adding to their skills, now made and sold guns, either staying on in the village or moving into town and expanding production. And the irony of the situation was that rural Bihar required both products; it needed machines and machine-made goods for improved farming and modern living, and firearms on a large scale to deal with a host of troubles, primarily agrarian unrest.

2. The Decline of Caste Society

Bihar is often seen as the most caste-ridden of all the states of India. Even dispassionate observers argue that although caste sectarianism is everywhere in India, it is in its worst form in Bihar; and that view can be substantiated. Caste riots, the gunning down of untouchables in shocking numbers, severe hostility between the upper castes and the backward castes over the question of reserving government jobs; the violent display of caste-solidarities at every election, the operations of caste cliques within the teaching community, among the students at the universities, and among officials and employees of state administration; cliques even among journalists and trade union officials. Caste sectarianism, then, runs very deep within the rural aristocracy, among the peasants, in the political parties and among the intelligentsia.

Yet how today's Bihar society runs itself cannot be appreciated on the basis of general evidence. Of course, the evidence offered by the state by no means completes the list above. Indeed, the deeper we probe, the more the evidence is seen to be complicated, even sometimes contradictory. Before inferences are drawn, we should first examine how history has influenced Bihar society.

Before the British established the Raj, the people here had lived for centuries, at least for 1,500 years, as a caste society, a society reduced to a state of immobility, with a finely graded hierarchical, unchallenged and almost unchangeable structure. From there they turned along a different road; they started to move—and continued to move—towards a Western-type society, of course in their own way and at their own pace. They could not leave caste behind in their march; it has always accompanied them. Nor in the past were fanatical inhuman practices of caste society like *sati* (the burning of the widow to death on the husband's pyre) and human sacrifice and religious murder and the selling and buying of *naukars* or *ghulams*, slaves, easily or quickly rooted out.

In the beginning the Raj was reluctant to tamper with the internal structure of the subject society. Even when courts of law were set up, locally accepted customs were what determined judgments on personal and social matters. But 'respect' for the social order was not all that the Britishers showed. Once they settled down, they began to organize the army and the administration—administration for revenue and law and order, later also for roads, railways and post and telegraph—for which native hands could be easily and cheaply hired. And whose, from the native multitude, could these hands possibly have been? In southern and western India it could only be the Brahmans; and in northern and eastern parts (including Bihar) the Brahmans together with the Kayasthas, Rajputs and Bhumihars. That is, men from the same castes who kept themselves above everyone else and denied absolutely scholarship and precedence, even literacy, to all other castes—castes who, by the constraints, made themselves the self-styled sole claimants to lineages of superior blood and of the greatest mental skills. Even the sepoys, the ordinary soldiers, in the army regiments created by the English East India Company were largely Brahmans and Rajputs.[1]

So the early British administration and army hired people from the upper crust of Hindu society, creating no disorder at that time. But if we look only at the Services, as many historians do, we would be missing important parts of the colonial picture. For jobs were not all that the conquerors created. They had, particularly in Bengal to which Bihar was then joined, introduced certain land regulations by which the social order was disturbed more than ever before. Most subversive of all was the regulation of the Permanent Settlement of land revenue—put into force less than 30 years after the Company took over the administration of Bengal from its Mughal governor in 1765—which made the peasants poorer than ever before. And with no mitigation of their abysmal condition in sight, thousands and thousands of them fled their villages. They were mostly lower-caste peasants bred traditionally to do manual labour. So when tea plantations and industrial factories and docks and mines were thought of, it was these dispossessed peasants, a large number from Bihar, who turned up looking for work. This probably represents roughly the colonial picture: high-caste men taking jobs in the administration and the army—as clerks, petty officials, soldiers—and low-caste men in the industries and plantations, as manual workers.

Jobs in industries and plantations could not have attracted men from all ranks of caste. It could be said that the methods of recruitment, the way the labourers were moved (innumerable people died on the way to workplaces because of the overcrowding, epidemics, hunger and beatings in the inland river boats or sea ships which took thousands of Biharis to the West Indies); the way they were locked up in barracks as prisoners under guard, to be herded every morning to the workplace and back after dusk—in a word, the barbarities of colonial capitalism—kept people, particularly those of the upper castes, away from such undertakings. But more than these barbarities, what kept the upper-caste men away was their disdain for manual labour. In all societies rankings between manual and mental labour are found, but in India's caste society they were tightly formal, inflexible, rigidly ordered. (Even today very few upper-caste owners of land would choose to go to their fields to guide the plough.) So, high-caste men went into jobs that required mental and martial skills, skills that were most valued in the caste society.

But there soon was to be a mass reaction against the monopolization of the new administrative and military jobs by those who dominated the caste society. In time the agitation, more particularly by the major intermediately ranked castes, grew so intense that in some provinces the colonial recruiting authorities had to restrict the entry of certain castes (like the Brahmans of South India and the Kayasthas of what is now Uttar Pradesh) in order to break up their concentration and bring in men of other castes.[2] Apart from averting disturbances about job monopoly, the colonial authorities must also have been aware of the danger of one caste forming cliques within departments, to the detriment of administration.

There would then be a race among castes for jobs. Hindu society had long begun shedding its initial prejudice towards Western education. In certain areas of Bihar, at first, 'modern' schools enrolled very few children, for their parents saw them as institutions designed to subvert Hindu society by converting pupils to the low religion of the Christians. And in this race, caste looked like becoming stronger, almost imperishable. Every caste of worth (worth judged by its numbers or the status of its members as holders of land) organized itself into an association or a conference and set itself two main aims: (1) reform within the community (which meant caste) such as establishing solidarity of a single caste by abolishing the sub-castes, through, primarily, mixed marriages between the sub-castes; and (2) promotion of new education and employment among the castemen. Every major caste was to develop and run a chain of schools and colleges, a drive that continued in Bihar well after Independence.

This caste-based *modernization* went apace. It continued even after the Indian National Congress, established as an innocuous forum at the initiative of a Britisher in 1885, changed its character to speak about the 'Indian nation' and self-rule in the first quarter of this century. It was yet another proof of the acceptance of caste as something natural that even nationalist-minded Congressmen saw no contradiction in associating themselves—openly and actively—with the organizations of their respective castes. To them nation and caste were two distinct entities, neither standing in the way of the other. Thus every Congressman had a dual membership—until the mid 1930s when the Congress made a rule that its members should dissociate themselves from caste or religious bodies and put nation above all loyalties. After that caste went underground.

The colonial period

During the colonial period, many things changed. First, the British opened up Hindu society and split it along the line of old cleavages. Each caste closed its ranks; casteism assumed an organized form. The interests of different castes clashed: as casteism grew, the hierarchical caste society began to fall apart. Then the colonial society, in the process, also produced new status symbols. To be a petty official of the Raj was in itself to have status. It needs pointing out here that the processes of disorder that the Raj unleashed did not lead to total rejection of the old value system. Thus, although a job with the Raj could gain one's status general recognition, there would simultaneously be a claim made to belong to the rank of Brahmans or Kshatriyas. The same castes, then, which clamoured for education and jobs for their men, also gave themselves Brahman or Kshatriya origins; they produced their theories of how, originally, such Brahmans or Kshatriyas had been pushed lower down the Hindu social scale by the conceit of the upper levels of society. And in order to prove their higher-caste roots they started to wear the sacred thread (insignia of the twice-born, or Brahman caste) and became deeply orthodox and puritanical, a phenomenon now known as Sanskritization. Yet, despite the return to higher Hindu culture, the general direction in which all castes were moving was clear ahead. The truth was that in the colonial society the basic principles of social ranking had begun to change. The accident of birth could not alone now be fundamental to a Hindu's existence. Hindu society had been led into an altogether new pattern of employment, a pattern that free India keeps developing further.

What was the form of caste society? It mainly consisted of villages. And typically in a village there was a majority of families of agriculturists (they did not work their fields if they were of an upper caste); others were artisans—carpenters, ironsmiths, goldsmiths, weavers, potters—or servicemen—barbers, washermen, priests—and they all worked for the agriculturists in return for annual or periodic payments in grain after the harvest. These relationships could be confined to a single village or extended to a cluster of villages. For the artisans and servicemen, the clientele was fixed, and both they and the clients inhabited the same small part of the world; neither went beyond those boundaries. There were, no doubt, traders and towns; they could not have existed without a surplus of village production; and, besides, the village needed to import things like iron and salt. Yet relations with the outside world would never break up the village, as developments under British rule, initiated, doubtless, for purposes of colonial plunder and political control, were eventually to do.

The fact that this social division of labour underwent no change for several centuries made the people born into it develop and foster a belief that it was unchangeable: that caste was integral to Hindu civilization, a divine dispensation, a law of Nature. Every Hindu unshakeably believed in the hierarchy, no matter what rank he himself might belong to—high, middle or low; even now, in the villages of Bihar, people describe the caste rules as *dharam* (a popular form of the word *dharma*), duty, almost religion. Untouchability, for instance, is seen in this light. The ideology was constructed and rammed into the minds of the people by the Brahmanical texts. It was not that minor shifts did not take place; evidence has been found of changes of occupation by rebellious individuals or groups in past centuries. Yet caste society stayed stable enough to absorb such occasional shocks.

As for the division of labour, one feature that was remarkable in this context was that of its gradual refinement, its tendency towards stricter specialization. To take illustrations from contemporary Bihar: those who produced vegetables were the caste of Koeries; the selling of vegetables was given to another caste, the Turhas. Those who dug earth for salt would be called Noniyas, those who worked the earth for house or canal building, Beldars; the workers in iron were Lohars, the workers in aluminium and bronze, Thatheras. Finer expertise, however, did not transform the methods and techniques of work: the Noniyas and the Beldars used the same tools for earth digging, as did the Lohars and Thatheras for metal working.

In our opinion, the character central to the production system of caste society was the Lohar, the ironsmith. Indisputably, it was a system run on the unity of agriculture and handicrafts, at the village level. And who else was supposed to bring this unity about but the ironsmith? He made and repaired the simple tools; he was in charge of the Hindu farm technology. Today, those who do not believe caste society has changed should go to the villages to have a look at what has happened to the ironsmith. New agricultural technology has hit him as perhaps it has no others, and forced him to look for a living in other ways. And with the displacement of the provider of the unity of agriculture and handicraft has come the slow squeezing out of other artisans and of the servicemen. For in the new system of modern mass-production technology are contained the seeds of the disruption of the old agriculture-handicraft interdependence. Indeed, modern technology counts much for its expansion on the severance of that local unity–it begins by eliminating the old.

Today, like the ironsmiths, other craftsmen and servicemen are also fast moving into the towns where a few of them run small shops, selling their skill; but the towns do not need, and cannot absorb, all of them. With numerous factories making aluminium and stainless steel and china kitchenware, who needs the Thatheras? The washermen are redundant because of the prevalence of synthetic fibres and the electric iron, and the barbers after the advent of the safety razor. Even the Brahmans cannot now make a living by conducting religious services because *pujas* (special worship to which kinsmen and acquaintances are invited by the householder-patron) is now very rare, nor by officiating during marriages, since marriages have a restricted season and do not now bring in much *dakshina*, the gift of money, clothes and grain, from the fathers of the groom and the bride.

Men separated from their trades are compelled to try *any* type of occupation (other than those, of course, of scavengers or other untouchables) which means a great change. Also much has changed for those few who are lucky enough to have traditional skill-shops in towns. A carpenter running a cottage workshop in a town hardly bears any resemblance to the Badhai, the caste woodworker of the village. The fundamental difference arises from the fact that the town carpenter does not produce for a fixed clientele for fixed fractions of the harvest; he is there, with his labour and a little capital, in the market, where anybody from any place or caste can walk in to buy his products. Besides, he himself buys the raw materials and tools from the market. Likewise, a washerman in his town laundry does not wash only the clothes of a few dozen of the village patrons but of hundreds of customers drawn from unspecified castes and origins—and on the terms and conditions determined by the market, not merely for subsistence remuneration. These men are only using their ancestral skills. But today these skills have a positive use, they are not fetters; and they are becoming better skilled by using powered tools and such machines as hair-dryers and washing and drying machines. Their sons are no longer tied to the family trade but can move into other jobs and trades.

In short, society is going through a period where caste is becoming detached from occupation; when what Marx described as 'anarchy in the social division of labour' has set in. The two taboos on manual labour and business, inviolable until recent times among the upper castes, are breaking down, mainly because of high unemployment. But this has caused a crisis.

By turning towards industrial work, the upper castes have blocked the way for lower-caste aspirants. Thus, while a change in their attitude to labour is doubtless tending to weaken caste society further, it is at the same time retarding the process of separation of caste from occupation in the lower orders. There are complaints, often true, that the upper-caste men who have pushed their way into jobs in the mines and factories are proving to be shirkers; from the coalmines of Dhanbad, for instance, there are reports that productivity and efficiency have suffered because the upper-caste workers avoid doing the work for which they are paid. But, then, traditional disdain cannot vanish all at once. In these coalmines, until recently, there was a clear division: jobs in the accounts and administrative offices were held by upper castes while jobs in the pits, underground where the coal seams are blasted and cut out, found only lower castes as takers. Now that the pressure of unemployment is severe, men from the upper castes are seizing the underground jobs too—and, so far, not adapting to the labour involved.

The fall of caste

The fall of caste society began when the British established themselves in India, and has continued ever since. It would be absurd to think that caste society could now restore itself in the countryside or reproduce itself in the towns. There can be no self-contained segments of population in the villages, consisting of clients and servants, because there is no longer an organic link between agriculture and handicrafts. Old towns will grow; new ones will be built at the bazaar-centre of every cluster of villages. In future society, too, there will be status ranking, probably to some extent by reason again of birth, but whatever it may become, future society will not see again the unhumanly-religiously-ranked social order of caste.

But caste is centuries old; it is part of the Hindu's unconscious. Caste society has been put on the road to destruction: but caste itself will take longer to burn out, for several reasons. Endogamy is one reason; it continues to strengthen kinship ties within every caste, to preserve the 'blood'. Marriages are still arranged by fathers. In the towns (and here we again draw on our observations on Bihar) fathers do now show some inclination to seek the consent of son or daughter before finalizing the marriage, but this does not mean that there is freedom of choice. Reaction is inevitable, and marriages independent of paternal will are being more and more reported and accepted. Yet a fair number of such marriages also turn out to be endogamous, since the social life and exchange of visits by young people are still largely confined to caste circles. The girls particularly remain restricted, with no freedom to go out alone or even to move out of the home other than to go shopping or to attend a social occasion at a close relative's home. Girls, until recently, even in town families, were not accorded higher education: and when they began to be sent to colleges they took a degree only for the degree's sake, and were not allowed to take a job. Now all girls, except in poorer families, attend college, and the family ban on their employment outside the house is much relaxed. Already a few cases of girls choosing lovers and husbands from college or workplace, independently of caste considerations, have been reported. Should the nascent feminist movement in urban Bihar gather strength, it could deal a severe blow to caste.

Concepts of society

People in rural Bihar have their own concepts of society and act in accordance with them. Though there are many, four concepts could be said to be the main ones: *samaj* (also *biradari*), *gaon, ilaka* and *desh. Samaj* is not 'society' as we translate this word into English: people in rural Bihar mean it as 'caste'. *Gaon* is the village where one lives; and *ilaka*, the neighbourhood, the district around the village where one lives. And *desh* is the outside, greater world or, now, the nation. Loyalties in rural Bihar follow that order—from caste to nation. Allegiance would go to caste if pitted against the rest of the village; it would go to village rather than the neighbourhood. This order can vary, especially at the lower levels, and in extraordinary conditions. For instance, people of a particular caste in a village could unite more firmly with their castemen in the surrounding villages (*ilaka*) than men of other castes inhabiting the *gaon*.

Caste, with its strength of tradition, is highly important. In the past every *samaj* used to have its own customs, to breach which was beyond imagination, because observance was his *dharam* or God-allotted duty. To discipline breaches the *samaj*, like the tribes, had its councils of male elders who constituted the court for hearing the parties and deciding the nature and degree of punishment—a fine in terms of a goat, or other animal, or some grain, or excommunication from the *samaj* in extreme cases. The councils have kept the *samaj* tightly cohesive down the ages. It was owing to the sense of oneness instilled by them that, following the expansion of colonial administration, which opened up avenues of social mobility, every *samaj*, particularly the major ones, rushed forward with massive backing from its ranks to demand its share. No forms of mass organization other than of caste were known to the people; caste had to be fought with caste.

Struggles to get government and legislative posts by castes whose members feel themselves 'left behind' continue to this day. The old caste associations have died out or are not very active; the *samaj* councils of elders no longer operate, and individuals of a *samaj* are freer to take decisions about themselves, their families and their occupations: the observance of custom has been much diluted. Even the caste associations formed to fight for jobs in the colonial administration are defunct. Yet the *samaj* is far from dead. For the sense of oneness has not been blotted out: *jat-bhai* (members of one caste are brothers) is a living consciousness. People act in accordance with this consciousness—not only in times of anger. A man does not see it wrong to favour, help and stand behind fellow castemen: indeed, he regards it as a sacred duty.

This *jat-bhai* consciousness, this demanding and doing of one's duty towards caste, is what has made each caste into a political community. Political, because each caste is constantly striving to establish its superiority over others, contesting them in all fields: at the *gaon*, village, the *ilaka*, one's part of the district, and the legislature, in administration, universities, trade unions and media. Electing a *jat-bhai*, a fellow casteman (or, for that matter, working to get a *jat-bhai* to the top at the university or in an administrative department) is looked upon as doing one's caste duty—be it the election of the chief executive of the village council or the chief executive of the government block level (*ilaka* level) committee or of the member of the State legislative assembly or the state chief minister. And the sense of political community-for-itself is sustained in no small way by the demographic structure of the village or the sub-district. In a village or sub-district several castes dwell together, thanks to the structure bestowed by caste society. But in every village there is a dominant caste—dominant not only because it is numerically the single largest, but also because it holds much of the village land. This dominant caste has stood above all other castes, exercising an authoritarian control over them. Quite often, by virtue of its numerical strength and economic power in nearby villages as well, a single caste is found to be dominant in the whole sub-district. No wonder, then, that it is very common for the people to know a village or sub-district by the name of its dominant caste. They will describe a village as a *Rajput* or *Yadav* village—when the Rajputs or the Yadavas are dominant. So, apart from the ideological roots of caste as *dharam*, religion, duty, law of Nature, what makes its political organization easier to form today is that its members live in proximity to each other.

Such social composition was not planned, but probably came about naturally as Hindu agricultural society expanded horizontally. When much of the land was still wasteland, families came to clear and settle, then the children married, the families grew in number, new families built huts around the huts of the patriarch and kept on expanding until it was thought proper for some of the members to move out and establish a new village; and villages grew in number. (Even today, in any village, one's kinsmen form a sizeable segment of one's caste; rather, they form the core of the caste, for blood ties are put above all other bonds.) Thus, historically the wasteland was populated by men of one caste living together in a village or the area about it. Today it gives them strength. It gives them power. And it makes them feel that in that particular village or sub-district it is they who decide matters, who run a *raj* of their own. Caste dominance, in practice, thus brings an extra-governmental force into being; and the government, through the caste lobbies in the administration and in parliamentary politics, appears on the scene generally to add to this force. In the villages and the sub-districts, therefore, people of other castes live in virtual terror; before doing something quite trivial they have to consider whether they may incur the displeasure of the dominant caste.

A minor illustration, as narrated by a young man from the intermediately ranked Koeri caste: he was (when much younger, thirteen or so), playing *carrom* one afternoon at a place run as a kind of open public club, with a few newspapers and a *carrom*-board and a chess board. The club was close to his village, which fell within a sub-district dominated by the upper-caste Bhumihars. With three others, he was in the middle of a round on the *carrom*-board when a few Bhumihar boys arrived at the club, and one of them, without saying anything, reached over the shoulders of the players and picked the striker off the board. Then, the players sitting around the board were quickly motioned to leave: 'Be off. We are going to play now.' The Bhumihar boys then took the quietly vacated seats, jerked the coins out of the corner pockets and settled down to play.

Behind the high-handedness of the dominant caste boys, as well as the corresponding submission by the other boys, at the *carrom* table there was, as our young friend felt from his vivid experience, social history and extra-governmental power to control things in the sub-district. And if you were only ordered away from a *carrom* table, you could consider yourself lucky; there are worse things these forces can inflict upon you and your family. You could be destroyed by unjust police and court cases; they could throw you out of the village, raze your house to the ground. You might even lose your life.

The caste wars

Bihar is known for its caste wars: in several sub-districts, more particularly to the south of the Ganga, they are never-ending. These wars, with ironsmiths' guns and factory-made and, sometimes, smuggled foreign guns (in the hilly or riverine sub-districts the commanders moving on horseback) are fought for local dominance. Armed groups of one caste attack a village of the rival caste knocking some people down and then going away, sometimes kidnapping one or two villagers. A retaliatory raid soon occurs to recover lost prestige.

Yet the caste wars, though they are clearly political, have their origins in the economic structure of the society—just like the killings of agrarian labourers reported daily. A dominant caste stays dominant owing to the economic power it holds. It owns the land, and now has sums of money from contracts for government development schemes (seldom implemented) and from welfare schemes. The men of this caste determine the wage rates in the local area, the mode of sharing the crops, conditions of work, the rates of interest on loans: they decide whether the children of lower castes can attend common schools or go to school at all: they forbid unemployed labourers from emigrating in search of work; they take their pleasure with the women of the poorer lower-caste families; they bar people from the polling stations during an election; they resent being answered back.

In March 1977, immediately after the end of the 19-month internal Emergency imposed by Indira Gandhi, much blood was spilt in Bihar. Agrarian labourers, especially untouchables, were killed in large numbers by armed landowners in the villages where they were dominant. During the Emergency, Indira Gandhi's government promulgated a 'Twenty-point economic programme' some of whose 'points' related to the uplift of the agrarian poor, and made incessant propaganda for the programme over the government-run radio and through the censored press. The landowners became agitated but so long as the Emergency lasted they kept quiet for fear the government would have them arrested. They bided their time and struck out at their labourers as soon as Indira Gandhi lost power.

The confrontation between the agrarian poor and the landowners—about which more will be said in the following chapter—is one stream of disorder in rural Bihar. The other stream is that which activates movements for and against job reservations on the one hand and caste wars on the other: it carries along with it mainly the upper castes and the major intermediate castes and splits them. In 1978, the government formed in Bihar after the fall of Indira Gandhi, following the lifting of the Emergency and the elections, introduced a policy of reservation of 26 per cent of its jobs for the 'backward' castes (and women of all castes). The announcement brought upper-caste youths on to the streets. Patna and other towns saw angry demonstrations: a series of violent clashes between the outraged upper-caste youths and the youths from the benefiting 'backward' castes (led by those from the major intermediate castes, like the Kurmis and Yadavas). Considering the high level of unemployment, the outrage was not at all surprising. The upper-caste youths demanded that the criterion for reservation of jobs should not be caste but financial condition; they argued that a significant segment of the upper-caste population was just as poor and disadvantaged as the 'backward' castes. Indeed, the government move agitated the whole of the upper-caste population, who strongly backed their youth. Since education had become more general and jobs scarcer, families were bound to be concerned if their young educated members sat at home without work; the crisis was correspondingly deeper in a society where young men are expected to take up family responsibilities very early. That the criterion for protective discrimination should be other than caste is a view shared among others, by such leading Indian sociologists as M.N. Srinivas and the late I.P. Desai. Their argument is that caste-based reservations have only consolidated caste—giving it 'a new lease of life', says Srinivas—and, have denied opportunities to the poor among the upper castes.

Parliamentary politics in Bihar have undergone a change through the 'reservation war' of the late 1970s. Karpoori Thakur, the chief minister who introduced the policy, has lost much of his reputation and support among the state's upper castes, who seemed to have vowed never again to vote for him or for candidates known to be close to him. He lost an election for the first time in 1984, after winning since 1952. A veteran politician, he had taken part in the freedom movement and later risen as one of the key leaders in the Socialist Party. The party had split several times in the years following Independence, and Thakur stayed with this or that faction. In our view, what the non-Brahman movement did in the southern and western states of India, the socialist movement (it was indeed a movement before it became completely electoral, and factionalized) took up in the northern and eastern states, and particularly in Bihar. The aim, fundamentally, was to achieve social dignity for the castes ranked below the four upper (or *dwija*, twice-born) castes. Every male child in the upper caste family had to undergo a ritual called *upnayana* at which he was given a sacred thread to wear all his life across his shoulder. At this ritual, the son was declared to have taken a second birth. Hence the upper castes were called *dwija* or twice-born. Southern India had only the Brahmans as the high caste; in northern India and Bihar there were four of them: Brahmans, Rajputs, Bhumihars and Kayasthas. The socialist movement in these parts, therefore, instead of directing its attack only at the Brahmans developed as a campaign of the non-*dwijas* against the *dwijas*.

In making his reservation policy, Thakur felt he was only putting into practice his socialist commitment to uplift the non-*dwijas*. If anything, the measure was, he felt, overdue. The ideologue of India's socialist movement, Ram Manohar Lohia, had wanted the militant struggle of the non-*dwijas* to spread; together they formed the majority of the country's population and yet, he pointed out, they were the people who were kept down, and had practically no share of power or social benefits. According to his scheme, more and more non-*dwijas* must rise in every field. Lohia undoubtedly was one of the most acute Indian politicians. Though the literature he produced was flawed and fragmentary, he still remains a source of inspiration for socialist groups.

Preferential opportunity for the *backward* castes, including the untouchables, was, however, not the only thing Lohia wanted; this was only a component of the socialist revolution he was dreaming of. Yet all the movement his ideology achieved was the upward mobility of a few major intermediate castes in Bihar—sections of the Kurmis, the Yadavas and the Koeries. These castes were already rather more developed than the other non-*dwijas* on the social ladder. When Lohia's movement arose they remained as a significant force until the end of the 1960s, by which time they had factionalized miserably. In the meantime, the abolition of Permanent Settlement and the coming of the green revolution had turned a section of the population of these castes from tenants into prosperous peasants (as it did, of course, sections of other castes); prosperity gave them social dignity. The *dwijas* were also beginning to grant them a grudging respectability. Clearly, though, the battle to establish social dignity had not ended. The proof lay in the overwhelming support given by the non-*dwijas*, led by the major intermediate castes, to Thakur's reservation policy.

Conclusion

Having outlined the changes that have occurred in the structure of the old caste society it is relevant to examine briefly how these changes have contributed to the formation of classes.

We saw that the colonial economy and its political administration created a new pattern of employment. A middle class of entrepreneurs grew with the new growth of colonial industry and commerce. Not many of them, however, belonged to Bihar. They were usually Marwaris, the traditional North India trading caste: they made investments in mines and commerce and even bought up bankrupt land estates in Bihar.

The lower middle class comprised mainly petty officials, clerks and lower-rank officials in the army regiments. For a long time the members of this class were drawn exclusively from the upper castes. In sharp contrast, the tea plantations, docks, mines and factories collected the agricultural labourers, or the peasants who had lost their plots of land to the moneylenders or rent-receiving landlords, or who had insufficient land. They belonged to different castes, but nevertheless were at the bottom of Hindu agrarian society. (A large number of them also came from different tribes of the Chotanagpur plateau. They, too, were an impoverished peasantry.) Thus, the nascent working class was composed of men from the lower castes and the tribes, forced out of agriculture by rent-receiving non-cultivating landlords, big and small. Throughout the colonial period this class of rent-receiving non-cultivating landlords had grown abnormally in size due, primarily, to the decline in the number of the peasant proprietors through indebtedness and inability to pay rents and levies, but also because of the sub-dividing of rent-receiving tenures.[3]

Not all the field labourers and poor peasants who went to work on the plantations or in the factories and mines would, however, lose their links with the village. There was a working class whose tail was, as it were, tied to land. Except for the tea gardens, where usually the labourers migrated with their families, workers everywhere had families awaiting remittances or expecting their arrival on certain important occasions. At the tea gardens, too, the labourer did not lose his connection with agriculture, since the plantation owner allotted him a piece of land on the garden for him to cultivate for food. But then neither had members of the middle class broken away from the village, coming as they did largely from the families of the landlords, or well-placed peasants (tenants or proprietors).

In post-colonial Bihar, the revocation of the Permanent Settlement freed a large section of the peasantry of all castes, and the popularity of new farm technology brought prosperity to a small number of them. With the displacement of the ironsmith came the downfall of the old caste society. The unbreakable link between caste and occupation at last broke down. Artisans turned into field labourers and field labourers into industrial workers. The government's policies of promoting education and reserving jobs for the untouchables and the tribals—and later also the backward castes—also contributed to the detachment of occupation from caste—as much as did the open competitive examinations for recruitment in the professions. About the reservation of jobs for the *backward* castes, however, one point has to be noted. The major intermediate castes saw in this policy not merely an opportunity to raise their social status, but also a way of getting as many of their men as possible into the bureaucracy. Having become prosperous, the top sections of these castes wanted to be able to manipulate the levers of governmental power in times of danger (often in circumstances of revolt by the agrarian labourers). After all, the officials of the upper castes had done precisely that in the past. In the countryside, therefore, the might of governmental power would go towards reinforcing the extra-governmental authoritarian power that a dominant caste enjoyed in a particular village or sub-district.

Occupationally, the sizes of the working class or the entrepreneurial and professional classes in Bihar remained very small and their rates of growth were low owing to the slow pace of industrialization in the state. Unemployment was very high. All this had blocked the out-migration of population from the village: people of all strata in the countryside would hanker after land, or at least try clinging to what pieces they had. And in the village, the concepts you acted in accordance with were the old ones; they were your faith. You could not dare, even if you wished to, to walk out of the bounds of the *samaj*, your caste—in the village you did not have the kind of anonymity and cosmopolitan liberation that the town provided. So you always voted the way our *samaj* leaders wished you to, married off your daughters in the *samaj*. (Marriage of daughters of non-conformists and heretics was, indeed, a very great problem.)

Nevertheless, in the past 20 years young men from upper castes have begun working where only the lower castes worked, in the mines and factories. Today the working class in Bihar, therefore, has in its ranks people from all castes, as have the salariat and the professional groups. Old caste prejudices do adversely affect the solidarity of these classes. Yet the awareness of a common identity is stronger.

Part Two
Under the Raj

3. The Rising of the Chiefs—and Some Different Aims

When the British arrived to administer Bihar, in the 1760s, the region was in a state of political confusion. Though the Mughal emperor still ruled India from Delhi (it was he who gave the formal permission to the East India Company to administer Bengal, Bihar, and a small portion of Orissa) the long rule of the Mughals had faltered, with the result that their revenue administration had broken down. The Mughal officers in Patna, Bihar's capital, no longer paid much attention to the collection of taxes, and they no longer bothered who, among the native chiefs and *zamindars*, was contributing regularly their annual payments to the Mughal Crown and who were not. Quite a few of the chiefs had stopped paying.

Amid this confusion, which lingered on, no matter how hard the Company's book-keepers worked, some of the chiefs (like the Maharaja of Hathwa) even began to cultivate ambitions to become fully independent, recognizing no imperial authority whatever, either Mughal or British. They ignored all the company's demands to pay taxes. The Maharaja of Hathwa refused to yield, asserted the independence of his chiefdom and fought battles over it against the Company's troops.[1] Though the peasants suffered under the Mughals they did so mutely. The rebellion of chiefs like the Maharaja of Hathwa remained veritably a private rebellion: the peasant masses quietly (or actively, by enlisting in the chief's army) supported the rebellion for the chief's sake.

Peasant participation was remarkable, though, in the First War of Independence of 1857, fought less than 100 years after the British arrived in Patna. In this great insurrection (for a time the British even began to have doubts about whether they could continue to hold the region from Bengal through Bihar to Delhi) the number of rebellious chiefs was considerable. These were the chiefs who the British had 'harassed', and even removed from their estates, for tax arrears; but this time they were not fighting for the independence of their particular chiefdoms but to drive the British out of India. There was mutiny in the regiment of the Company's army, whose soldiers were, after all, from peasant families. And peasants and mutineers in the countryside battled, against the British, under the leadership of the chiefs. But the time when the peasant masses of Bihar would organize themselves for their own struggle still lay in the future.

God's message to the tribals

In Bihar, the Company had to face the 1857 war before it could recover from the shock of the Santhal insurrection. That also had struck like a hurricane, though causing upsets in a much smaller area and population, for then only the Santhal aborigines had been involved. Other Biharis—civilized, superior, looking down upon the tribals generally—had stayed away. Nowadays, every historian dealing with the colonial period in Bihar attaches the Santhal revolt to his historiography of the Freedom Struggle. But the Santhals, up in arms two years before the rest of Bihar went through the First War of Independence, did not have the benefit of even a regional solidarity. Of course, the non-Santhals who lived in the villages among them—the shepherds, the ironsmiths, the potters—had backed them, but their number was too small (and numbers were important in a war). The Santhals were actually on their own, with their own aims, their own leaders: they didn't wage war to rehabilitate Delhi's Mughal emperor which was the aim in 1857: the Santhals wanted a 'government of our own' for the territory they had come to populate and cultivate; and they marched behind a leader who would proclaim that Thakur, God, had ordained him to go ahead and establish a Santhal *raj*.

The land area the Santhals wanted for themselves was not the site of their ancient habitation, but was altogether a new area, measuring 1,366 square miles, dense with rocks and jungles, put on the revenue map by the zealous officers of the Company. It was beautiful, green country, sprawling in eastern Bihar, among the Rajmahal Hills where the Ganga turned a little way north to enter Bengal. The Company officers had given this charming country a charming Persian name: Daman-i-Koh, Skirt of the Hill. Daman-i-Koh came into being in 1823: it was marked off with boundary posts. The officers first asked Paharias, the tribal community living atop the Rajmahal hills, to come down, make clearings and cultivate, but they did not, saying they preferred the highlands. (Many of the Paharias, even today, live on the top of those hills.) A search for other cultivators was made, and finally, the Santhals were brought from various places—the Santhals, who were already being acclaimed by the Company officers who had observed them as a 'race of most industrious cultivators'.

In this invitation the Santhals saw a way out of the coercive world of their *zamindars*. From Cuttack in Orissa, from Singhbhum, Manbhum, Palamu, Ramgarh, Bhagalpur and Chotanagpur of Bihar, and from Dalbhum, Midnapore, Bankura, Barabhum, Pachet and Birbhum of Bengal they migrated to congregate in Daman-i-Koh. There were no *zamindars* here. Daman was a government estate where the officers would collect the rent directly from the peasants. For the Santhal it was not a bad deal. He had to pay nothing at all for the first three years, and a 'nominal' rate for the next three, and 'such rate as the Santhals themselves agree' to pay for a further five years. About 3,000 Santhals arrived in Daman by the end of the 1830s; within the next twelve years, there were 83,000 of them. Daman as a scheme of finance-raising would prove a great success; and very soon, Pontet, the revenue superintendent for Daman, was being recommended for a salary increase. From Rs.6,600 in 1837-38, the revenue from the new country had soared in twelve years to Rs.58,000.

But immigration also attracted others. Into the jungles of Daman, now studded with Santhal villages in the clearings, slithered, from parts of Bengal, the petty moneylenders. The Santhals fed on rice, maize and seed-oils; the moneylenders fed on the Santhals. A 'phlegmatic race' was what the English called the Santhals, and that was how the moneylenders found them. So, to begin with, they lured the peasant to come and take two rupees, four rupees, asking him to repay whenever he pleased; they invented his needs for him. And the Santhal, a great respecter of obligation like all tribal people, brought the moneylender bags of grain and baskets of fruits, without ever looking at the tilted balance and the home-made stone weights; without ever caring to know that in the towns he could get double, ten times, sometimes thirty times the rates his creditor paid him; and when through such ways he accumulated loss after loss and took loan after loan; and when, at the end of the year, Pontet's subordinate appeared in the village to demand rents, there was no one in the world for him to turn to for help.

And Pontet's subordinates did not just collect the rents. They usually extracted more than was due. Unlettered *junglees* no more understood the scribbling on the rent receipt books than what the moneylender entered in his credit ledgers. There were, no doubt, courts with magistrates where the Santhals could go to lodge cases against the moneylenders or the assistants to the superintendent, but that was expecting too much from the *junglees*. And, besides, the courts were either at Deoghar or Bhagalpur, both miles away. Yet a time was bound to come for *junglees* to begin to understand things. They started complaining; a petition against Mahesh Dutt, most hated of all Pontet's subordinates, was sent bravely to Pontet. Taking his own time, Pontet, when he was ready to hear the case, found there to be no case at all: inexplicably, the complainant had taken back his petition. Complaints against moneylenders were continually coming up before Pontet. And Pontet, in whom (according to his superiors who wrote in favour of raising his salary) the Santhals had great trust, dealt with these complaints in his own inimitable style. He would send for the moneylender, and, after giving him a scolding and warning, close the case.

In the rebellion that followed in Daman in 1855, Mahesh Dutt (who had been promoted to a police sub-inspector) was the first to die. The peasants tied him up with a rope, and Siddhu the leader slew him with his own sword. After him, it was the turn of the moneylenders. Mobs like informal armies advanced in all directions in a devastating mood; moneylenders were slashed and killed; palatial houses were ransacked; an indigo factory was burned down; two Englishwomen and three West European men got in the way of the marching rebels and all five were done to death; the Company's troops were faced fearlessly without firearms, furious peasants were shot down in scores. The battle for Daman dragged on for several months. Thousands of the rebels never returned to Daman after the Company forces were able to regain control.

The commended, efficient Superintendent Pontet, the officer in whom alone the *junglees* were said to confide, was, in the official records of the Company, now blamed for his inefficiency in dealing with the peasant complaints and, what was more curious, for his failure to get any forewarnings of such a massive insurrection. Pontet lost both his image and his job in Daman. But one officer's bad luck was unimportant compared to the fate of the several thousand Santhals who could not liberate a jungly country they had made their own. Before they declared war they had (informed, it was said, by means of a circulating twig of Sal) milled into Bhagnadini, the village of young Siddhu, and of his brothers, Kanhu, Chand and Bhairab. There, Siddhu, on the night of the full moon of 30 June 1855, as ten thousand Santhals watched intently and reverently in silence, proclaimed that he had a vision: Thakur, God, had appeared in his hut and instructed him that Daman must be cleared of all outsiders, that moneylenders and policemen be immediately slaughtered, and that Superintendent Pontet be also slain. And Siddhu and Kanhu declared themselves to be *subahdars*, governors, of Daman and allocated to themselves powers to collect rents from the peasants. One week after these proclamations the war and the slaughter began; and Pontet hid himself in a fortified palace—the residence of the railway engineer at Rajmahal—and soon escaped, never to return to Daman.

A land of their own

The Santhals could never establish sovereignty over Daman. Incontestably, Daman was a nation without roots, without an ancient culture associated with soil, air, water, hills; a jungle recently studded with villages and not a nation at all. But the war was fought for 'Daman for Sanhals', because feelings of attachment to the place had grown among those who populated it. At the root of the war were, no doubt, the peasants' aspirations to be free to grow crops without having to set aside more than a nominal levy for the 'Authority', whoever that may be. But this aspiration became inextricably entwined with feelings, hardening gradually into conviction, that the Santhal could not be free as long as 'others' remained inside Daman. So began the campaign to throw them out.

But this conviction was not bred by Daman's local conditions alone. There was an idea unfathomably older; it had astonishingly survived centuries of displacement, migration and exhaustion of resources, followed again by migration, which had become very dear to the Santhals: the idea of nationhood. Their own name for themselves was not 'Santhal' but 'Kherwar', and they believed that the Kherwars had once been free men with a country of their own called Champa where they lived blissful lives, hunting, growing crops, giving a token of grain to the tribal chief. This yearning for Champa (though the name is not now so often mentioned) presented them with their cause and has continued to guide the Santhals' actions in one form or another. In the decades following the 1855 revolt there then emerged Kherwar 'prophets' who called upon the Santhals to become purer by abstaining from animal food and liquor, and whose oracles promised them sovereignty.

There was no doubt, said the prophets, that the land belonged to the dark-skinned people of the Kherwar community, because the soil was dark; the white men would go back home where the soil was white! One of them, who was called Bhagirath, preached that 'No human being created the earth or sends rain and sunshine; no human being has cleared or ploughs our land but ourselves; no human being but ourselves has a right to a share in the produce.' Bhagirath then proclaimed himself King of the Kherwars, and told them he would fix an auspicious day for them to gather together and drive out the non-Kherwars from their land. Meanwhile, however, British officers sought him out and put him in prison.

Even today the idea of Champa moves the Santhals. The name now in currency is Jharkhand, Land of Jungles. But it is not only the Santhals but all tribes who yearn for it in one degree or another: the basic idea of having a country free from alien occupation or plainsmen still, however, remains. There is a map of the cherished Jharkhand which shows the whole of Chotanagpur plateau and Santhal Parganas district. This district has now been broken up by the Bihar government, not without political reasons, into four smaller districts. The map extends to cover some districts of the neighbouring states of West Bengal, Orissa and Madhya Pradesh. Within the region outlined, the tribals claim to have a majority, a majority made up not of one tribe but different tribes together: today no single tribe aspires to a country of its own, and does not consider it practicable. In the British time, however, every tribe fought for a country of its own: the Kols, 23 years, before the Santhals rose, and afterwards the Cheroes, the Chuars, and the Mundas.

The Mundas around Ranchi, which was to become the centre of the Jharkhand movement in the 20th century, waged war in the 1890s, with the slogan: 'The Queen's (Queen Victoria) raj is ended: our raj has begun.' Their dream, like that of the Santhals, was to expel all aliens from their land. And their leader, again like that of the Santhals, was a young man who claimed he had seen a vision of God. He told his people that when the Sirkari (government) troops pressed their triggers only water, and not bullets, would issue from their guns. Birsa the leader, son of an uprooted Munda peasant, converted as a child to Christianity, educated in a Mission primary school, retired when 20 years old to a hillside village, Chalkad, and announced that on a day not far off the whole area, the whole world, would be destroyed by God's will and Chalkad would remain, the only spot blessed and untouched. (Some chroniclers of the Birsa movement suggest that he got the idea from the story of Noah's ark.) From the villages, long lines of distressed Mundas, bundles of rice on their shoulders, moved out with their families towards Chalkad. They put all their trust in Birsa; they believed he could perform miracles. Birsa, within a hut at Chalkad, coated his skin with a mixture of turmeric powder in oil and, leaving the front door half open, dazzled the mass of credulous peasants assembled outside by saying he, with God's blessing, now had a body purely of gold.

There was one new enemy in this Munda war, which involved the arrest of Birsa at Chalkad, his imprisonment for two years, his release, and his reorganization of the Mundas and a fierce engagement of bows and Sirkari guns at Domabari Hill, named thereafter as the Mount of the Dead. (Birsa was rearrested and his death from cholera shortly after in jail resulted in a continuing disbelief in the official cause of his death.) This new enemy, apart from the moneylenders and the landlords, was the Christian missionaries. When the missionaries first arrived in Ranchi they saw the tribals being cheated, bullied, and pauperized. They extended assistance to them by writing and taking their complaints against the moneylenders and the landlords to the courts (where the Mundas had ever feared to go) and by having the cases argued and decided in their favour. At the time, to the beleaguered Mundas, the missionaries seemed no less than holy men sent to liberate them. But a short time later the missionaries revealed their own purpose; the aborigines had no choice but to agree that becoming Christian was the only way to survive under the given circumstances. The conversion in the Chotanagpur region broke all records, and was the largest conversion ever in the history of Christianity in India.[2] All worked towards it; the Lutherans, the Jesuits, the Roman Catholics. The Jesuits alone increased the number in just four years, beginning in 1885, from less than 2,100 to 67,000. One man, Father Constant Lievens, a young Lutheran, was to become the most famous for single-mindedness. 'He made his assistance in land matters conditional upon conversion to Christianity. He not only insisted that individuals must become Christian before he would help them, but in many cases he insisted that the entire village must first become Christian. . . . '[3]

But at the next stage, Lievens and his ilk slipped up. In every village, there were cultivated strips of land that the Munda community used to set aside for the religious services of their native faith. After the mass conversion to Christianity the missionaries began to argue that since they had now renounced their native faith, those 'religious village tenures' should be made over to the Mission. This was the last straw; the Mundas had, after all, adopted a new religion for a productive cover, and no other reason. From then on, the estrangement between the Mundas and the missionaries only deepened. The missionaries ceased to help the peasants in courts, drew themselves closer to colonial officialdom, and now worked to remove anti-British disaffection among the people. When the Mundas launched their war of liberation, Birsa the prophet, to smite the missionaries, chose Christmas as the 'auspicious day', and the churches, the missionaries, and the Christians as targets.

4. The Wrecking of the Countryside

The collection of land revenues

The English East India Company, after taking over from the Mughal governor the administration of Bengal, Bihar and a part of Orissa, got down to the devising of ways to gather land revenue. This presented a problem. For all that the Mughals gave them was the charge of administration; there were no real records and the territory and the people were completely unknown to the Company's officers. In the Bengal-Bihar-Orissa region the Mughals, despite their long rule, had never ordered a land survey or maps of the estates' boundaries. The Company staff had no equipment to carry out a survey, and, in fact, working principally for a commercial business, its officers knew almost nothing about surveys or agrarian matters.

The Mughals had, for this area, had taxes collected by a new kind of official, called a *zamindar*. These *zamindars*—'drawn from every level of society'[1]— were permitted, in lieu of salaries, to retain a proportion of the collection, and also to have some rent-free strips of land, and allowed to collect for themselves certain levies, like transit duties, and to lease out pieces of arable wasteland. The *zamindars* had to serve the Mughal Crown when so ordered and for that service were supposed to keep a body of armed retainers, cavalry, elephants, boats and, for major areas, cannons also. Initially, therefore, the East India Company could see no way other than to work through *zamindars*.

But not all the *zamindars* were ready to work for the Company. Some like the Maharaja of Hathwa, tried to break free; others opposed the new conditions imposed by the Company. One such condition in particular caused great confusion. The Company was against an annual settlement of revenue with the *zamindars* and insisted on having a five-year settlement, believing that a longer and more stable arrangement would go a long way in inducing the *zamindars* to bring more of the wasteland into cultivation and thus develop their estates undisturbed. The five-year settlement (1772–77) was not expected to run into trouble. As it happened, however, a number of estates passed from the established *zamindars* into the hands of speculators and 'upstarts' who practically turned the settlement into merciless plunder. Rents and levies, at whatever rates the new collectors set, were extorted from the peasants, often at gunpoint. Since the collectors had powers to order confinement of defaulters, peasants were imprisoned. Compared to these collectors, the *zamindars* appeared much the lesser evil.

Even when estates were in the hands of speculators, however, the *zamindar* still retained his office and his entitlement to rent-free plots, his powers to receive tolls, customs and excise. He could also allocate rent-free plots to his subordinates and employees in the rural police, the revenue services, and so on, and receive fees from them for the plots leased to them. He was also entitled to a ten per cent share of the collection made by whoever had received his estate from the Company. Under the five-year settlement, then, the peasants had to bear a double burden. The hopes behind this kind of settlement were thus belied; the rapacious new collectors paid little attention to developing the estates (though in certain cases they were reported to have leased for trivial rents the best strips of the wasteland to close relatives and friends). The *zamindar*, reduced and ignored, and jealous of the new collector, obviously had no interest in developing the land.

The annual settlement was reinstated, after the discrediting of the five-year settlement. This time, too, several of the new collectors were able to buy their way into tenures. Freed now even of formal responsibilities to develop the estates, their exploitation increased. Whatever one had to accumulate could be done only in one year, for there was no guarantee of getting an estate again at next year's settlement. After a second failure—annual settlements were made successively for four years—the Company's officers decided it might be a better idea for rent collection for the whole of Bihar to go to one single person. The choice went to Kalyan Singh, the Maharaja of Patna, in 1781. But this arrangement, too, quickly became fallible: the Maharaja alone could not collect the rents as he had no Bihar-wide network; what he could do was to sub-lease the estates to the *zamindars*, speculators and 'upstarts', if not the same then a similar lot; the story for the peasants came full circle.

Permanent settlement

It was to bring order and stability to the countryside that the Company finally introduced the Regulation of Permanent Settlement in the Bengal-Bihar-Orissa region in 1793. Under this regulation, the amount that the Company would receive every year from the tenants as rent was fixed permanently at the level of 1792. The idea behind this was that, freed from the uncertainties of an annually increasing State demand, the tenants would devote all their energies to the development of their estates. It would involve great financial loss since land was then a major source of revenue: the Company officers described it as a 'sacrifice', but argued that about one-third of the land in the region was still wasteland, and that periodic settlements militated against its reclamation, development and settlement. Said Lord Cornwallis, the Governor-General:

I may safely assert that one-third of the Company's territory in Hindustan is now a jungle inhabited only by wild beasts. Will a ten years' lease induce any proprietor to clear away that jungle, and encourage the *raiyats* [tenants] to come and cultivate the lands, when, at the end of that lease, he must either submit to be taxed ad libitum for their newly-cultivated lands, or lose all hopes of deriving any benefit from his labour, for which perhaps at that time he will hardly be paid? I must own that it is clear to my mind that a much more advantageous tenure will be necessary, to incite the inhabitants of this country to make these exertions which can only effect any substantial improvement.[2]

But agricultural expansion through felled jungles (the same idea that would, about 40 years later, lead to the creation of Daman-i-Koh and the settling of the Santhals there) was not all that Cornwallis had in mind. Above all, a frozen tax level would make the landlords, indeed the whole of the subject people, believe the British rulers to be most reasonable and just; it could go a long way to keep them happy, and their thoughts away from provocation to insurrection. In the words of the then Secretary of State for India, the sacrifice of revenue might (among other things) be regarded as the 'purchase-money paid for the diffusion of a general feeling of contentment among the land-holders, their increased loyalty to a Government in whose continuance they would have acquired a personal interest. . . . '[3]

And this sacrifice of land revenue, said the officers, was also based on sound principles of capitalism. In fact, it might not prove a loss at all, because the landholders who were to benefit would make investments in developing the land, and towards the general development of the estates; idle resources would begin to yield, employment would be better, productivity would grow and from such all-round growth, the State, the English, could not but derive benefits, for taxes would flow in abundantly in forms other than that of land revenue. For one obvious loss there were, therefore, a hundred hidden gains. What was more, the fixed tax would be strictly collected.

The landholders were, accordingly, ordered to deposit their revenue fully, regularly, and punctually each year. There was no room now, said the officers, for the defaults that had been common during the time of annual or periodical settlements. Though the Mughal methods of forcing landholders to pay had been abandoned, there would be a Sale Law providing the officers with powers of strict enforcement. If there was a slight delay in paying, parts or all of a landholder's estate could, under the Sale Law, be seized and auctioned, the purchase money going towards setting off the arrears.

To the landholders the Permanent Settlement, however, had by one stroke made them owners of the soil. Under the Mughals,* to be a *zamindar* was to be

---

* On the subject of these Mughal methods, Hunter wrote: 'In order to enforce the payment of revenue [the Mughal viceroy's deputy in Bengal] ordered a pond to be dug, which was filled with everything disgusting; and the stench of which was so offensive as nearly to suffocate whoever approached it. To this shocking place, in contempt of the Hindus, he gave the name of *Baikunt*, which in their language means Paradise; and, after the *zamindars* had undergone the usual punishments, if their rent was not forthcoming, he caused them to be dragged, by a rope tied under their arms, through this internal pond. He is also stated to have compelled them to put on loose trousers, into which were introduced live cats. By such cruel and horrid methods he extorted from the unhappy *zamindars* everything they possessed.'[4]

a holder of the office of a tax-gatherer, and no more. The land belonged to the emperor, the paramount power. Under the Mughals all kinds of people had made their way into the office of *zamindar*; semi-independent chiefs, businessmen from the town, sycophants in the courts of nawabs or local rulers, government officials—even *kanungoes*, revenue officers, and *patwaris*, village accountants, and the employees of the *zamindars*. The British transformed all these into proprietors of land and believed that, in the absence of spiralling State demands, looking on the land as their own, the *zamindars* would settle down to act as dependable agents of progress.

At the close of the eighteenth century the scene thus underwent a significant change, which led to more changes in the nineteenth, and even into the twentieth, century. People of the region were buffeted in the initial decades of the Permanent Settlement by laws heaped upon laws. To interpret and apply them, a collector was posted to every district; and *diwani adalat*, civil courts and *faujdari adalat*, criminal courts, were set up. The peasant in the villages was bewildered by these institutions, transplanted here from England. Bound immemorially to oral tradition, it was impossible for him to imagine that written-down things could govern everyday life. Some conscience-stricken British protested that the new arrangements had only driven the peasants deeper into misery; and that Cornwallis had fathered the scheme of Permanent Settlement because he, coming from landed English aristocracy himself, had a natural bias towards landlords.

In 1928 a Royal Commission on Agriculture in India was formed, to investigate the impediments to agricultural growth in all the provinces. The same year the Commission visited the province of Bihar and Orissa (separated from Bengal for 16 years by now) and summoned A.D. Tuckey, the province's director of land records and surveys, and—135 years after the Permanent Settlement—asked him this question:[5]

> *Commission*: With reference to the terms of the Permanent Settlement, is it a fact that there has been a proclamation on record that even the rents (from the tenants) should be permanently fixed?
> *Tuckey*: I do not know. I know that there are a number of officers who have studied the question who think that that was the *intention*, but I do not know whether there was a definite proclamation to that effect. (Emphasis ours)

And thus was revealed, years later, during which time it had caused social tragedy in the countryside, the Permanent Settlement's most wicked—but not inadvertent—omission: statutes about the rents payable by tenants to the *zamindar*. While the tax payable by the zamindar to the State had been made unalterable, nothing had been laid down about rents. Therefore, rent became entirely at the whim of the *zamindar*, levied, and increasable at his pleasure. But an ever-rising annual rent was not all that the *zamindar* extracted from the peasants. There were *abwabs*—the most recurring word in the history of *zamindari*—or cesses. Every day the peasants were pestered for money: if the *zamindar* had to remunerate his servants and attached artisans, or to repay a loan; or when there were religious festivals or fairs; when someone from the *zamindar's* family set out on a pilgrimage to the Hindu or Muslim shrines; if someone died in his family and burial or cremation and funeral rites had to be observed; when there was a birth in his family or if the *zamindar's* daughter was getting married. The occasions were infinite in number; and it was always the *abwabs*, extracted from the peasants, that mainly helped to pay for them.[6]

Further exploitation by the zamindar

Cornwallis's arrangement was that the *zamindar* would fix the rates of rent with the consent of the tenants, and in consultation with the Company's district collector, but the *zamindar* did not bother to do either, and neither did Cornwallis take any steps to enforce the arrangement. One order laid down that no *zamindar* could levy 'new *abwabs* and was liable to pay as a penalty three times the amount of the *abwab*, if discovered'. But the old *abwabs* remained and the levying of new ones also went apace, for, first, no *abwab* was specified; the British officers could thus always plead ignorance of their origins. Secondly, the district collectors had no village rent rolls in their offices, and the *zamindars* could extort old and new *abwabs*, calling them all traditional.

In the rules of Permanent Settlement it was also said that *patwaris*, village book-keepers, would be appointed in the village to maintain registers of the accounts of the *zamindari*—rents, *abwabs*, payments, arrears, expenses—and to build up a record of rights listing each tenant and the size and location of his landholding. It was the *zamindars* who were asked to appoint the *patwaris* and give a list of the recruits to the collector concerned. In two of the Bihar districts, Purnea and Bhagalpur, *patwaris* were recruited; but there was little or no progress made in others. The *zamindars* from two districts, Saran and Tirhut, even voiced total opposition to the scheme, arguing that the *patwaris* might cause more problems by 'misleading' the tenants, they said than they would solve. In Bihar, therefore, the scheme was virtually allowed to die following this resistance, and the tenants were denied their first chance of having a written record of their status.

A *zamindar* would give his tenants no *patta*, lease paper, on which the type and the terms of the lease and the rents payable were entered. The tenants did not even have receipts for the rents they paid. Insecurity and fragility of tenure thus guaranteed their servility to the *zamindar*. The more the *zamindar* kept, in his own interests, to the oral tradition, the more the tenants wanted to break with it, because of their experience with the British, whose magistrates, judges and officers considered only what was written down when deciding their fate. A record of status with respect to cultivated land became a basic concern of the tenants. Throughout the whole time of the *zamindari*, 163 years, the tenants kept pressing for *pattas* and receipts.

Without any records, ejection went unopposed, but instead of putting a stop to it, the British, in the years following the Permanent Settlement, passed several orders and regulations that gave the *zamindars* more power. The *zamindars'* standard plea was that the tenants were evading rents and would pay only under duress. Unless they had these powers, they said, they might not be able to pay the taxes themselves. The British, fearing a shortfall of revenue, and inextricably dependent on the men of their making, gradually transformed the *zamindars* into a force for evil.

If a tenant failed to pay punctually, the *zamindar*, with his new powers, could prosecute him in a court of law; eject him from his land; distrain (and for this no court orders were required) the tenant's crops, cattle and other personal assets, and cause them to be auctioned to cover the arrears; he could arbitrarily raise the rent and if he refused to pay could detain the tenant in his office until he accepted the new rate, and order the tenant to pay within three days and, in case of default, have him flung into prison. The *zamindar* was also empowered to enter a tenant's house with a police officer, by breaking down the doors, even going into the *zenana*, the women's quarters, in search of goods and gold to seize. A judge of the time, A. Tufton, observed that a tenant's house after a *zamindar* had ransacked it looked 'as if a most daring robbery had been committed'.[7]

Written records, written orders and regulations, and court proceedings all proved new aids to the exploitation of the peasants. Yet the records they most needed in order to establish their tenant status always eluded them.

We read in the discussion, again, between the Royal Commission on Agriculture and Tuckey, 135 years after the Permanent Settlement:[8]

Commission: Would you say that, in a considerable part of this province, the relations existing between zamindar *and tenants are a serious obstacle to agricultural development?*
Tuckey: Yes, I should.
What is the nature of (the tenants') insecurity?
The *zamindars* do not usually grant rent receipts, and if they grant them they do not grant them in the proper form, and if a tenant can at any time be sued for three years' rent, although he has paid it, and the *zamindar* in nine cases out of ten can get a decree for it, well, the tenant is not going to make improvements.
He can insist upon a proper receipt?
In theory yes, but not in practice.
Has the fact that proper receipts are not given to the ryots *(tenants) by the* zamindars *been brought to your notice?*
Yes, in hundreds and hundreds.
With regard to the granting of receipts, may I know whether it is possible for the ryot *to go to court and obtain his relief there, and compel the* zamindar *to take his receipt?*
It is possible for a court, on the complaint of a *ryot* within three months of the date from which the receipt should have been issued, to take up the case under section 58.
He can sue the zamindar *in a court of law?*
In theory, but not in practice; he has not got the power.
Are you prepared to say that the zamindars *of this province are powerful*

*enough to go round the public offices and courts and influence them to such
an extent that the* ryots *do not get proper justice?*

It is not a question of going round to the courts and influencing them. It is
largely a question of the power of the purse. The *ryots* have not got the money
to fight the *zamindar* up to all the various appeal courts, unless they can
combine, which as a rule, they cannot. In some few cases they do combine,
and then the *zamindar* is in a very unhappy situation.

*Do they send money to the landlords through the post office in the form of
money orders?*

Not very much, I believe. I do not know very much about that; it is usually
refused, I think.

That was in 1928. But within the 135 years of its enforcement the Permanent
Settlement was marked not only by the main feature—insecurity of tenure—but
also by the damage inflicted on certain old communal arrangements upon which
the population of the village used to rely for the production and distribution of
the fruits of the soil within its boundaries: arrangements such as the common
right to forests or rent-free grants to the artisans. In the village, irrigation used
to be a joint responsibility. In the chaos and disorder caused by the Permanent
Settlement individual suffering stifled the peasant's sense of community. With
the centralization of powers, the old village councils, the *panchayats*, were
already becoming less effective.[9] The British administrators asked the
zamindars to allocate certain specific funds out of their revenue for the improvement of irrigation; but rarely did any of them even repair or maintain the small,
indigenous waterworks.

And as the Permanent Settlement continued, the *zamindar* was not the sole
exploiter of the peasants and the labourers. Between him and the peasants there
developed a number of exploitative layers. Subinfeudation began with the
zamindar himself leasing out his estate, or part of it, in portions, thus creating
a group of rent-receivers below him. If the portion was small, the tenure-holder
sub-leased it to a peasant (obviously at a higher rate than he was paying to the
zamindar). For larger portions, the tenure-holder might prefer to lease to
professional moneylenders or well-off, non-cultivating upper castes. These
moneylenders or prosperous upper-caste men would then find peasants to work
the land for an annual rent or a share of the produce. Throughout the period of
the Permanent Settlement the number of non-cultivating rent-receivers continued to rise.

The condition of the agricultural labourers was even worse. Their wages did
rise slightly over the years, but the rise in prices always kept their real wages
low. Among the labourers, the *kamias*, or bond-men, were at the bottom of the
pile. The *kamia* slaved, usually for generations, for a landlord (a *zamindar* or a
rent-receiver) who kept him perpetually in debt to him and gave him all that he
(the *kamia*) needed. In 1885, for the first time, a law was made, called the Bengal
Tenancy Act, which in theory guaranteed a tenant the right to the occupancy of
the land after he had *continuously* tilled it for 12 years. In 1908, also for the first
time, a Chotanagpur Tenancy Act was passed, to apply to the tribal region of

Bihar. This banned increasing of rents without an order from a government revenue officer. And even in the rest of Bihar, through the Bengal Tenancy Act, to increase rents was prohibited except on certain specific grounds.

Yet, when certain amendments to the tenancy laws were presented to the Bihar Provincial Assembly in 1937, the prime minister of the Congress Party-run ministry, Sri Krishna Singh (the chief minister of a province was then called prime minister) observed that 'the incidence of rent in Bihar is higher in comparison to other provinces of India'. He also commented on the fact that over and above the high rents, *abwabs*, extra levies, were demanded of the tenants; and that on an average the *abwabs*, were as high as 33 per cent of the rent. All rent increases made by the *zamindars* between 1911 and 1930 were annulled by the amendments, which also held out promises to establish fair rents for the tenants in all cases, as for instance in the areas where the land had declined in quality due to soil erosion.

But certain powers (powers given by the authors of the Permanent Settlement to the *zamindars*) still remained. In the middle of the processing of the amendment bills, there was a compromise. The Congress, in government for the first time, acted in what would become its standard political fashion in the years following Independence: speaking for the poor but acting for the rich. Their powers retained, the *zamindar* could continue his exploitation: throwing out tenants at pleasure, distraining their goods, cattle, crops and valuables and selling them; taking away land legally, on the plea that the strip was wanted for the *zamindar's* self-cultivation or for a fresh lease to another tenant; never in fact allowing any tenant to complete 12 years of *continuous* tilling of the same plot and thus never allowing the peasant's lifelong ambition of owning a piece of land to be fulfilled.

5. Farewell to Bows and Arrows

The Jharkhand movement

In the twentieth century, the politics of freedom in the tribal region of Bihar entered a new mode. Good lessons were bound to issue from the bad wars that every tribe had fought in the past century: wars against the moneylenders, the landlords, the British, even against the Christian missionaries. Now that the way of arms was abandoned, the tribes planned to struggle for freedom together instead of singly. There would be no leaders like Birsa or Siddhu rousing the people by convincing them that 'Our God' willed it; while sentiments would remain the same, the people would no longer form small, ferocious factions.

The new mode flowed from the new, Western education. It was the tribals attending the English schools who, identified as the tribal middle class, became its exponents. But it was not Western education alone that bound together the tribes' semi-intelligentsia. There was (and here, Christianity in Chotanagpur also had a role) a common new religion uniting them, and mission officials to back this unity. Furthermore, the conditions existing in the region provided unity as its basis: all tribal people saw every immigrant from the plains as a common enemy. These were the conditions and sentiments that had produced the nineteenth century revolts; now they would create the movement for Jharkhand, Land of Jungles, the homeland for which claims to separate 'nations' were surrendered. And the man who emerged as this movement's greatest leader was Jaipal Singh, a Munda from a village of Ranchi, the town which the British had made Bihar's summer capital, because of its cooler climate.

Jaipal Singh was not a founder member of the Jharkhand movement, about 25 years of organizing effort having passed before he felt motivated to join. As a boy he had attended a mission school in Ranchi. The principal was impressed by his talents and arranged to send him to England to take an Oxford degree, after which he left for Ghana on colonial service. Back in India a few years later to work for a petroleum company, he then became finance minister of the princely state of Bikaner. It was while serving the prince, it is said, that travelling by train to Ranchi, some British, who were discussing the living conditions of the tribals, said to him: 'You are educated and experienced. Why don't you work for the welfare of your tribesmen?'—a conversation that Jaipal himself was often to recount to his fellow workers in the Jharkhand organization.[1] This casual suggestion, he said, provoked and shamed him into giving up everything to achieve a tribal homeland.

A year or so after the formation of the first Congress ministry in Bihar, in

1937, Jaipal took over the leadership of the just-founded *Adivasi Mahasabha*, Great Assembly of the Tribals. Several forums were set up and disbanded before the movement finally settled on the *Mahasabha*. First, the Christian students' conference in 1910; then the Chotanagpur political conference in 1915; and after that, the Chotanagpur *unnati samaj* or Chotanagpur development society; all of these had the 'socio-economic development' of the tribal region of Bihar as their main objective. Such an objective in itself contradicted the administration's claims that the region had already developed; that its rich mineral resources, such as coal and iron ore, were being exploited. The advocates of 'development' refuted this by arguing that such exploitation had only relegated the tribals to the lowest rungs of the working class—for instance, as cutters and loaders in the coal mines. And in agriculture the financial ruin following the activities of the landlords and moneylenders was there for all to see. In their view, the tribals could never develop unless they had a province of their own, an autonomous homeland, though not secession. Before the *Adivasi Mahasabha* came into being, the earlier forums had tried to put these views across. In 1928, when the members of the Simon Commission on constitutional reforms in India arrived in Ranchi, the Chotanagpur *unnati samaj* presented them with a memorandum demanding a separate province for the tribals, to be separated from Bihar.

The opposition

Educated Biharis, especially the upper-caste Hindus (in politics, government service, and the professions) already had a fixed view of Chotanagpur. Chotanagpur to them was a region where Hinduism had suffered losses occasioned by a foreign and low religion. Some of them, in frustration, even began to describe Chotanagpur as 'a Christian country'.[2] Everything that happened there appeared to them as acts of intrigue by the missionaries, the European residents, the converts and the British administration. There *was* intrigue by some European residents (who morally backed the tribals) against the immigrants, or by the missionaries, when obsessed with achieving conversion targets. Denouncing the way conversions were achieved was understandable, as was the denunciation of the idea of some of the British that the British government should work in concert with the missionaries as a 'body of men fighting on its side'.[3] But what had these intrigues to do with the demand for a separate tribal homeland? The answer lay within the question: the demand flowed from the intrigues!

Jharkhand was a 'Christian conspiracy'. Once the educated Biharis had painted that picture, the painters themselves showed their deceit, for the picture portrayed the tribal on the stage and a white man supplying the words from behind the curtain; it represented Jharkhand as an artificial thing. In doing so, the human urge to be free was totally unrepresented. So it transpired that if the Biharis were concerned about certain European ideas or activities this concern was born out of anything but love for the tribals. They had tended never to accept the tribals as human beings: they were no more than 'junglees', dull-witted, lethargic, unclean, incorrigible and worthy only of servitude. The reality was that the Biharis were worried about people other than the tribals. They were speaking for the few millions of immigrants from the plains of Bihar, who had by then settled in Chotanagpur as *zamindars*, moneylenders, petty traders, government officials, mine workers, employees of the courts: people who, wherever they settled in the region, proved themselves particularly skilful at cheating and squeezing the natives; and who, when the natives set about organizing themselves, looked desperately to men with a voice at the provincial centre, in the city of Patna, for support.

The question of Chotanagpur's separation soon came up before the first provincial Congress ministry. And one of the grounds of its rejection was the presence of the immigrants, who it was claimed were 'Aryan' and akin to the 'people of Bihar' and the language they spoke. The prime minister of Bihar, Sri Krishna Sinha, argued: 'Taking the area as a whole, Hindustani or Hindi is the language of the vast bulk of the people of Chotanagpur, closely followed by the aboriginal tribes.' According to him, 3.2 million people there spoke Hindustani; only two million used aboriginal languages.[4] Like other educated Biharis, the Congress premier's argument ignored the history of immigration: it made no mention of the fact that the tribals had lost much as a result of immigration. He simply counselled resignation to the loss.

The history of Chotanagpur had various protagonists. The greatest among them were the rajahs. It was the rajahs of Chotanagpur, tribals themselves, who were believed to have opened up the territory to all kinds of plainsmen in the late medieval period. Their motive was personal. They wanted feudal grandeur. They had long been rajahs, it is true, but thought they did not seem like rajahs. This self-awareness of inferiority occurred when they compared themselves with the Hindu or Mughal princes of the plains. They set about bestowing magnificence on their princehood: they created a *durbar*, a court; they recruited officials to it; married out of tradition into the feudal Hindu families; asked Brahmans into the land to conduct religious services; and made extravagant purchases from Hindu, Muslim and Sikh traders from the plains to embellish their palaces. Understandably, unable to afford the services and the goods, they paid in land tenures. The court official, the attendant, the Brahman, the trader, all of them descended on the tribal society as landlords, as its princes proceeded to make themselves *real* princes.

It had started long before the British arrived. When they took the reins, conditions got worse, for they set revenue as their top priority; the number of landlords swelled and their cruelties reached a climax. Before the Chotanagpur rajahs sought feudal grandeur, all that the tribal peasant was expected to pay was a little tribute to the rajah of the day. Now he was forced to part with most of what he produced, as land rent and extra levies, which were entirely new categories of payment. Worse, the upstart landlords from the plains, besides extorting rents and *abwabs*, forced the tribal peasants to work on their stretches of agricultural land and in their households for many days in the year. It was from such barbarous immigrant masters that the Christian missionaries, eager for a moral foothold, elected to save the Mundas and other tribals in the last quarter of the nineteenth century.

Whenever the demand for Jharkhand was pressed, educated Biharis in and outside Congress pointed to the immigrant plainsmen: the response remains the same to this day (as does the accusation of a Christian conspiracy). The same Biharis, when they had to justify Bihar's separation as a province from Bengal, which, without a public movement, came about in 1912 after 18 years or so of a newspaper war between the Bihari and Bengali middle classes, would say that the people of Bihar had little in common with the people of Bengal; Bihar was being exploited, and its development neglected, in favour of Calcutta and other regions of Bengal, because of the prejudices of the Calcutta-based regime. Biharis were kept out of government jobs and the professions. Much of what was said about Bengal and the Bengalis, the tribals of Chotanagpur could say about them. Yet such an echo would be termed false: in Chotanagpur, Bihari eyes saw only the immigrant Biharis, not the natives. Some immigrants wrote as follows to the Government of India, opposing Jharkhand: 'The inhabitants of these (Chotanagpur's) districts are closely akin to the people of Behar. . . . The non-aboriginal population of Chota Magpore—so far as their spoken language, habits of life and social and religious customs are concerned—have no difference whatever from the people of the neighbouring districts of Behar.'[5]

Apart from the force of this Bihari cultural and linguistic *unity*, the tribals asking for Jharkhand ran a political risk. Those were the days of the movement to free India from the British. India had been created; national feelings were now very strong. The tribals, too, wanted the British to go. So, Jaipal Singh, then towering above all tribals in Chotanagpur because of his background, put forward a suggestion to the Congress leaders. He pointed out that he stood for India's independence and was ready to join hands with Congress to fight for it together. But, he said, there was one condition: Congress must agree to the demand for separation of Chotanagpur. His demand was turned down. To Congress, he was told, everything other than India's independence was secondary; let us first have national freedom, other things can wait; and the line of argument against Jharkhand changed accordingly. Creation of new provinces, said the premier, Sri Krishna Sinha, was beyond the powers of a provincial government, or even of the government of India of the time: it was a matter that 'entirely rested with the (British) Crown'. Such propositions as Jharkhand were, therefore, Sinha said, beyond the range of 'practical policies' in the then existing circumstances, as the 'ideal of reconstituting our provincial governments cannot be carried out until the Indian people have acquired full control over the Central government.'[6]

6. On the Move

The conflict of priorities

In the 1930s practical politics was a vogue expression in Bihar. Prime minister Sinha placed the separation of Chotanagpur beyond the range of practical politics. One newspaper wrote, after the provincial elections of 1937: 'The responsibilities of office have a great sobering effect, and we have little doubt that if the Congressmen in the Bihar Assembly decide to accept office they will have to abandon many of their pet theories. . . . In other words, they will enter the region of practical politics.'[1] Discussing the dearth of state finance, a non-Congress, Bihar politician, a Constitutionalist, lamented how the Permanent Settlement of land revenue had blocked the flow of resources from agriculture. 'But then', he said, 'revocation of the Permanent Settlement is not yet a matter of practical politics.'[2]

Generally, the expression stood for ordinary pragmatism: action possible under the given conditions; having first the things within your reach. It was said to be particularly necessary when running a ministry, making laws and taking decisions: you could not have at one and the same time the support of all classes of people. There could be no two opinions, said the advocates of practical politics, about the fact that 'changes' were needed for the making of a new society, but that did not mean instability and disorder and mob violence and destruction had necessarily to precede it. Everything, they said, had to be done in a constructive way.

It was hardly surprising to find that the voices of conscience belonged to the classes opposed to change. 'Practical politics' turned out to be the language of reaction, spoken by the *zamindars*, the immigrant oppressors in the tribal region, Constitutionalists, and Congressmen. But the Congressmen claimed that their concept of practical politics differed from all the others. For Congress, practical politics was not an ideology of no change. Congress stood for change; and when it referred to practical politics, it simply meant that as long as the British were there only so much change could be induced as was permitted by them. The Congressmen referred to it to make the people see their limitations, to bring home to them that though they had a ministry, they did not have the government. And, said the Congressmen, no matter how hard they tried, a fundamental change could not be brought about under those conditions. The Congress election manifesto of 1936 concluded: 'For the vast millions of our countrymen the problem of achieving national independence has become an urgent one, for only independence can give us the power to solve our economic and social problems and end the exploitation of our masses.'

Therefore, the tribal, the peasant in the Ganga plains of north and south Bihar, in fact everyone, would have to wait until India's independence, the future starting point of total revolution, for problems to be eliminated; all must follow the Congress programmes of action and look forward to the departure of the whites. At election meetings, the peasants wanting to attack the cruelties of the *zamindars* were told to put nationhood above all else. Addressing one such meeting in Patna, Nehru said that the candidates opposing the Congress in electoral constituencies were 'guided not by national interests', but included many who were denouncing the 'extremism'—attempts, they said, to bring instability and disorders—of the Kisan Sabha. This drawing of the line within the Congress bolstered up the *zamindars* who felt more and more that with enemies like Congressmen they did not need friends. As the *zamindars* (excepting a few diehard, frenzied individuals) and the Congressmen (except, of course, the socialists) clasped hands behind the curtain, Congress increasingly became averse to change. Inside the party, the socialists and the Kisan Sabha men saw through it and protested vigorously from time to time; they wanted quick action against the *zamindars* ; they agreed that the cause of national independence was supreme, but that people could not just wait in hope; there were things that could not be put off. The Kisan Sabha had already committed itself to the abolition of the Permanent Settlement, but the Congress, committed to practical politics, would not go beyond things possible under the given circumstances. In the election manifesto of 1936, the Congress made no reference to the Permanent Settlement. It said only:

> [The Congress] stands for a reform of the system of land tenure and revenue and rent, and an equitable adjustment of the burden on agricultural land, giving immediate relief to the smaller peasantry by a substantial reduction of agricultural rent and revenue now paid by them and exempting uneconomic holdings from payment of rent and revenue. . . .
>
> The question of indebtedness requires urgent consideration and the formulation of a scheme including the declaration of a moratorium, an enquiry into and scaling down of debts and the provision for cheap credit facilities by the State. This relief should extend to the agricultural tenants, peasant proprietors, small landholders and petty traders.

In Bihar, it was not just that the *zamindars* had begun manipulating Congress in the 1930s; they had done that from the very outset. They were among the founders of the provincial unit of the Congress in 1908. They attended the All-India Congress Committee sessions as Bihar delegates wherever they were held. When Gandhi came to Champaran in 1917 to investigate the excesses of the European indigo planters, they supported him, not because they sympathized with the oppressed peasants, but because the planters (though fellow landlords) were foreigners. It was not surprising that men of *zamindar* families became firmly placed within the Bihar Congress. To be a leader in those days certain abilities, such as writing and speaking English, being articulate, displaying a sober social self-pride, were essential, and no section of the people were better placed than the upper-class upper-caste men to develop those abilities by first acquiring Western education.

Yet it must be recorded here that, despite the fact that they were a creation of the British, and still in a relation of interdependence, and despite the fact that they, in most cases, would never want to cease to be landlords, there were many among the *zamindars* who were as strongly guided by patriotism. More particularly, small and middle-rank *zamindars* were influenced by it; and their patriotism had much more devotion and strength than that of the individual feudal rebels of the early British period in Bihar, or that of the *zamindars* in the forefront of the 1857 war. In the second quarter of the twentieth century, these *zamindars* would be known as 'Congress-minded'; but they had not detached themselves from class interests. They wanted the status quo: to be landlords even in free India. According to their philosophy, nationalism did not imply destruction of landlordism; the two were not incompatible or irreconcilable.

The *zamindar* influence with the Congressmen put the Kisan Sabha in a strange situation. The *zamindars* had men inside the party, and they also funded it. (As the daily *Indian Nation* often reminded people, *zamindars* 'fuelled and lubricated the Congress machine'.) At the same time, leading Bihar Congressmen were associated with the founding of the Kisan Sabha. Sri Krishna Sinha, who became prime minister in 1937, served as the Sabha's first general secretary. For quite some time Congress and the Sabha worked together to represent the peasants. But as the Sabha gradually moved forward into the villages, the Congressmen stayed behind. To be a 'Sabha-ite' now was to be 'dangerous'.[3]

Sahajanand and the Kisan Sabha

The Kisan Sabha had come into being in rather a strange way. Neither Swami Sahajanand nor the oppressed tenants of Bihar had consciously worked to form it. The Swami was not even a Bihari, but came from a village of Ghazipur district in the neighbouring United Provinces, not Uttar Pradesh state. Born into a minor *zamindar* family, growing up under elders who touched no food before bathing and bowing to the sun at day-break, beginning his studies under teachers who involved him in yoga exercises for several hours each day, in worshipping Shiva, and in the public recital of Tulsidas's *Ramayana*, he did well at his studies, and very early on married a young wife, who died leaving no child. Sahajanand, still a boy, already motherless, immediately after widowerhood left both school and home, when he was just sixteen, determined to become a monk. After a year of wandering, he arrived in Banaras. There, at one of the innumerable Hindu sect monasteries, he was tonsured, discarded the clothes of a village boy for a saffron robe and took the *guru-mantras* to enter the order.

After a two-year pilgrimage on foot to the great Hindu shrines, the young swami, back at his monastery in 1909, buried himself in the Vedic texts. For years he also studied the works of the schools of Indian philosophy, assiduously listening to lectures, interpreting grammar and the Shastras. He was still studying when he broke his solitude briefly in 1914 to travel to Ballia town, in Eastern

Uttar Pradesh, not far from Banaras, to give end-of-the-day lectures at a conference of the Bhumihar Brahman Mahasabha, the Great Assembly of the Bhumihar Brahmans. The Bhumihars were a landed upper caste, providing the largest number of *zamindars* to Bihar, but were socially ranked below the Brahmans and the Rajputs, which to them seemed to be a disgrace to their caste. Therefore, they had started calling themselves Bhumihar Brahmans in order to remind people that originally they had actually been Brahmans. At some point in history, they claimed, a section of the Brahmans, abandoning the priestly pursuit, turned to the cultivation of *bhumi* (land), and had thereafter been described as *Bhumihar* Brahmans. For the Bhumihar Brahman Mahasabha this was the greatest issue of the time, particularly because the Brahmans rejected the theory and would not accept them as Brahmans.

Ballia proved a revelation to Sahajanand, as he himself noted in his autobiography. He belonged to the Jujhautia sub-caste of the Brahmans, but this sub-caste, unlike most others, could intermarry with the Bhumihars. To the young swami, this was proof enough of the Brahman origin of the Bhumihars. After Ballia, he set out on a long tour; he went to Darbhanga, Bhagalpur, and Munger, areas in Bihar heavily populated by Brahmans and Bhumihars, to collect evidence of marital kinship between the two castes. At the end of his research, he wrote a book *Bhumihar Brahman Parichaya* (The Identity of Bhumihar Brahmans), 400 pages in length, which aimed to refute the Brahmans' view of the Bhumihars.

Within a short space of time, Sahajanand became the hero of the Bhumihar Brahman Mahasabha. He published two other books on the subject, and edited a journal, *Bhumihar Brahman*, from Banaras. But in the process, a change came over him. He was no longer like a monk, but someone moved by the problems of the human world outside the monastery. The caste status of the Bhumihars was the starting point; afterwards, other influences gripped him—the national movement, for instance. By 1920, travelling a lot to the rural parts of Bihar and Uttar Pradesh, lecturing and talking to people of all classes, reading newspapers, Sahajanand became convinced that Gandhi was right. He was particularly fascinated by Gandhi's advocacy of *swadeshi* (home-made) goods as a substitute for foreign, and also by his campaign of non-cooperation with the British government, asking peasants, for instance, not to pay rents.

Sahajanand now thought of joining the nationalist movement. There was no question of his giving up the fight to establish the Bhumihars' status as equal to the Brahmans'; struggles, including that for independence, could go on simultaneously at different levels. Once, shortly after he felt the urge to participate in the struggle for independence, Gandhi stayed for a while in Patna. Sahajanand first heard him speak at a small informal gathering and quickly sought an interview and asked Gandhi a number of questions; and by the time he left, noted one of Sahajanand's biographers, the young swami, at just over 30, became a Gandhi fanatic. He wore homespun dress, began to work at the spinning wheel and the spinning needle, and suggested that everyone should spin and wear *swadeshi*. He took part in the Congress programmes, went to jail, went back into action when released, and it was in the course of these activities that he came to understand the peasant agony a good deal more, and learned that the big *zamindars* were *raj-bhaktas*, loyalists of the Raj.

At the lower level, too, the struggle intensified. The Brahmans became more rigid and, as though to prove to the world the inferiority of the Bhumihars, the Brahman priests stopped going to Bhumihar homes to perform religious services. A slap in the face! The Bhumihars felt disgraced. Sahajanand, provoked, called to them to become priests themselves and perform their own religious services: forget the Brahmans, he cried. In a short time, in a few places in Bihar and Uttar Pradesh, *pathshalas* (schools) and *ashrams* (hermitages) sprang up to provide the teaching the religious books, services and hymns necessary for any Bhumihar to become a priest; these institutions were to keep growing in number. In Bihar's history it is known as *purohiti andolan*, the priesthood movement, and dated from 1924. It held a fantastic attraction, particularly for the young men of the Bhumihar caste, for it offered great possibilities for shattering the Brahman arrogance.

But Sahajanand's brainchild had its troubles, even within the Bhumihar Brahman Mahasabha. The rich and powerful Bhumihars trembled with anger, not because they were against cultural war with the Brahmans, nor because they were inimical to the activities or general philosophy of the Mahasabha, for they were, after all, its leading patrons, but because they were totally opposed to Bhumihar youths becoming priests. They saw the vocation of a priest as a lowly, demeaning, beggar-like vocation, the taking up of which, instead of inflicting injuries upon Brahman pride, wounded Bhumihar self-respect. Among these opponents was Sri Krishna Sinha (in those days it was not considered immoral for a nationalist to be actively associated with the organization of his caste) who derided the training of priests at a meeting of the Mahasabha.

As his participation in the Congress movement grew, Sahajanand had come to feel that the larger *zamindars* were *raj-bhaktas*, loyalists of the Raj, and he began to be convinced of this after the opposition they organized against the *purohiti andolan*. Leading the opposition was Ganesh Dutt Singh—a powerful *zamindar*, commonly regarded as the greatest caste leader of the Bhumihars of Bihar. He had long been a minister of the Imperial provincial government before the elections under limited democracy in 1937 had carried him off to the position of leader of the opposition in the provincial assembly. As the *production* of Bhumihar priests proceeded apace, Ganesh, soon to be Sir Ganesh, one day sent for the swami. In his sitting-room, in front of his courtiers, he showered abuse on the swami: 'You always lead the Bhumihars along the wrong path. First you encouraged our young men to leave their schools and colleges and take part in the Congress activities so that they ended by rotting in the jails. And now, you are working to destroy those that remain by preparing them for the job of beggars!' The swami, too, lost his temper. A person like Ganesh, the swami jeered, had no right to have any say in these matters; he had sold out to the foreigners. Quoting a pithy Hindi saying, he said: 'Someone who strangles the nation to aid the British ought to take water in the cup of his palm and drown himself in it.'

From then on, Ganesh and Sahajanand became great enemies. Ganesh, from a Bhumihar caste chief, would develop as the leader of the Bhumihar *zamindars*, and Sahajanand, from the hero of the Bhumihar Brahman Mahasabha, became the tribune of the Bihar peasants. In Bihar society there were already conflicts arising from *zamindari* that cut across castes, and this was now reflected in the Mahasabha. In 1927, during his unflagging campaign for religious tuition for Bhumihars, Sahajanand established an *ashram* at Bihta, then under an hour by rail from Patna. There he listened sympathetically to the tenants from various, mostly lower castes who, politely disregarding what the *ashram* was meant for, and finding a holy man had come to live in their area, approached him from the nearby villages to tell him their tales of woe. He tried to do whatever was possible for them, like advising the *zamindars* to relieve some of their pressure, and the *ashram* at Bihta soon became known as a centre of disaffection. Within months of its inauguration, circumstances compelled Sahajanand to form a local peasant body, the West Patna Kisan Sabha. No sooner did the *ashram* start encouraging peasant unrest than some rich and powerful Bhumihars, who had been aiding it financially, thinking it was advancing the interests of their caste, stopped supporting it. The swami reacted with typical earthiness: 'I piss on such dirty money.'

Out of his Banaras monastery emerged an ideologue of the Bhumihars, a determined nationalist and a peasant sympathizer, but the monk in him was not yet dead. After a burst of activity at the Bihta *ashram*, which saw complaints reaching the landlords and government officials and some follow-up by them, the swami went into seclusion. He spent two years of solitude at different places in Bihar and Uttar Pradesh. Then he returned to the world. And he heard now a good deal more about the machinations of Sir Ganesh to have his way in the Mahasabha. The Mahasabha was holding its 1929 conference at Munger, in Eastern Bihar; Sir Ganesh was at the helm, and the swami had not been invited.

The swami went to Munger but stayed away from the venue of the conference. Word travelled that he was there, and some of the delegates came to persuade him to join; no, he said to them. He was, however, the jewel of the Mahasabha movement and a large number of delegates clamoured to know why Swami Sahajanand had been kept out. Sir Ganesh shouted back from the rostrum that the working of the Mahasabha did not depend on any single person: so much commotion followed that Sir Ganesh hurried down from the rostrum and disappeared from the conference. Some delegates then went back to the swami and brought him to the conference, to an ovation. He walked up to the rostrum and gave a speech proclaiming that the Bhumihar Mahasabha Brahman had outlived its usefulness and stood dissolved from that day forward, forever.

And in the winter of the same year, at the great annual cattle fair at Sonepur, across the Ganga from Patna—a fair where peasants from all parts of Bihar crowded in to buy and sell cows, bullocks, buffaloes, ponies (and elephants, for the *rajahs* and *zamindars* a status symbol) and lived in make-shift huts for days, sleeping beside heaps of animal dung—some leading Bihar Congressmen, together with the swami, announced the birth of the Bihar Provincial Kisan Sabha for the protection of the interests of the tenantry.

Charismatic leaders

The cause that Sahajanand now championed as president of a province-level peasant organization—the wish of the peasants to give as little as possible for their produce, against the greed of the *zamindars* to extract as much as possible—was the one that the leaders of the nineteenth century tribal insurrections, Siddhu the Santhal and Birsa the Munda, had defended with arms. In some ways, Sahajanand, Siddhu and Birsa resembled each other: each carried the peasants with them, as if by a spell. No other way of 'organizing' the peasants could have, perhaps, been possible in those times and in these parts. The people were extremely religious; only provocation by messengers of God could move them to action. What the leaders therefore seemed to represent was the primary stage of peasant consciousness.[4]

This consciousness was orthodox, backward-looking, limited. Yet it represented, in itself, no small development of the peasant mind. The peasants still believed that God could destroy the Evil and build the Good, but they had gone one step ahead in believing that God alone could not do it; that, to get back to a life of happiness, to end their woes, they too had to make an effort. It was with 'direct' messages from God who made an Appearance that both Siddhu and Birsa had been able to persuade the masses of tormented tribals to act. Sahajanand claimed no vision of God, but the very fact that he was a Hindu monk in monk's clothing with shaven head, linemarks of sandalwood paste across the forehead, the two-piece saffron robe, a hollowed, long, thin bamboo staff—and the fact that he had been touring the countryside lecturing on Hinduism held a magic in itself for the peasant in the plains of Bihar.

And, like Siddhu and Birsa to their own tribal 'nations', Sahajanand was a fearless, devout Indian patriot. Each of them wanted, and made people want, freedom. There was, however, a distinction between them: the Santhals and the Mundas were told they could never be free unless all outsiders and immigrants were thrown out of their land; the question of the freedom of the peasant was inalienably linked to the aim of independence for Daman-i-Koh or Ranchi. In the plains, this idea had been appropriated by the Congress: first, India to ourselves, and then everything will follow; all liberation pivoted on national liberation. This idea produced 'practical politics'. Sahajanand, as he saw more and more of social conditions, became staunchly opposed to it. Independence of the nation should be our highest aim, he argued, but it would be callous to postpone aims like putting an end to the oppression of the *zamindars*.

Even though all three, Sahajanand, Siddhu and Birsa, had a halo of religion around them, there was much more to the movements than that; none of them saw himself as a messiah, there was a design in what each did, a worthy technique; each had closely experienced the tragic living conditions of the peasant. Moved and agitated by that experience, each searched for a way to awaken the peasant out of his fatalism, and succeeded by using recognizable symbols that could excite the peasant. Siddhu, as well as his three brothers, knew what kind of Thakur had descended from the sky over his hut; Birsa plastered himself from head to toe with an oil and turmeric mix in order to mesmerize the

Mundas with a golden body. They invented a mystique. In Sahajanand the mystique was contained in the saffron. As Sahajanand himself once said: 'This saffron robe has been deceiving people for a long time. Let it be used at least once for their good.'

The Kisan Sabha

About the time that the Bihar Provincial Kisan Sabha was founded at the Sonepur cattle fair, the worst disaster ever threw the peasants off their feet. Already reeling under the weight of the *zamindars*' demands, the peasants were struck with horror as they found, during the Great Depression, which shook economies the world over, that the country-town merchants in Bihar (as in other parts of India) were no longer interested in buying grain or any other agricultural produce. Grain prices fell and fell, year after year, month after month to end, in December 1930, at a level two-thirds of that offered in October 1930;[5] and between 1929 and 1931 the price of rice-paddy, then the main crop, fell by half, a reduction that plummeted overall grain prices to the level of the 1890s. It was disastrous for those tenants who, when the returns from the grain market had risen earlier in the century, had agitated for 'commutation' of rent, paying the *zamindars* in cash rather than in grain.

But rents were to be extracted in every way possible. All the petitions with which the government's district offices were inundated, all those entreaties for remission, reduction, or even suspension, of the rents, fell on stony ground. 'Throughout the Depression', it was found, 'the land revenue collection was almost always more than 90 per cent of the total demand.'[6] If the *zamindars* were able to turn over 90 per cent of total revenue demanded to the government, it does not need much imagination to see how unmercifully they scoured the countryside for money. As some accounts of the period show, the peasants raised money from the moneylenders, and cut down on basic expenses, for if they did not pay the rents they might fall into arrears which, at the *zamindars*' arbitrary rates of interest, could soar in no time and bring the *zamindars*' men to distrain the defaulter's assets and throw him on the street. But even if a peasant managed to pay his rent he was given no receipt. The same old, tragic story, now running through the melodrama of Depression: meetings held by the Kisan Sabha cried out for valid receipts, but, first things first, they cried out more for the remission or reduction or suspension of the rents, and still more particularly for a reduction which corresponded with the fall on the market in grain prices.

In Shahabad district the issue of canal irrigation rates agitated the peasants during the Depression. One of the oldest canal systems that the British had built, on the Sone river in southern Bihar had, no doubt, benefited the peasants by increasing their productivity. The government, whose officials collected the canal rent directly, had steadily raised it year by year. As the Depression set in productivity lost its meaning. The peasants wanted their rent for irrigation reduced but they could not summon enough courage to fight for it on their own. They did make some feeble individual efforts, but the British officers turned down the appeal. All that the Kisan Sabha and the Congress had to do (and actually did) was to send teams into rural Shahabad to ask the peasants to assemble at selected places to offer evidence, or sign the mass petitions. After that the Kisan Sabha and the Congress demanded the reduction of the canal rates to the level of the 1890s since the grain prices had now dropped to that level. (The canal rent per acre in the 1930s was five times than in the 1890s.) The demand was rejected by the government, and the rejection was accompanied by a threat that if the peasants refused to pay the rates fixed, the government would proceed to confiscate their properties.

In its initial years the Kisan Sabha pursued no action. It almost wholly concentrated on public meetings addressed by its leaders, especially the swami—often provocatively and, on investigation (like the one on the tyrannies of the rajah of Tekari and the rajah of Amawan, both in Gaya district in southern Bihar, written jointly by the swami and a second-rank Sabha leader, Pandit Jamuna Karyee) reported on by teams or committees to publicize local griev-ances. But considering the times, those speeches and meetings and probe reports, rather than proving useless as tools of protest, yielded a positive result. Pockets of peasants became activated, and the concerned *zamindars* hurriedly sent alarm signals to the government officers.

With peasant awareness growing, the Sabha tried other means. At Tekari, where the rajah was demanding payment of all arrears together with the year's rent—an impossible demand—a large demonstration was held to oppose it. Later, demonstrations were organized in several other places in the province. The issues were almost the same everywhere: high rents in the days of Depres-sion, *abwabs*, the manner of division of the crop between the *zamindar* and the tenant where produce rents prevailed, the rapacity and excesses of the *zamindar's* employees and retainers, increasing rents for deteriorating soil in the areas badly affected by floods and soil erosion and other natural influences—and, of course, the constant denial of lease records or rent receipts.

There was agitation also by the sugar-cane growers around Dalmia's sugar mill at Bihta, where Sahajanand's *ashram* was. When Dalmia, his head adorned with the boat-shaped white Congress cap, had first arrived at Bihta to make his investment, he seemed to have made a good impression on Sahajanand. He had a mission, said Dalmia to the swami, and the required zeal: he wanted to open a sugar mill in Bihta because he, a nationalist Indian businessman, wanted to eliminate the European company running a sugar mill there and exploiting the cane-growers. It sounded excellent to Sahajanand, and he assured Dalmia of his full co-operation. He helped Dalmia to get the land for his mill, while Dalmia, the 'missionary' capitalist kept sending small donations to Sahajanand's *ashram* to strengthen their bonds. But Dalmia, when his mill was on its feet, stunned everybody by paying the cane-growers much less than the European 'exploiters' were paying. The swami was furious and the peasants retaliated; the ox cartloads of cane ceased to arrive at Dalmia's mill gate. Not long after the boycott, the 'patriotic' businessman, on his knees, agreed to pay the peasants higher rates. And the swami stopped accepting Dalmia's donations.

But twisting Dalmia's arm was one thing, bringing the *zamindars* to heel another. The *zamindars* were, no doubt, growing afraid of the Sabha, but its activities, even the mass rallies, had not brought the peasants much actual gain. The situation on the ground called for stronger action. In some parts of the province peasant militancy was beginning to develop, but Congress continued to practise its practical politics. Although they were among the founder members of the Sabha, leading Congressmen isolated themselves from its activities, dealing only superficially with the peasant question. With the Sabha going more deeply into it, it was inevitable that the two should go their separate ways.

Amid isolation and desperation, the Sabha had to move into direct action. This, in the first place, was resistance to ejection by the *zamindars*. Peasants in areas of growing militancy squatted on strips of land which they had tilled long enough to be entitled to own; for the first time, on a big scale, the tenancy reform laws were actually applied in practice—by the peasants themselves. This squatting was called *satyagraha*, insistence on truth, Gandhi's famous weapon of non-violence. But, as things turned out, on the actual spot, the truth-seeking peasant squatters, face to face with the retainers of the *zamindar*, freely employed clubs, farming tools and cutting weapons to chase off the *satyagraha*-breakers.

And when, at peasant rallies, the swami on the speakers' rostrum, raising his own hallowed bamboo staff in the air, cried, *'Latth hamara zindabad'* (Long live our Staffs) it turned into a war-cry. The peasants doggedly held on to the land they considered their own, and recaptured the pieces of land the *zamindars* on one pretext or another had taken away from them in the past years. Even the court orders declaring the squatting 'illegal' could not make them leave. The *zamindars'* men who came armed with orders for evacuation were greeted with cries of *'Latth hamara zindabad'* . The Congressmen were much alarmed, and made it known that Congress was not a party to such activities. Such was their concern that there were moves to throw Swami Sahajanand out of the Congress Party. The Premier, Sri Krishna Sinha, had, through official intelligence, discovered to his amazement and shock that much of the land in the province which the *zamindars* should have got 'legally' vacated was 'in actual cultivating possession of tenants' whom (such was the effect of the action) the *zamindars* were 'steadily attempting to dispossess.'[7]

The executive committee of the provincial Congress called a meeting to censure the swami for 'incitement to violence'. The swami, himself a member of the executive, remained uninformed about the meeting: he resigned in disgust from membership of Congress. It was a period of heightened tensions between the two organizations: Congress, after a year in government, was congratulating itself on various amendments to the tenancy laws which it had got passed through the provincial legislature; and meanwhile the swami was issuing books and pamphlets and touring the countryside saying that nothing would come out of this pile of legislation; that all the amendments would be useless because they had evolved from a great compromise between the Congress and Sir Ganesh, the *zamindars'* leader. It was also a period when the men of the Congress Socialist Party, the organization of social democrats created under the Congress in 1934, and the communists and the radicals from the Forward Bloc Party, were working jointly under the banner of the Kisan Sabha in a determined effort to give the Sabha a leftist, direct-action, orientation; while the All-India Congress Committee, understandably influenced by the views expressed by the Bihar delegates, passed at its Haripura session of February 1938 a long resolution excerpted here:

> In view of certain difficulties that have arisen in regard to the Kisan Sabha and other organisations in some parts of India the Congress desires to clarify the position and state its attitude in regard to them. The Congress has already fully recognised the right of kisans to organise themselves in peasant unions. Nevertheless it must be remembered that the Congress *itself* is in the main a Kisan organisation and as contact with the masses has increased, vast numbers of kisans have joined it and influenced its policy. The Congress must stand, and has, in fact, stood for these Kisan masses and championed their claims, and has worked for the independence of India which must be based on the freedom from exploitation of all our people. . . .
>
> While fully recognising the right of the kisans to organise Kisan Sabhas, the Congress cannot associate itself with any activities which are *incompatible* with the basic principles of the Congress and will not countenance any of the activities of those Congressmen who as members of the Kisan Sabha help in creating an atmosphere hostile to Congress principles and policy.

The case of the untouchables

The Congress had adopted an identical approach to the question of untouchables. Just as it abhorred any other organization politically appropriating and stimulating action by the peasants, so it reacted to endeavours by others to organize the untouchable labourers. Not only was Congress, according to the Congressmen, itself 'in the main a kisan organisation'; it also had to be the one and only organization for the untouchables. In fact, the Congress was run by upper-class upper-caste men and its love for the untouchables was suddenly born out of the announcement in August 1932, of a Communal Award by the British prime minister. This divided Indians eligible to vote into separate electorates, mainly on the grounds of religion: Hindus, Mohammedans, Depressed Classes (as the British preferred to call the unclean castes) and Europeans. The Congressmen instantly reacted against the Award; they particularly disliked making the Depressed Classes into a separate electorate. The Award, they loudly protested, in dividing the Indian electorate had divided Hindu society itself. When did the untouchables stop being Hindus? they asked the British government. (The question, when did the Hindus begin treating untouchables as a part of themselves? was flung back at the Congressmen even then.)

Less than one month after the announcement of the Award, a period of intense Hindu unrest, Gandhi began a fast-unto-death, determined not to let the untouchables have a separate electorate: neither he nor the Hindus would care if the Mohammedans had one. As the Hindu Mahatma started to spend his days without food, there began an unending procession of Congress leaders to the residence of Bhimrao Ambedkar, the brilliant and unyielding exponent of basic rights for the untouchables, an untouchable himself, educated, a powerful polemical writer. The Congress leaders wanted him to agree that a separate electorate for the untouchables should be revoked. They begged him to consider the Mahatma, starving and stricken with grief; they told him of the deep pain the Award had caused them, and they took a vow in front of him to wipe untouchability from the face of India. In the end, Ambedkar yielded, after which the famous Poona Pact was signed between the two sides, and forwarded to the British government for approval.

In the changed arrangement, in place of a separate untouchable electorate, in which all the electors as well as all the candidates in the constituencies were untouchables, there would now be 'reserved' constituencies where only the untouchables would be entitled to run the election, but the electorate would be mixed, comprising people of all castes living in a constituency area. It was obvious from this that the Hindus were not opposed to men from the unclean castes becoming public representatives or politicians: what had horrified them about the Communal Award was the thought of untouchables needing only the votes of the untouchables to elect themselves, of the untouchables turning into a self-dependent political community, whereas if the untouchable contestant had to seek support from a mixed electorate he would never be sectarian. If he looked only to the unclean castes for votes, he ruined his chances. There was no doubt that those Congressmen, by persuading Ambedkar to accept the new scheme, scored a great Hindu coup, and proved themselves worthy owners of the machinating, far-sighted, high-caste mind. For never, even in free India, could an untouchable politician develop whose political fate was not in caste Hindu hands, in the landed dominant castes of the constituency; like a kite he could fly, but only if a superior hand did not cut the supporting string.

After the pact, Gandhi broke his fast. The very next morning there began an untouchability Abolition Week all over India. On its fourth day an All India Anti-Untouchability League was formed, whose head office would be in Delhi and whose branches in the provinces sprang up at an amazing rate. It was, as it were, a marathon festival of Hindu brotherhood; the days witnessed an astonishing amount of Congress activity. Untouchable labourers were conducted with ceremony into temples, places which had been *sacred* since time immemorial; were brought to join communal singing of devotional songs in the villages; asked to communal banquets; taken to participate in rural games and to receive prizes; ushered to the common wells in the villages to draw water; asked to stand and watch as caste Hindu residents in the village swept the labourers' quarters; and persuaded to send their children to attend schools on Congress scholarships. The list of achievements mailed to the Delhi head office by the Bihar provincial board of the Anti-Untouchability League was never-ending. Bathed by this newly sprung fountain of love, the poor labourers must have felt quite stupefied.

But Gandhi urged the Hindus: remove untouchability, *purify* yourselves. When he came to Patna two months after the great Bihar earthquake of 15

January 1934 (which killed about 20,000 people and levelled almost 76,000 square kilometres) Gandhi said the calamity was 'a divine chastisement sent by God for our sins' and particularly, the 'sin of untouchability'.[8]

Some hints that very few Congressmen and Congress-influenced Hindus wanted to undergo this sort of self-purification were apparent from the progress report of the Anti-Untouchability League's provincial board itself. Covering the very first year of its work, 1932-33, the report said: 'District committees of the League were formed in fourteen districts, in the fifteenth the matter was under consideration; committees organised district conferences in seven of the fourteen districts; 236 temples were opened to untouchables; a new temple was opened for them, another was under way; about 600 untouchables entered schools [mixed?—it is not clear in the report] no fewer than 3,000 untouchable students were sent to five girls' schools and 113 day or night schools; regular sports teams were formed amongst untouchables; a football championship was held with awards of a silver shield and medal; 646 wells opened up to untouchables, nine new wells dug for them, 14 other new ones were under construction.' So it went on. Judging from the report, the uplift of the untouchables took two distinct lines: one, of the symbolic, short-lived communing during the festival of Hindu brotherhood: and the second, which was revealing and dangerous, and emerged as the line of expediency by patriotic Hindus, was that of separate temples, separate schools, separate sports teams, and separate championships and separate wells of water. The same people who had so frantically opposed a separate electorate for the untouchables would end as advocates of the idea of giving them a separate life—almost caste apartheid!

Almost all the untouchables worked as landless labourers: men, women and children. There were people of other lower, but touchable, castes who also worked in this way, but the untouchables were the majority. They were on the lowest rung of the village social ladder. Moreover they had been nailed there: not one step could they move up. It was futile, for instance, for any of them to think of opening a grocery shop or a betel stall if he had the resources; only the untouchables would buy from him. Occupations were closed to them, and so were the Hindu homes.

But there were moments when the Hindu doors half-opened, for example when the Chamar leatherworker waited outside with shoes made to order or when the Dom scavenger came to deliver the baskets and trays woven by him with strings of bamboo. These baskets and trays, in addition to being in everyday use in the Hindu kitchen, were indispensable to all such pious occasions as marriages or religious festivals. Goods brought by these craftsmen were, no doubt, washed before use with buckets of water—but not the shoes: clever people, these Hindus! And, for example, when women were in labour (and in the large extended families of those days there were frequent births) it was the Chamain, the leatherworker's wife, who was called in as midwife; she was led into the female quarter of the house, past other rooms, to deliver the child or children who, even as toddlers, learned not to touch her. She was also remembered at the time of a marriage when she cut the women's fingernails and toenails and applied henna to the soles of their feet. In so far as prohibited entry into the house was concerned, she was, for instance, luckier than the wife of the Dom basket-maker who, like her husband, was never allowed in. But birthpangs and marriages were the only occasions and after these the doors were slammed shut.

A separate, peripheral, dehumanized existence of a whole segment of the population—yet rooted in a Hindi society which could not do without them, but which did not want them near it.

Together with the lower, but touchable caste labourers, the untouchables were classed under three broad categories:[9] *naukar* or *ghulam* or slave; *kamia* or semi-slave, and *majur*, free workers. The slave, man or woman, could be bought and sold for a few rupees: a down-and-out person, deeply in debt, could sell himself or his child as a slave to his creditor in the hope of clearing the debt. The semi-slaves (the same *kamias* about whom we learnt something in Chapter 4) were, technically, recruited to operate ploughs for a whole year, on a contract—a contract without papers which, in most cases, inevitably lasted longer than a year and eventually coiled around them like a python. Hindu society refused to rid itself of untouchability. Gandhi could do nothing about it. The Congressmen did not bother about untouchables once they had manoeuvred them into a politically powerless, subordinate, role. Towards the close of the 1930s, the Kisan Sabha had acquired a leftist orientation, and had been distanced from the Congress; but even the Sabha could not reach out to the untouchables. Although it was Sahajanand's omnibus definition that a *kisan* was anyone from a landless labourer to the petty *zamindar*, the Sabha, plodding along with an overload of peasant problems on its back, was never to be able to pay close attention to the plight of the landless labourers. Contradictions were obvious in Sahajanand's definition itself: for among their employers, the landless had not only the petty *zamindars* but also the larger tenants, who had the attitude, hard to change, of employers. So the Kisan Sabha could do no more than pass resolutions urging the *zamindars* and tenants to fix reasonable wages, write off the debts and improve the working conditions of the labourers.

Of course, the Sabha's priorities were with the tenants. It wanted tenants and landless labourers to work together to fight the *zamindars*. 'Both the peasants and agricultural labourers [ought to] realise', the Sabha reminded them, 'the great and growing need of their united front against all the powerful vested interests which have been crushing them both for ages past.'[10] The appeal was fruitless because the labourers were not yet awakened. There probably was only one occasion when, under the Sabha banner, landless and peasants had joined together; but even then, the landless did not fight as labourers. The issue was not of wages or debts or working conditions. It was the agitation, famous in Sabha history, of Barahiya Tal, a vast expanse within Munger district which in the rainy season was submerged by the floods of the Ganga. The water receding left a thick deposit of fertile alluvial soil to yield rich winter crops such us wheat. A number of tenants there had been turned off their strips of land by the *zamindars* on various grounds, mainly of outstanding rents. Among them, also, were those landless servants who had, choosing their masters' moments of magnanimity, begged their way into tiny tenures.

Tenancy laws had proved of no help to the ejected. The Barahiya Tal agitation, which the tenants, led by the Kisan Sabha, doggedly carried on for some time, also laid bare the emptiness of the Congress ministry's amendments to the tenancy laws; the *zamindars* were never forced to put them into practice. And, though small gains resulted from the leftist militancy in the Tal (some tenants grabbed back the strips they were ejected from) actual relief to the peasants was to be given only by the abolition of the Permanent Settlement in 1956, about 20 years after the Tal agitation had started and about six years after the death of Swami Sahajanand.

But the Tal remained an exception. Unity between the peasants and the labourers could not be forged by the Kisan Sabha. And when, in the mid-1940s, one or two organizations of and for the landless labourers began to be formed in the province, the Sabha leaders reacted against it. Rahul Sanskrityayan, a close associate of Sahajanand's, Marxist, USSR-returned and Russophile, one of the founders in 1939 of the Bihar provincial unit of the Communist Party of India, a Hindi writer of great renown, especially as a travel writer, essayist and polemicist, gave a bitter judgement on the organizations of the landless. These organizations, he said, had been fathered by the *zamindars* of Bihar with the aim of dividing their main enemy, the peasantry.

Rahul's essays give the reader an insight into how the Sabha was then thinking about the labour question. Unless the Permanent Settlement ended, Rahul concluded, there could be no solution to the problems of the agricultural labourers. Although he was aware that there were formidable problems: mainly, of wages and land, he argued that for the peasants to be able to receive higher and reasonable wages, they needed to be disburdened of the heavy demands of the *zamindar*; that alone could pave the way for improved farm practices, better investment, good returns from the land—and higher wages.

As for the distribution of pieces of land for cultivation by the landless, it was neither easy nor possible at the time, Rahul opined, because in most districts of the Bihar plains, and more particularly in the districts of North Bihar, there was barely any land vacant or existing as wasteland; the land use in these parts (Rahul based his view not on any researched data but on his personal observation) had almost reached saturation point. If there still were strips of land in these parts—and they, of course, were immeasurably vast taken together—which could be made available to the landless labourers, they were what the *zamindars* had come to possess fraudulently. Or—and here Rahul's suggestion was very strange, revealing his ignorance of tribal life and politics, and of the questions of land and peasant freedom in that part of Bihar; ignorance, in a word, about the tribal sensitivities—the landless labourers from the plains should be taken *en masse* to settle in Chotanagpur 'where the aborigines populated villages which were quite sparse'.

And here the writer presented his Marxist theory and vision: 'The rights of the peasants and the agricultural labourers, no doubt, demand sympathy, and another way to change them has to be found. But we must bear in mind that we cannot bring about all revolutions in one go.'[11] Of course, the problems of the labourers could finally be solved only under Communism which, in the 1940s,

Rahul said he foresaw would come sooner or later.

We shall see in the following pages the shape things took in the Bihar countryside after Independence.

Part Three

Roads To Freedom

7. The Jesus Path

The rise of liberation theology

Enlightenment, renaissance, moral renovation of Hindu society—that was how the Christian missionaries spoke of their mission in colonial India. But the Hindus as a whole, even as voiceless colonials, never looked upon the missionaries except with suspicion and contempt. So, in setting out to renovate, the missionaries concentrated upon the tribals and low-caste Hindus, communities exterior to and oppressed under Hinduism, people whom the missionaries described as those who actually had no religion. To these people, and indirectly also the Hindus who shunned them, the missionaries brought many new things from the West: schools which, unlike the Hindu *pathshala*, or even the Muslim *madrasa*, not only gave lessons in religion and in rudimentary arithmetic, but also taught geography, the sciences, and Western ideas as well as the gospel. They also brought printing presses (for the first time) which published in regional languages, the actual local dialects whose script, grammar and alphabets were developed by these same devoted missionaries. And, with the growth of these schools and printing presses, several changes were to come to colonial India.

Historical evidence has it that for the missionaries, *renaissance* in India could be based on two beliefs: one in Jesus, another in the Raj. Among the non-British missionaries there were some who did not work towards establishing native allegiance to the Raj. The colonial government, realizing this, made it obligatory for missionaries coming to India from countries outside the British empire to sign a 'neutrality pledge', in which they had to promise never to interfere in the political matters of the colony. But the rest, particularly the British, had set allegiance-building as an aim. They constantly reminded the colonial government, records inform us, that it should let its officers 'co-operate' with them in order to eliminate chances of insurrection by segments of the native population. The schools, the printing presses, other schemes of development, and the large scale conversions, were steps towards the consolidation of the Raj. By the beginning of the twentieth century, however, unintended consequences flowed from these actions. Indians acquired political awareness and started to oppose the Raj.

After Independence, the missionaries were not wanted, conversions dwindled, the government of free India put visa restrictions on their entry, and there was a Hindu backlash. What was more, simultaneously with these external blows came an attack from within; the new cry was: Indigenize the church. The native men within the Indian church said it should be run by Indians: the foreign missionaries—whose total number, in 1947—British, European, and American—was put at 5,000, must go. To back up their demand the natives disclosed the fact that the foreign missionary had never endeared himself to them. He had never shown an inclination to mix with his Indian fellows: he had always led a separate life, in a well-appointed bungalow with European or American standards and food habits, rarely socializing. He had controlled all the funds and was the boss of the institutions under his charge. In short, said the natives, the foreign missionary had been a benevolent autocrat giving order from the 'Little Europe' or 'Little America' of his residence.

The foreign missionaries went away. But the decolonization of the Indian church produced no revolution. In the years to follow, the Indians who formed the establishment of the Indian church, discovering no great role for themselves in society, settled down to running institutions such as hospitals, schools, colleges, and properties, chiefly in land. But decolonization of what is now known as the Third World, which unfortunately mostly installed self-serving and repressive local regimes allowing Western exploitation through imperialism created a crisis everywhere for the church: a crisis of relevance. An establishment as orthodox as the Vatican also began to change, though very cautiously. At the Second Vatican Council in the mid-1960s, Counter Reformation was pronounced at an end: it was time to have a 'new positive dialogue with other faiths'. The Pope himself set the seal upon the new orientation, which was described as *modernization*, almost a religious revolution.

With this change, the Jesuits (once the vanguard of the defence of the Catholic faith) opened up. In the thirty-first General Congregation of the Jesuits in 1965, held at about the time of the Second Vatican, a new mood for change was observed. At the thirty-second General Congregation, nine years later, the Jesuits decided to go forward in the direction of 'revolutionary changes', to continue 'to do battle against the ravages to humanity brought about by unjust structures'. For them to be accepted in a pluralistic society, the Jesuits felt that 'something charismatic and central to the world condition needs to be deliberately sought out and assiduously pursued'. More precisely, 'given the signs of the times and the emphatic appeals of social movements in many parts of the world [our legitimacy] can be found in solidarity with the poor and in a minority battle for the rights of the disenfranchised. . . . '

But, later, Vatican authorities were to cry out in horror as they saw some of the Catholics going too far, especially in the countries of Latin America. These Catholics allied themselves with the revolutionary movements there and preached an ideology—which its practitioners called 'the theology of liberation' after the Peruvian priest, Gustavo Gutierrez, wrote a book with that title in 1971—that drew inspiration from the godless ideology of Marxism. Since 1984, the Vatican has been making serious attempts to stamp out liberation theology, but without much success.

In India, too, liberation theology influenced a section of the Jesuits and sections also of other Catholic orders such as the Society of Medical Mission Sisters. This was a society established in 1925 by a nun in Rawalpindi to help

Pakistani women. It is now trying to reach the poor after realizing that its hospitals, providing specialized medical care, attracted only wealthy patients. Liberation theology has not yet generated much literature in India, but its Indian proponents hope to evolve an Indian theology of liberation to suit local conditions. In 1977 a book, *Jesus and Freedom* was published, which its author, Sebastian Kappen, a Jesuit writer who also gives occasional lectures, described as the 'fruit of more than a decade of anguishing search for relevance' of the Christian faith. What is needed first of all, says Kappen, is 'lifting' of Jesus from the cultic, dogmatic and institutional morass where He had been dumped ever since the fourth century when Emperor Constantine of Rome proclaimed Christianity Rome's state religion, a proclamation that reversed the Jesus movement which was 'predominantly of the poorer classes in Palestine and the Greco-Roman world'.

Looking at contemporary India, Kappen finds capitalism holding the reins of the national economy (though feudalism in some form or the other does persist) and generating a culture of consumerism, a culture where a man's concept of happiness consists in 'having something which his neighbour does not have'. Kappen deals at length with forms of exploitation and cruelties and the failure of all the Indian political parties—even of the left—to put a stop to them, and proceeds to lay down what could perhaps be a Christian manifesto. Capitalism, he says, can be destroyed by 'socialization'—Kappan avoids the world Socialism—under which 'society as a whole determines, at the various levels of its organisation, the ownership and use of the productive forces'. Kappen's vision of a new society is of one with decentralized power and decision-making, with 'initiatives from below', not with the State ruling by 'dictates from above'. Since India is a vast country with many religions, races and regional cultures, each having 'its own distinctive genius', Kappen would want the new society to allow each of them to grow and bear fruit'.

As for ways to accomplish this vision, there have been, admits the Jesuit writer, movements in the past to oppose existing conditions. Such movements have had the Marxist parties 'in the vanguard', but there was also *Sarvodaya*, the Gandhian movement, which championed the cause of the oppressed, 'especially in Bihar', and there were also 'critical individuals and groups', some to be found even within the Congress party. Keeping this in view the Christian strategy, according to Kappen, should be twofold. First, the Christians have to create a 'new socio-political movement of liberation', which has to be peaceful, adopting only methods of strikes, demonstrations, non-cooperation and civil disobedience. Secondly, there should be alliance with others. The disciples of Jesus have to 'make every form of legitimate protest in the country their own'. Although they should not be identified with any of them, they should not ignore the faction-ridden, feuding radical movements (an allusion presumably to the Naxalites); they should offer 'critical collaboration' to the factions on issues where there is sufficient consensus and also try to provide a common platform where radicals of different convictions can meet and sort out their differences.

Life in Jamsaut

Within the huddle of the low clay huts at Jamsaut, the socially unclean Musahars appeared to be leading an infinitely carefree life. Their little naked children squatted and played in the dust of the narrow lanes. There was dust wherever you looked in Jamsaut: in matted heads of hair, on faces, on bodies, on the clothes, in the windowless hut, on the floor and on the walls, upon the bed and on the hundred-times mended and patched counterpanes, on the cooking pots and aluminium dishes buckled by use, and on the palms and fingers with which food was put in the mouth. The Musahars were completely at ease with their squalor.

They, unlike Muslims, were pork eaters, but still Hindus in the Hindu eye. They didn't need to buy pork—no butcher, in any case, sold it openly for fear of hurting Muslim sensibilities. Every family raised its own local poor, dark-grey breed of pig. The pigs were housed in a little covered hole by the hut, and they fed principally on human faeces, or at times on pickings from a litter heap. In the hot season the Musahars went out in groups in search of fish; they went long distances looking for drying puddles on public land. Finding one, they trudged about in the mud for hours grabbing the little finger-sized fish that failed to hide themselves under the diminishing water. In the landowners' fields, after harvest, the Musahars explored the holes for field rats and the grains which these sizeable little animals gleaned and stored in their holes. Rat meat was also relished in Jamsaut.

Jamsaut, where 130 families lived, the Musahars among them the single largest number, was an extension—the labour quarters—of Nargada, the village where the landlords and peasants lived, located about ten miles west of Patna, approachable through metalled roads. On a day of ceremony at a Nargada employer's, the Musahars from Jamsaut could enjoy an excellent meal. Whenever there was a wedding, a childbirth, a funeral or a Hindu festival in Nargada, the Musahars eagerly left their huts that day, each equipped with a dish, a *lotah* (water jug) and a bucket. It did not matter who was having the ceremony in Nargada; all Musahars felt it their right to invite themselves to every dinner party thrown in the village. No host (charity being part of sincere Hindu religious practice, perhaps) turned away these shameless, determined beggars. Better, the host would decide to make them do some work before letting them have their meal. And so they worked the whole day, the women and the children, too, carrying loads from one place to another, arranging things for the reception and seating of guests, picking up the leaf plates and earthen glasses after every round of eating, before they were allowed the meal; after which they got back to such work as the host directed, and at the end returned to Jamsaut, after the guests had left and the festivities were over, with bucketsful of leftovers which saw them through the next day.

Sometimes, during the wedding season, some of the Musahars did the job of carrying the heavy gas lamps overhead in the groom's procession to the bride's house; for this there was a meal, and also a remuneration of a few rupees. This as well as the family pig-breeding, fish-gathering, grain-hole exploration, rat-catching and self-inviting to Nargada dinners, was what the majority of Jamsaut residents did aside from their main task as field labourers for the employers of Nargada. Several of them had, in fact, borrowed money and grain, or, the same thing, been lent money and grain, to turn themselves into bondmen. A bondman was given on a daily basis less than a quarter kilo of parched coarse grain or of gram flour as breakfast and stale rice for his main meal, and two to four annas, 12 to 25 paise, as a money wage. If a man was bonded his wife and children were treated as tied too; they got their meals by serving the same master.

Women among Musahars worked much harder than men. After a few glasses of alcohol which they brewed in their huts from the hazelnut-sized sweet fruits of the indigenous mahua tree, the men sank into sleep, sometimes away from the huts in the open air, or quarrelled with their wives if they were having their 'booze at home'. The women needed no drink to shout back; they screamed that the world was right in believing that the Musahars were a lazy, useless lot. It was the women who were more articulate in dealing with the Nargada's landowners than the men. But to some of the men, confidence came by way of drink. For, beginning with home-brewing for private consumption, they found their huts turning into liquor shops after a time, with customers arriving from near and far. Though the business could not but be small, it brought in a good deal more income than a bondman could ever imagine having from his master, and enabled the alcohol brewers to rebuff their masters.

This closed, exploitative corner of the world, where Jamsaut's labourers knew nothing more than obeying their in Nargada masters, where resistance was unknown, was opened up by the logic of action on the part of the larger society, which sowed the seeds of resistance by sending customers for mahua beverage down to Jamsaut. Thus they created a demand; and customers were driven into addiction for their own personal reasons. It was unimaginable that addicts could have anything to do with the labour-landlord relations in the village, to which they came just for drink, but by buying drink, they aided the brewers by improving their financial position, which affected labour-landlord relations.

But the market for home-brew was not the only external factor inducing changes. There were a good many other conditions that caused servitude and ignorance to begin to crack. The village was only three miles from Danapur, a large suburb of Patna, so when there was a demand in Danapur and Patna, chiefly for building construction workers, it attracted hands from the nearby villages, among them Jamsaut. The town could offer other daily wage jobs, such as the loading and unloading of goods for stockists on the market, or the plying of cycle-rickshaws. The wage rates in the town, though still very low, were higher than those in agriculture and though the employers in the town, too, liked to keep a worker as a slave, there was some freedom to quit one's paymaster if his attitudes became unbearable.

Town life also affected Nargada deeply. Young men from the landowning families were readily educated, for they were free from financial responsibilities, their fathers having enough income from agriculture for them to graduate. There are about 100 houses in Nargada, and today very few of them are of mud and thatch. The brick houses belong to those who became engineers and officers and employees of the government, or small contractors, even one or two small factory owners. These people mostly live outside the village, although their bond with the village remains since they have not sold the farm land they own there (cultivation being supervised by the father or a brother not successfully educated). They can be said to have, in a way, been urbanized.

The richer among them have bought more land in the village. But with them living away in towns, several things have changed in the village. Of central importance is change in the way agricultural land is handled. It is not suggested that the vogue for new farming technology, which, indeed, with its tractors, high-yielding plant varieties and chemical input, has arrived in Nargada, is responsible; the handling of land is now different in the sense that a substantial part of Nargada agriculture is under contracts. An increasing number of land-owners go for quick hard cash, rather than wasting the year organizing the tilling, sowing, weeding, harvesting, stacking, transporting and sale of the crops.

It was the poorer peasants, and the better-off among the Musahars who, adding loans from other people to their savings, came forward to bid for pieces of land offered for annual lease. They longed for good extra income from the leased strip, over and above their usual earnings. But though the new system did bring them a margin of profit, it was not a very good deal. The landowner dictated the terms. He set the rent every year. The tenant had to pay full rent in advance in December for a farm plot that would be made over to him only the next May. It was an oral contract; the owner was at liberty to cancel it any time before May, should another tenant offer a higher rate. If the tenant hired the owner's tractor for ploughing the plot, hire charges could be arbitrary. The same arbitrariness hit the tenant if he hired the owner's irrigation. A tenant could take two crops from Nargada's soil in a year: rice and wheat or onion for which the owner demanded differential rates for supplying water from his tubewell. For the rice season, he charged a flat rate—of, say, 300 or 400 rupees an acre—which, too, had to be paid in advance. A flat rate was established because in the rice season, which was the rainy season, the tenant would not use the tubewell much since, barring a drought, rains would do most of the job. Therefore, the energy consumption of the tubewell would be negligible, giving the owner a clear profit. But for wheat growing, irrigation was charged on the basis of the energy meter reading at the tubewell—at double the Bihar State Electricity Board's unit rates—for the owner calculated that the tenant would be using the tubewell a lot in the absence of rains in winter and early summer.

Winds of change in the outside world which were inspired by a gradually industrializing economy, and which pulled sections of land labourers and landowners alike into the towns, connected village with town, and established the importance of money, had begun to promote changes in local relations of production. The bondage of the Musahars was loosening; some of them earned enough to be able to avoid sinking into debt—even by selling mahua brew! Yet, the transformation was not very spectacular. There were still several bondmen in the village; they continued living upon the food allowed them for their daily work, and the presence of a landowner still filled them with fear. Even those who made a living, or at least supplemented their income by doing other jobs, such as brewing, working as coolies in towns, leasing a farm plot, barely fitted the description of 'better-off'. Almost all the Musahar children remained far from schools, and their fathers continued to go out hunting for fish in muddy puddles and for rats in field hide-outs. There was still dust and squalor everywhere in Jamsaut, raggedness and hunger. That was how the progressive Catholics, when they first came to the village seven years ago, found the Musahars.

The coming of a Catholic mission

In labour quarters of Jamsaut, there were also people of other castes living, including the Yadavas, Koeries, Kahars, Badhais, Kumhars and four others. A few of them had regular jobs in the towns, also tiny pieces of agricultural land, and they had built brick houses for themselves in Jamsaut; but most of them were as poor as the Musahars. Sharing a common plight, they had grown to be not so rigid or excitable about the Hindu code of conduct as were the landowners of Nargada, almost all of whom were Murkis (an intermediately ranked caste). They were also lower in the caste hierarchy, although they were touchable and ranked above the Musahars; a few of them, the Yadavas and Koeries, were intermediately ranked. Yet they had given up observing the rules of untouchability in dealing with the Musahars, though even they did not freely mingle or eat with the Musahars.

When the Catholics arrived in the village with plans to run a camp school, they didn't go to Nargada. They sited it within Jamsaut, specifically within the Musahar segment, thus avoiding even the streets where other castes lived. The Musahars, the Catholics quickly decided, were the poorest of the poor and most in need of non-formal education. Eyebrows were raised, both in Nargada and the rest of Jamsaut, but no real obstacles were put in the way. Disapproval came in murmurings: 'The Musahars are a lost cause' and 'Whatever you do, Father, they won't mend their ways'. Some Yadavas and Koeries of Jamsaut approached the Catholics with a suggestion that the school be run somewhere within the segment of the touchables; for their children, they whispered frankly, could not go to the Musahar segment to study. That did not mean, they went on, that the Musahar pupils were to be barred; they could attend a school which might be set up on the verandah or in front of a touchable household. Politely, the Catholics turned down the suggestion.

Leading the Catholics was a Jesuit teacher, Father Philip Manthara, in his early middle age, from a middle-class family in Kerala, impressed by the awareness of rights among the poor in that south-coast state. He came out to Bihar in 1962, but also lived on teaching assignments in Darjeeling, Calcutta and Delhi, finally settling down at St Xavier's, a reputedly elitist public school in Patna. He was driven to work for ordinary people, slum dwellers, and village labourers, after being moved by their utter helplessness, and was later inspired by the liberation theology issuing from Latin America. It was he to whom the poor touchables of Jamsaut came with the suggestion about the school site.

Manthara, while he did say no to them, assured them there was no intention to keep any child or any group out. He asked them to send their children to the Musahar school, following which the touchables said nothing; but two or three weeks later the teachers were amused and gladdened to see the first group of touchable children hesitantly walking down to the school. The new pupils were of an age when commitment to the Hindu code of conduct is only skin deep; and their parents, once they let their little ones attend that school, could not stop them from sitting and playing and laughing and teasing and quarrelling and making friends with the 'nasty kids'.

Later, the Catholics were to think up other ways to cement the fellow feeling among children. They introduced games and sports in the village, inducing the children of different castes, without ever pressurizing them, to get into a team, so that joy over a victory never became a celebration of caste valour. There was the particularly fascinating three-legged race: one foot of an untouchable boy was tied to that of a touchable boy when they ran and, if they won, they equally shared the pride. In mid-March of 1985, by which time the advocates of liberation theology were working in several villages in the area, games were held which drew children from various villages, one of whose important events was the three-legged race in which some Kurmi, and even one or two Brahman, boys participated, joining ankles with the untouchables.

In order to further decrease the sense of caste and to facilitate growth of awareness and solidarity among the poor from childhood, the Catholic teachers employed Paulo Freire's pedagogical techniques. Questions were taken from everyday life and answers found by the pupils themselves and thought over again and again, in a cycle of reflection-action-reflection (it had a ring of the dialectical-materialist theory of knowledge). The children were set to learn, for instance, the outline history, geography and economy of their village through these techniques, as well as the alphabets and arithmetic. One day the teacher might ask every pupil to go and talk to the old people of the village and find out from them what they knew about how the village came to be established, how it got its name, how it grew into the shape it had today; and, back in school, pupils were asked to narrate things they had learnt from the old villagers. Likewise, the pupil's attention was directed to the agricultural fields. Whose fields are these? What crops are grown in them? Who works the fields? Who takes the harvest? And why? The pupil was also asked to describe his house. How many rooms has your house? Of what materials is your house built? Why is it made of, as you say, only mud and thatch? Of what materials are the houses across those fields, in Nargada, made? Why are they made with, as you say, brick, cement, sand and stone? Why the difference?

When the teachers—Manthara stayed for weeks within the Musahar segment, accompanied for some time by a Sister—began non-formal education for the adults under the Government of India's national adult literacy programme the same question-answer techniques were used. Again, the Musahars had educational priority. Manthara, paying no attention to the touchables' annoyance, spent day after day with the Musahars, eating and sleeping the way they did, speaking broken Magadhi, the language of south-central Bihar, to make it easier for them to communicate with him, though both sides could speak and understand Hindi. In the dark, bespectacled, bright-eyed Father, who was of average height and usually dressed casually in trousers and light-coloured *khadi kurta* (a homespun long shirt), the Musahars saw no Christian agent bent on conversion; the subject, in fact, was never brought up. In spite of the indignity they were subjected to by the Hindu society, the Musahars looked upon themselves as Hindus. In another village where the Catholics work the untouchables insisted on parading their self-identity by organizing the celebrations during great Hindu festivals—such as Diwali, the festival of lights and fireworks—separately, and by installing clay images of gods in their segment. It was an orthodox expression of indignation against the orthodox Hindus in the village who never let them join their festivities. In the eye of the Musahars of Jamsaut, the Catholics were with them in a 'good cause'; to mould the Musahars in ways acceptable to the Musahars themselves, to reform them, help them stand on their feet and live with self-respect. They felt that the Catholics never intended to change their religion, nor could the Musahars, indeed, ever yield to such a change. Even Mathura Das, 78, the chief landowner of Nargada, who was looked upon by other Kurmis as the caste headman, felt sure, though he had certain reservations about the activities of the Catholics in Jamsaut, that the aim of Manthara's team was not to convert the Musahars.

Mathura Das spoke about the team, and Manthara particularly, with respect; he thought them quite sincere, enlightened, philanthropic, hardworking. Das (at least in public) took the line that there was nothing wrong in their endeavouring to better the lot of the downtrodden. The Kurmi chief also, in terms of faith, placed himself outside the Brahmanical Hinduism; his was, he stated, a family of Kabir-panthis, followers of the faith founded after Kabir, a great medieval poet and social reformer. All this reasoning, however, could not remove the doubt that he, like other well-off caste Hindus, might be ready to pounce upon the Catholics at the very first opportunity under the pretext of saving Hinduism, for as well as being a Kabir-panthi, Das was also a practising Hindu. So far he had not spoken against the Christians, but one or two Hindus had once or twice been heard shouting about the Musahars being led into the Christian faith; and though these shouts had been put down to the influence of drink to which the protesters were known to be addicted, it could equally be true that, in a state of drunkenness, hidden Hindu suspicions revealed themselves.

It was the Catholics' stance that religion was personal belief and, if one were to follow this, their own faith in Jesus was unlikely to conflict with the people's faith in Hindu gods. Certainly, such a stance could go a long way in overcoming Hindu suspicions. Yet this could perhaps also mean that the practitioners of liberation theology were never to be able, while working to reconstruct this Hindu society, to propagate or discuss what Jesus stood for and how he, as Sebastian Kappen wrote, founded a movement in Palestine and in the Graeco-Roman world 'predominantly of the poorer classes'. And if they ever felt uninhibited enough to do that, then the Hindus, even those of the lowest rank, might be inclined to produce their own heroes of the great epics, *Rama of Ramayana* and Krishna with Arjuna in the *Mahabharata*, and say they too led a war against oppressors and usurpers, against Sin and Evil. Who in such a case could be the source of inspiration—Jesus or Rama? This is bound to present itself, sooner or later, as a great ideological obstacle to the Catholics. An Indian theology of liberation cannot evolve without the resolution of this contradiction.

And even if the followers of Jesus come to accept the use of ancient Hindu epic-heroes in awakening and inciting the oppressed to struggle to change their present conditions, the question remains: How far would they be willing to go in the equally important struggle against superstitions and the Hindu dogma? For such a struggle the Catholics might perhaps find themselves too handi-capped. First, they would not want to do anything which might be misconstrued as anti-Hindu, and secondly, being believers themselves, however intellectually convinced, they might think it undesirable to provoke questions relating to the Supreme and the Unseen. Disguised as personal belief, any blinkered vision would last and cripple initiative in the oppressed.

Manthara and the buffaloes

The Musahars were beginning to love Manthara. He demanded nothing, did not force them to do anything; and when he put a baby on his lap and caressed it, forgetting the filth and dirt on its body, real affection seemed to glow in his eyes. Oddly, Manthara never asked them why they lived in such a fashion, why they did not have a daily bath: he accepted the Musahars as they were; he accepted the squalor, the stink, the pig droppings, the rat meat, the choking air of the tiny shacks, the drunks, the wife-beaters. But not everyone in his team could be unmindful of the filth in Jamsaut. One Sister, when she had been there a few days, on one of her first mornings, saw a very dirty child who, innocently, without being beckoned, was attracted to her. Finally it climbed on to her lap, cheerful, playful; horror gripped her soul, though nothing showed in her face; later she discovered that the baby's greasy fingers had left marks on her dress. She told other members of her team of her revulsion and said she felt ashamed of her feelings and ought to free herself of them. But she could not help asking why the team was making no effort to teach these people elementary personal hygiene and sanitation.

The team had a discussion. Everyone was asked to reflect. And in the course of discussion the question acquired a different frame, touching the very root of the problems: why they kept themselves dirty. Did they keep themselves dirty? The Musahar streets had no bathing amenities; the residents could not buy soap, they had no other clothes to change into after a wash, they let the single dhoti or sari they were wearing gather layers of dust and sweat and large greasy spots; they let their hair grow matted for want of oil. Besides, they had no reason to stay clean and washed, for they were never, after all, asked to dine in clean homes, or invited to a social gathering: when they came out of their shacks it was to work or search for food, in the fields as ratters, or in the muddy puddles.

No one expected a Musahar to remain washed and clean. And the Musahars themselves realized there was no reason to be so; they were happy and unwashed in their own little world. Others in fact recognized a Musahar by his shabbiness. Living thus they displayed resignation to their fate, the Catholics reflected. And, the Catholics believed that since resignation was bred by the conditions of exploitation, their shabbiness could be seen only as an accident of history; it was not, and could not be, a permanent part of their lives. Musahars were human, no different from any of us; their bodies were covered with dust, but not their souls. If the will was awakened to change their condition then even the squalor would go. But at the outset, you had to take them as they were for should you bring pressure upon them to come near you only after having washed, or to invite you into their huts only after the floor had been swept and the counterpanes made of rags had been washed bright, you would get respect but not love; they would never feel relaxed in your company—never be themselves. The Musahar would accept you only after you had accepted them. It would be at a much later stage that questions of cleanliness could be raised. Before that, from the very first day, the Catholic animator could silently begin to influence them by his own example, by bathing and washing his clothes every morning in the Musahar street.

After staying a few weeks, the Catholics went away, but the contact with Jamsaut was not broken, nor was it even after the adult literacy programme was concluded. Today the people, the homes and the streets of the Musahar segment are much cleaner, and there are a few people who can read and write—and speak without fear or hesitation. Some of the women there are no less active and vocal, sometimes more so than the men. Women generally, despite being heavily burdened with work, are found to be more enthusiastic about meetings and discussions; they see, in what the Catholics have begun prospects for male reform in Jamsaut, a reform they believe to be a sure step to bringing happiness to the whole family.

In the campaign against the alcoholic brew, the women—overcoming reticence after the first few discussions—spoke out against their wayward husbands. They began to tell how the brew was causing ruin, by telling of instances like the one of a man who, one evening after the booze, staggered several yards away from the village and then plumped down and slept the night there. Although brew-selling did irregularly bring in some extra rupees, selling was no less ignominious than drinking, the women said, corroborated by some prohibition-minded Musahars. The addicts, they said, who frequented the Musahar home often began, when no longer sober, to make uninhibited abusive speeches to the world at large or to each other, or to the brewer; and they tried to take liberties with the women of the family. Raids by the police (there was not enough money in the business of bootlegging in Jamsaut to keep them sweet) also brought shame to them; at the sight of the Khaki uniforms in the village, the Musahar would run away; the policemen chased them, but whether or not they were able to grab hold of any, they searched every shack and destroyed possessions and flung insults at the cowering women.

The campaign against brewing in the Musahar street was wholly educational. No fermentation pots were ever broken by the Catholics; no committee of Musahar elders took the brewers to task; no brewer was threatened. Discussions were held in which such questions as: Why do you make liquor? How much profit is in it, do you calculate? How much of you profit is spent on the actual, basic needs of your family? How much of it do you think you use wastefully? How do the customers and the policemen behave towards you, your wife, your daughters or daughters-in-law?–were asked. The replies were to come from the brewers, and others were asked to examine dispute or corroborate them in the presence of everybody; then the further views of the brewers were sought, without forcing any opinions upon them, and the points were re-examined in the assembly.

The Catholics held that no people or person could be reformed by force. All changes were to come through pedagogical methods: it was not desirable, or even possible, for an ideology to impose itself on people. It was to be a learning, not a teaching process. But, just as the two questions of cleanliness and prohibition showed, it could not be just a matter of faith. It seemed all right in theory; in practice, imposition could not always be avoided. On the matter of cleanliness, the Catholics were convinced that squalor and shabbiness were bad things that should be removed, and their initial acceptance of dirt, aimed at establishing affectionate intimacy with the Musahars, and the example they set by washing every morning in the Musahar street were steps towards achieving the goal of cleanliness. Similarly in the case of alcohol, the Catholics started with the assumption that brewing and drinking were evil, and began to find ways to end it. The ends were in the minds of the Catholics, only the means had to be found.

What was imposed could be welcomed. It is generally felt that people should live in clean surroundings and should not harm themselves by addiction to alcohol. But the Musahars had entertained no such ideas until the Catholics arrived in Jamsaut. 'Pedagogy of the oppressed' had therefore its own limitations. It would be too idealistic to believe that the oppressed could change the world they lived in simply by asking questions; the answers—though certainly not all of them—must be prompted from outside, from more conscious and revolutionary minds. No doubt, the people are their own strength, and living in a changing world they are certainly the best people to know how to tackle some of the local problems. They show remarkable wisdom at times, but fettered by tradition they are unable to think far ahead. They might be able to make suggestions but they cannot produce an ideology of transformation independently. In Jamsaut, elements of the idea that brewing alcohol and becoming addicted to it were bad might already have existed, as the fact that the women and some men were enthusiastic about the prohibition drive showed. But the task of linking prohibition to people's dignity and self-respect by provoking them to consider the daily humiliation that was inflicted on them by customers and the police was left to the wiser organizers, the Catholics. The magnitude of this task is evident from the fact that it was four years before the breweries closed.

But all wise pedagogy would not have made the brewers close down their shops had no alternative source of income been thought up. With the breweries, as with the wage-labour in the towns, some of the Musahars had risen a little way in the world. They had been able to save themselves from drowning in the landowners' pits of debt. Also, the urbanizing landowners themselves had loosened the system of classical bondage. In the village, generations were not tied to a master for, say, borrowing 20 rupees or five kilos of rice. Yet there were several Musahars who, having no choice, became farm servants for a year or more. During the Emergency, Indira Gandhi's economic reform led to the freeing of most of the bondmen of Jamsaut, without any obligation to pay their debts and, unlike hundreds of other villages of Bihar, Jamsaut was not subjected to retaliatory tyrannies by landowners in the first post-Emergency months.

It was the Emergency government's scheme, continued by the succeeding ministry under the opposition, that the freed bondmen would either be provided with financial assistance for self-employment or with a supplementary income. The former bondmen of Jamsaut, however, received nothing from the government offices, or from any state sector bank. As friendly feelings grew between the Musahars and the Catholics, the unassisted labourers spoke to them about it, citing instances from other villages where former bondmen had been aided to rehabilitate themselves. The Catholics considered that the Musahars' concern was conducive to their self-development and self-respect, it fitted well with their vision. But it was felt preferable that the Musahars alone should be involved in looking into the matter. Discussions were held about the kind of proposal they could put to the officials for approval and assistance. What should they propose that would be feasible?

Buffalo was the majority opinion. To each the government should provide a buffalo; the former bondmen while doing jobs as free day labourers could thus have additional income by selling milk. On being told of the decision Manthara was pleased but also a little nervous, for he knew nothing about buffaloes himself. He had no idea of how a buffalo was looked after, where one could be obtained, or bought, how much milk it yielded every day, whether it could be a viable scheme for a Musahar who, though he must have seen and known much about buffaloes, had never had the luck to have one tethered in front of his shack. The Jesuit priest went to see the managing director of the Bihar State Milk Federation, V. Baghavan, whom he knew. From this government officer he learnt about buffaloes, and the possibility of the Musahars getting a loan from any of the state sector banks to buy the animals. Baghavan also told him that if the Musahars were to form a milk co-operative after buying the buffaloes he would get the society entered in the Federation-run dairy project for Patna, so the Jamsaut milk had an assured buyer 'in us'.

Nargada's aged aristocrat had his doubts about the soundness of the buffalo idea. Mathura Das was not, he said, opposed to the idea because it held within it the danger of the land labourers getting further out of control. He wanted these people to *develop*; he feared that the buffalo was not the right way. The animal might prove more a liability than an asset to a working family, for in order to look after it at least two persons needed to be around all the time, and that would mean, the daily wage in agriculture or outside being ten rupees on an average, a daily loss of 20 rupees. And the expert opinion too, according to him, was against buffaloes. In his anxiety about the scheme he had even written to the

National Dairy Development Institute, Karnal, in Haryana state, and also to a
nutrition research institution of Bombay. In the replies he received, he said, it
was clearly explained that buffaloes ceased being profitable after a time. The
replies also confirmed his doubts that buffalo milk was less nutritious than cows'
milk. Cows' milk, the Bombay firm said (he claimed), was very rich in Vitamin
A. 'How much our country needs Vitamin A!' lamented Das. He went on, 'The
other day there was a world conference on the blind where comparative statistics
showed that almost half of the world's blind were Indians. And, tell me, what
is the chief cause of blindness? Deficiency of Vitamin A! Clearly, the Musahars
are just interested in short-term personal gain; the government's dairy centre
pays higher rates for buffalo milk than for cows.'

It needed little imagination to put the objections of Nargada's biggest
landlord down to fears that the labourers might well get out of hand. But he only
thought about it and made enquiries; he never came out in the open to oppose
the scheme, or to put his arguments before the Jesuits, or to give advice to the
former bondmen who were, in the Musahar street, discussing the setting up of
the milk co-operative. Among the former bondmen the co-operative had really
aroused a great deal of interest. Every Musahar of Jamsaut wanted to be in the
co-operative, also a few from the touchable poor. When names were collected
for membership they came to well over 100. This being a very large number, at
the outset the Jesuits persuaded them to start with a small grouping, a group of
people accepted as the most needy, three or four of them coming from the
touchable poor families.

The co-operative had troubles with the officials in the beginning. Men in the
Block Development Office, who were to certify that the members were former
bondmen and needy, and in the bank, where the loan applications were submitted, delayed work at every step. It had been decided by the applicants that they
would not give bribes to get their papers past the offices. They would not even,
as is customary for people wanting to speed up bureaucrats nowadays, entertain
any of the officials with snacks and tea at one of the tea shops outside the office.
A way had to be found, though, to get the work done. The applicants sent
complaints to the higher authorities and then started visiting the office in small
groups every few days; one group met the officials concerned one day, to ask
them how their papers were moving, then another group would go down shortly
after to make the same enquiry. The intention was to be such a nuisance to the
officials by asking questions that the moment would come when the only way
to get rid of this nuisance was to hurry the pending applications through speedily.

Twenty-two people obtained buffaloes through bank loans. The co-operative
got itself attached to the Patna dairy project, and it was arranged that the project's
milk collection vans would come every morning to Jamsaut. But for the initial
period the arrangement could not work since it was the season of rain and mud.
The vans waited in Danapur town for the people from Jamsaut to take the milk
in tin barrels overhead. It was a trying time in another way. Their entry into rural
milk business had earned them the animosity of the *makhanias*, the traditional
milk sellers who brought milk from villages to the tea shops and confectioners
in town in tin barrels in the same way; the *makhanias* tried to frighten the

Jamsaut men out of the trade; they beat up Vishnu Dayal, the chairman of the co-operative, one day on his way to Danapur, but this intimidation had little effect and, after a time, the *makhanias* gave up their harassment.

Only keenness and hard work, helped by the absence of internal disputes, made the co-operative into a quite exemplary success, and one of the best co-operatives feeding the Patna dairy project. After the rains, the milk vans began to come regularly to the village and, paid regularly for the milk it supplied, the co-operative did its book-keeping very well, without any professional help. There was the secretary who was paid a salary, fixed at 33 per cent of the profits in a month, to see that everything worked all right in the co-operative. Once a week the men on the executive, elected by the lay members, met to discuss problems and to review the week. There was a general meeting every month where the secretary read out his report and presented the monthly accounts, after which the lay members spoke freely, either asking clarification, or to criticize things done or being planned. Questions and answers at the monthly meetings could sometimes be a lively affair, increasingly so as the co-operative expanded, reaching, from a membership of 22, upwards of 70 today.

Within the Catholic church, among the Jesuits as well as in a few other congregations, particularly the Society of Medical Mission Sisters. Manthara's work in Jamsaut, his pedagogical efforts and the establishing of a viable milk co-operative provoked informal discussions. The Society of Medical Mission Sisters, already in the process of a ten-year radicalizing to turn towards the poor, was running an elitist hospital in Patna and a Health Centre in Maner, 90 minutes' drive west of Patna. It was at this Health Centre that Manthara found some young active nuns as colleagues.

The Sisters, nurses by profession, had started going out to the villages about Maner, a small town, with the idea of providing the rural folk with a minimum of medical care and primary health education. They stayed nearly a month in a village, which enabled them to observe the situation closely in a part of the Bihar countryside. This exposure was necessary, for the Maner nuns, like Manthara, hailed from Kerala and, though wanting to work for the poor, knew nothing of the conditions of a Bihar village. 'It was our education first,' said Sister Chinamma, 35, the most active of the group of nurses by whose efforts bondmen of Gyaspur village, ten minutes' drive south of Maner, were freed and given bank assistance to run a milk co-operative like Jamsaut's.

The same roots—back home they were all in the same middle class—had drawn Manthara, the nuns, and a few others easily into a cohesive group. There was no regional sentiment behind the cohesiveness: it was just that they shared the language and life experiences of Kerala, and felt an instinctive affinity with each other, an affinity made stronger by the sharing of ideas generated by liberation theology. In Kerala, Marxist unionization had led to a qualitative change in the rural situation, enabling the agricultural worker to establish his self-respect and set his daily wage. The militancy of the agricultural workers, commonly disapproved of by Kerala's rural middle class, sometimes made even radical Catholics like Manthara and the nuns think that unionization had perhaps gone too far, in so far as it badly affected the financial position of the lower sections of Kerala's middle class: but the Catholics still found it a very inspiring example to follow and put into practice in a region like Bihar, where the land labourers quietly suffered. The general level of awareness of one's rights was very high in Kerala (many agricultural workers were newspaper readers). Some of the south-coast state's Catholics were among the first to be influenced by liberation theology. Defying their superiors, they had gone forward to organize the struggles of boat-and-net fishermen against the businessmen's trawlers. Kerala's political processes had strengthened the convictions of the progressive Catholics in Bihar.

Chinamma and other nuns encountered more active resistance from the agricultural employers in Gyaspur and around than did Manthara at Jamsaut. There was no violence, but, once, a rough drunken employer shouted abuse, staggered angrily into a meeting of the nuns and the bondmen and warned them to disperse at once, which they did. At the outset, the employers made it almost impossible for visiting officers, come to enquire into debt-bondage with the nun's help, to find out information. At two such investigations the bondmen themselves told the officers none of them were bondmen, they were free, for that was what their employers had ordered them to say and the officers asked questions in the presence of the employers. Finally, the nuns had to ask Patna's district magistrate to intervene personally as the superior officer. His enquiry succeeded in making the servants speak the truth, in identifying them and declaring them free.

Becoming a 'model village'

Through the buffalo scheme in Jamsaut, also in Gyaspur, the former bondmen hoped to increasingly reduce their dependence upon the owners of land. It was organizing an alternative source of income, finding a different way of living from service to the landowners. By earning from his own resources, the Catholics believed that every bondman would develop self-confidence and a sense of pride and stand firmly by the view that all people are equal; that no person's life is predetermined, and that he could meet his former master not as a master but as a man.

In Jamsaut, circumstances seemed to be leading the former bondmen to such an awakening. The co-operative was bringing a good profit, it now had a brick-built office of its own and in one of the rooms a lower-primary school for poor children was started. The co-operative had placed Rs. 15,000 as a fixed deposit in the bank. From the interest, a village youth, taken on as the sole teacher at the school, could be paid a token salary of 50 rupees a month.

Following its policy of incentives to the feeder co-operatives, the govern-ment's Milk Federation awarded both a bonus and prizes to the Jamsaut co-operative. The distribution of these was to be carried out at a ceremony at Jamsaut which Baghavan, the Federation's sympathetic managing director, would attend. Mathura Das and other former masters were invited. The seating arrangements at the ceremony became symbolic of a minor cultural revolution.

On the rostrum sat the untouchable Vishnu Dayal, a bond-servant of Mathura Das for the better part of his life, as the co-operative's chairman with Baghavan. Mathura Das was received with due courtesy and guided to a chair in the front row of the audience. The ex-*zamindar* made no protest, but his face showed his feelings about this reversal of the order and the audience noted it with amusement.

At Jamsaut and Gyaspur, however, one feature was absent: strife. There were no demonstrations, sit-ins, strikes, indignation meetings, no direct conflicts and no occasion for the emerging underdogs and the Catholics to think in terms of strife—a fundamental subject which worries all organizations. The followers of liberation theology in Bihar were not so politically naive as not to understand that strife was inevitable. Direct conflict, and possibly retaliatory violence, would come sooner or later. But, looking at the way change was coming about at Jamsaut and Gyaspur, it became manifest that the Catholics were moving with great caution. They seemed to measure every step by judging what reaction it might invite from entrenched rural forces, as well as in official quarters. Aware of the stock phrases that the government used, they scrupulously avoided doing anything that would lead the government to smear them as 'extremists' or Christian missionaries acting as 'foreign agents'.

Almost solely, so far, the Catholics had therefore relied upon pedagogy. Raising of consciousness would be slowly and quietly achieved. There was no question of ideological compromise; the vision of a liberated world stayed unaltered, only the tactics varied (though these, too, had to be fair). A group ever-fearful of a smear campaign could best be saved from it by regular discussion and involvement of the officers; after all, the Catholics told them, it was the government's development or welfare schemes (like the one for former bondmen's rehabilitation) in which they, the Catholics, had showed themselves to be interested; they even let the officers have the credit for their implementation. The coming of the schemes, by raising the income of the poor families, generated its own impetus in the growth of consciousness among the oppressed, primarily being brought about through liberation pedagogy.

Yet there was one danger in using officials. The emerging sections of the oppressed might come to depend too much on the government. The Catholics were tactically using government institutions to advance the cause they were wedded to, but that could not be said of the poor of Jamsaut or Gyaspur. The poor did not as yet have the vision of a liberated world that the Catholics had at heart; they were much too happy to see that (due only to the presence of the 'church people') high government officers were making extra efforts to have various schemes carried out, among which the co-operative was just a beginning. Other schemes, like providing a small plot of land to each member of the co-operative for growing fodder plants and grass, in which the forest department planted trees, and providing street lights in Jamsaut with solar-energy batteries, had followed—more were under way. The officers were paying frequent visits to Jamsaut; once the chief minister of Bihar had come with a group of officials. In the eyes of the government, Jamsaut, an untouchables' hamlet, was developing as a 'model village'—a showpiece of benefits the government had brought to the untouchables!

Accordingly, the Musahars were inclined to get things done only through officials. There was, for instance, some trouble after the government 'distributed' the fodder plots to the members of the co-operative. The plots formed part of the land that the government had acquired from Nargada's landowners for the purpose of building a mud embankment to protect Patna after a high flood of the River Sone had inundated the capital city in 1975. The plots lay below the rise of the embankment, and some of Nargada's landowners, though they had been paid the compensation, had in recent years illegally extended their cultivation back to those plots. So providing allotments to the members of the co-operative remained on paper only. Yet there was no protest, no agitation which, while aiming to force the landowners out of their plots, could have served to bring the consciousness of the oppressed to a higher level. The labourers looked to the officers to do the job and, indeed, it was the officers who did it.

If all the Catholic endeavours were going to end up just as some improvement in the living conditions of the poorest of the poor, this was not in any way bad, but it made the realization of the vision of revolution more distant. The risk involved in such a course was that the work would not move beyond the point where those left out by the nation's processes of development also received the benefits due; in other words, it could at best turn out to be, if precautions were not taken, a minor satisfaction about 'growth with justice'.

8. The Abbey in Bodh Gaya

The 18 March Movement

The 18 March Movement began with a big student demonstration before the Bihar state legislature on the opening day of its budget session of 1974. It became one of the greatest middle-class movements in free India, for two reasons. Though started by students, it rose above narrow campus demands, and was concerned with deeper issues of unemployment, rising prices and venality in public life. Secondly, after a short time, the movement came under the incorruptible leadership of Jayaprakash (JP) Narayan, a national hero of the independence struggle. This upsurge brought out thousands, sometimes tens of thousands, of people for spontaneous meetings or demonstrations in Patna or the outlying districts. The people, including women of every age, took part in the protest programmes because they felt the movement concerned them. They only needed to learn from the newspapers what programmes were presented by JP or the *Chhatra Sangharsh Samiti*, the Students' Struggle Committee, to pour out in large numbers on the appropriate days. Great was the public anger against the evil political system that had developed in free India and experienced in its worst form in the state of Bihar!

Revolt must be concentrated upon someone or something, upon an identifiable devil. The suffering caused by increasing unemployment, rising prices and growing corruption prepared the ground, and JP as leader generated their hopes: but the crowds would not have been out on the streets unless they had an obvious target. The unpopular current Bihar Congress ministry became their target, despite the fact that the three main issues of the movement were national problems caused more by central government than a state ministry. Immediate dismissal of the Bihar Congress ministry, and fresh elections to the State Assembly, were at the top of the movement's list of demands, and had been copied from the students' movement in Gujarat. This movement too, only a few months before the Bihar movement began, had led to the involvement of ordinary people and, ultimately, the dismissal of the Congress ministry and the dissolution of their state Assembly of that western state.

Indira Gandhi, as was her custom, painted a picture of the Bihar movement as just another conspiracy, opposing her and threatening the stability of the nation. Ironically, with the support for the movement growing daily across the country and all national opposition leaders (the Left parties excepted) associating themselves with it, the danger, indeed, of the electorate inflicting losses upon Indira Gandhi at every opportunity was very real. Her position was made worse by the famous Allahabad High Court judgement which unseated her as a member of Parliament for breach of electioneering laws in Uttar Pradesh. She remained unabashed by the judgement, did not resign and, on the same theme of conspiracy, declared a state of emergency in the country on 26 June 1975. JP and opposition leaders, students and other intellectuals she threw into jail, suspended all democratic liberties, and changed the laws to nullify the court judgement against her.

Indira Gandhi's propaganda apart, JP looked far beyond dismissal of a state ministry, which would, in his view, be only a beginning. The real objective of the 18 March Movement was revolution, *total revolution*, to be brought about, as he saw it, by fundamentally changing the country's economic, political, cultural and educational systems. JP, then 72 years old, was suspected of no personal involvement with parliamentary politics; he had left this arena shortly after Independence. For almost all his life he had sought for ways, other than through parliament, to bring about change. He had, indeed, tried several ways, before quitting them in despair. As a student in the United States he was converted to Marxism, following the Great October Revolution, but later Stalinist Russia lost him to Western social democracy. Back in India, he joined Congress, identifying himself with its Socialist group. After Independence, with the Socialists leaving Congress, he even stood as a Socialist nominee in free India's first general election to Parliament in 1952, and lost. Shortly thereafter he left parliamentary politics to be with Vinoba Bhave, a Gandhian saint totally opposed to Communism, who believed there was a surer way to revolution in India: the way of *Bhoodan* (Giving of Land). In this, landowners in every village would donate land to the landless, starting a process leading to *Sarvodaya*, prosperity for all, and *gram swaraj*, village self-rule. In this, people would help one another, settle their disputes by discussion and live in peace. JP led this movement with Bhave for nearly 20 years, though briefly, during this period, he was also attracted to the Nehru government's Community Development Programme whose objective was to build a countryside infrastructure with the people's involvement, to encourage the agricultural, educational, and cultural development of the village, an attraction which was fiercely opposed by his former Socialist colleagues, who regarded Nehru as no more than a leftist hypocrite.

In the revolutionary Marxist camps, Bhave-JP's *Sarvodaya* movement was regarded as nothing but a concerted effort to block the growth of political consciousness among the oppressed. They felt that the poor land labourers, receiving strips of land as gifts from the landlords, through *Bhoodan*, would feel only a sense of obligation towards their exploiters; they would continue to regard as charity what they ought to have taken as their right. The evidence for this view of *Sarvodaya* was found in its very origin. This was in the fear of an armed revolution which had been aroused by the five-year Communist battle in the Telangana region (in what is now the State of Andhra Pradesh in southern India) launched in 1946, first against the prince of Hyderabad, and after the army of free India had overthrown him, against the Indian state. *Sarvodaya* stood for peace, non-violence, fellow-feeling and the egalitarian use of natural resources—for revolution through love. So whenever the unrest of the rural poor broke out, *Sarvodaya* leaders became very concerned, and would at once depart for the affected area, to mount a peace offensive.

In 1971 it was for pacification purposes that JP had gone to Musahar, a village group near Muzaffarpur, in North Bihar, where the Naxalites were working among the landless. He stayed there almost a year, holding meetings both with the labourers and the landlords, appealing for peaceful change, telling the labourers that their use of arms could only invite greater violence by the state; advising landlords to change with the times; asking government officials to put the plethora of agrarian reform laws into actual practice. Yet his efforts had brought no real gains. There were favourable responses here and there, but they were not significant. The landlords remained obstinate. Musahari was a highly frustrating experience for JP; in the depths of his despair he began to think of abandoning *Sarvodaya*. *Sarvodaya* methods, based on appeal and entreaty, he now felt, might afford a little succour to the people: they could never lead to social revolution. For a revolution to take place, struggle was indispensable.

JP's vision of peaceful revolution

For one and a half years before the 18 March Movement started, JP had been meditating almost in solitude to find the right way to bring about change.[1] His new opinions, his beliefs about revolution through non-violent confrontation rather than through love, distanced him from Vinobha Bhave and finally led to a split between the two. This coincided with the student upsurge in Patna, where he lived, and elsewhere in Bihar—as well as in other states, notably Gujarat. In this upsurge, JP saw potential revolution.

So, when the students' leaders of the 18 March Movement appealed to him to lead the way, JP agreed, evidently thinking he should now act according to his convictions. But, there was another reason why he associated himself with the students. After the 1968 student and youth revolt in Paris, JP, following unorthodox Marxist ideologues like Marcuse, had become convinced that in these times of change the youth (Marcuse believed intellectuals generally), rather than the working class, was to play a leading role in preparing for revolution. As leader he called upon the students of Bihar to stay out of university for a year in order to work for *total revolution*. And *Chhatra Sangharsh Samiti*, the Students' Struggle Committee, formed in Patna prior to the 18 March demonstration, continued to have its active existence even after JP assumed the leadership; it had units in the towns and also in the rural parts. The central body of the *Samiti* also continued to have its original members, who were mostly members of the students' organizations of the non-Left opposition parties. Opposition students were in the district or lower-level committees as well, but students not attached to any political party had also enrolled. Statewide, in fact, it was the non-attached, independent students who made up the bulk of participating youth, and who looked to JP, rather than to the opposition student leaders, for guidance.

Though JP believed the student youth would play the preparatory role in revolution, that would not be realized within the 18 March Movement. For JP towered above everyone; he devised, or finally approved, the street programmes; and the ideas and the thinking he set out in pamphlets, or outlined at public meetings became the ideology of the Movement. In a way, it was a charismatic movement. In the public eye, JP was almost an ascetic, one who had conquered lust and ambition long ago (legend had it he had declined the post of President of India), and who dedicated his life to the service of mankind: a *sannyasi* who could think lofty thoughts, analyse things and present his ideas intelligibly. Little wonder then that the Movement was identified with JP and was interchangeably called either the 18 March Movement or the 'JP Movement'.

And JP set out to realize his vision of revolution by carrying both the youth and the people towards a higher aim than Assembly dissolution. He urged them to fight caste by encouraging intercaste marriage and cutting the sacred thread. He wanted more and more women to participate in the protest programmes, and warned that no one should give or take a dowry. His old *Sarvodaya* ideal of village self-rule was also published. But to move in that direction, he wanted people to set up *'janata sirkar'*, the people's government, at all levels, to take care of all local disputes and common problems. And then he laid out his concept of *total revolution* covering seven fields: economic, social, political, cultural, intellectual, educational and spiritual. Concrete features of the legendary *total revolution* were drawn, but only in part. The economic revolution, for instance, would encompass a broader mixed economy: enterprises both in industry and agriculture could be owned by the state, an individual, a company, a cooperative society, or committees representing the people of a village, a sub-district or district, or even by a combination of individual investors and a society or committee. Although in the economic revolution of his dream JP allowed the existence of a state sector, he had always been sceptical of its role in the economy of India. Nationalized industries or the public sector could not be equated with socialism, he argued, for they were run on the same capitalist principles as private enterprises, with no role for workers or customers other than as workers or consumers.[2]

All JP's ideas and exhortations, however, seemed to have little impact in a society that remained highly resistant to change. Few among the participants of the movements even committed themselves to taking or giving no dowry, and fewer still to the snapping of their sacred threads. Tragically, the complexities of caste, which hindered the movement, also affected JP. He himself was cosmopolitan, and most people saw him as genuinely so, yet it was impossible for someone in Hindu society to escape from caste origins. JP was a Kayastha; he never identified himself as such but the Kayasthas saw him as a Kayastha, and as a great man produced by their caste! This blinkered view explained to some extent the usually high participation in the movement of the Kayasthas in cities like Patna and Ranchi.

Like JP's other programmes, the *janata sirkar*, people's government, failed after a certain point. Nothing better revealed the class composition of the movement than this experiment of *janata sirkar*, for its establishment in the village was mooted without the participation of the land labourers, or by involving 'dummies' from within their ranks. In the village, the agriculturist middle class owned the movement, as, in the towns, did the urban middle class—government employees, teachers, lawyers, students, shopkeepers. The great majority of this middle class would never accept the social radicalism that JP preached. They were not prepared for a change of society overnight; they wanted to change the Bihar ministry, because they believed that would change unemployment, rising prices and venality which did concern them. That suited the opposition parties well, and also the leaders of their students' organizations comprising the *Chhatra Sangharsh Samiti*, who wanted the movement to go only to the point of sweeping Congress out of power.

It was some time before JP realized that the crowds were not following him along the road to revolution, and knew for certain that the *Chhatra Sangharsh Samiti* could never develop as an instrument of revolution. Yet he could not disband the Samiti or sack the opposition students' leaders who had filled it, because of the possible subsequent confusion. But the cause of revolution was never to be abandoned so, while letting the *Chhatra Sangharsh Samiti* continue to function, JP founded in October 1974 an organization called *Chhatra Yuva Sangharsh Vahini*, the Students-Youth Struggle Army. He was its *nayak* or commander, and it was planned to recruit 100,000 volunteers committed to the cause of *total revolution*. Though he adopted the name *Vahini* from Sheikh Mujibur Rehman's *Mukti Bahini* or Liberation Army of Bangladesh, JP's *Vahini* would work without arms. It was to have, however, the discipline, devotion, courage and fellow-feeling that made an ideal army. Against the target of 100,000, the *Vahini* could reach at most 13,000 on the rolls: the number who actually joined was much less. Most of the volunteers were independent young men, and the remainder were those from *Sarvodaya* who had sided with JP after his separation from Bhave. JP had barred anyone from the student or youth organization of a political party from joining the *Vahini*.

One thing that JP said about the *Vahini*, however, caused confusion among its volunteers. He announced that it would work as the agency to implement the decisions taken by the *Chhatra Sangharsh Samiti!* He probably said that to kill any suspicion that he was raising a parallel student-youth organization: he wanted to take everybody along. This was a tactic that, for a long time, stopped him from concentrating his energies on the *Vahini*. The contradiction in JP's stance was clear to the *Vahini* volunteers, though: if the *Vahini* was established on the logic that the *Chhatra Sangharsh Samiti* could never be the tool of *total revolution*, how could the *Vahini*, which was proposed to be such a tool, be given the responsibility of carrying out programmes announced by the non-revolutionary *Samiti*?

Thanks to JP's vacillation, the *Vahini* showed little activity for a year or more after its birth, in the middle of which time Indira Gandhi had clamped down a state of emergency. Before the Emergency there had been one activity in which the *Vahini* volunteers were involved: a programme for physical training (as *sainiks*, soldiers!) with morning exercises and parades in a park in Patna. This was organized by a retired serviceman from Akola, Maharashtra, Major Pratap Rao Jadhav, a tough, hardboiled disciplinarian. No one had requisitioned Major Jadhav's services: he came one day to meet JP in Patna and offered to organize physical instruction for the 'boys': JP had no objections. But soon Major Jadhav was found to be a follower of *Anandmurty*, an Indian mystic of ill fame, whose sect, *Anand Marg*, the Way to Bliss, boasted several members abroad, and preached weird notions of morals, body and soul, and politics. JP had to ask the Major to cease his self-assigned task without delay.

After that, exercises and parades were held on two more occasions—at two *Vahini* camps: subsequently no one bothered about physical discipline in the *Vahini*. These camps were organized during the period of Emergency (for the first four months of which JP was in prison) and there, apart from a few hours of physical exercises, the volunteers had lecture sessions and discussions. It was during discussions at the camps that the volunteers discovered each other's views, and differences between the *Sarvodaya* youth and the independent young members became sharp. Both sections looked up to JP as their leader and ideologue, and accepted his views about the inevitability of struggle, yet, the youths from *Sarvodaya*, trained to practise quiet and harmony, invariably resisted any suggestion of action. Later on, the divide between the two was to grow; even JP was unable to check it. For the independent volunteers found the *Sarvodaya* men not only reluctant to take up a struggle but also arrogant and comfort-loving, with their funds and resources for printing and cyclostyling. Their arrogance flowed also from their feeling that they 'owned' JP, and not the *Vahini* recruits. This feeling became evident every time they took their quarrels with the independent volunteers to JP and poured out venomous complaints in the absence of the other party. Not to be outdone, the independent followers also sought audience with JP to explain how they thought about a certain matter. JP tried not to be partisan, but on a few occasions he would berate groups of independent volunteers for rash acts or too rigid views.

If the independent volunteers found the *Sarvodaya* men easy going, compromising, arrogant, JP-worshippers, they in turn were disliked because of their adolescent ways; their habits of shouting others down during a discussion, of looking upon everyone with suspicion, of manipulating in order to have their way at any price; habits for which their impatience and romantic ideas would offer no cure. There was never anything like a split within the *Vahini*, but in later years all the *Sarvodaya* youths left in groups and individually, and formed their own youth organizations, together with those independent men who, too, were out of the *Vahini* for their own reasons.

After the Emergency

When Indira Gandhi ordered a general election under the relaxed Emergency in March 1977, the volunteers of the *Vahini* campaigned for the opposition candidates. She miserably lost the election, and the united opposition that assumed power in New Delhi dissolved the assemblies in Bihar and other states where elections were overdue. This fulfilled the main demand of the 18 March Movement. Once that happened, the movement died out: the scene bustled with leaders of the opposition parties and their students' organizations scrambling for election tickets. In Bihar, too, the united opposition won the elections, with 29 *Chhatra Sangharsh Samiti* men getting in. No one from the *Vahini* entered the fray, though its volunteers worked for the opposition.

But soon people began to complain that the coming to power of the opposition brought no change. JP, in despair, urged such steps as the stepping up of people's vigilance committees to keep a check on constituency representatives in the legislature. With the movement disbanded, he could perhaps do no more. Meanwhile, Bihar was rocked by one massacre of land labourers for being 'guilty' of trying to get benefits out of certain ameliorative schemes of the Emergency, such as freedom from bond service. The landlords had been waiting for the Emergency to end to launch the attack. To JP these atrocities were further evidence of the rural poor as vulnerable and defenceless, and showed how important and urgent was the task of making them stronger.

In August the same year, 1977, a newspaper recorded an interview with JP in which he said that he had come to believe that the weaker sections of society ought to be organized along class lines. The *Samayik Varta*, a Hindi fortnightly planned to be published from Patna by a group of socialists outside parliamentary politics, was to feature the interview in its inaugural issue. Some of the contents were leaked by word of mouth, even as the edition went to press, and everyone who heard them was startled. The *Sarvodaya* men were incredulous and thought that the interview must be garbled, for JP could never use Marxist or militant expressions like 'class organizations' and 'class struggle' which implied violence and hatred. They found that the interview was not the exposition of a single new idea: it covered a wide range of issues, and JP's stunning proposals had come in his replies to one or two questions, after which the interview had passed to other issues. JP had observed that he was no longer opposed to the idea of forming class organizations or separate organizations for the downtrodden. 'I now have no objections,' he said, 'even if it leads to class struggle in the rural areas. There seems to be no other way.'

The *Sarvodaya* men, alarmed, sought a meeting with JP. They could not summon courage to come straight out about it but told him they had heard that the *Samayik Varta* interviewer had put words into his mouth that could have very dangerous implications. The right thing to do in these circumstances, they counselled JP, would be to cancel the interview. JP at once asked the newspaper to send him a proof copy which he went through carefully and sent back, saying all was as he had said. When finally the copies of *Samayik Varta* with the JP interview were on sale, JP had to face a long line of excited questioners.

And JP explained. He talked about his lifelong search for the path of revolution, his profitless ideological quests. He had embraced Marxism, Socialism and *Sarvodaya* in turn, only to relinquish them. Ironically, it was in the twilight of his days that the road to revolution had come into sight. He had first seen it while working for peace in Musahari. There he became convinced of the futility of the *Sarvodaya* methods of change. They worked on the principle that

Man was naturally good: that even evil-doers could be changed. What society needed for vitality was love and affection between man and man, and the *Sarvodaya* workers, by pouring out love to everybody, could certainly build, on very strong foundations, a community based on love and mutual respect and common wealth. In the village, the practice of *Sarvodaya* would establish harmony and brotherhood; those who owned land would share property with those who did not; people of higher castes would treat lower castes as they would members of their families; all hierarchies would vanish. JP pointed out that he worked in Musahari along these lines. He went to the landowners, and to the men of the upper castes and reasoned with them. He appealed to their conscience and generosity and preached love towards the poor and the downtrodden—without results.

After that, he rejected the *Sarvodaya's* basic theory of *hridaya-parivartan*, change of heart, and began to advocate the line of struggle. The rich, JP now believed, would have no change of heart unless forced to. The strength of the poor must be organized to make the dominant class see reason, to deter the entrenched few from oppressing lower classes. The poor must awake, they must assert themselves.

But did not 'class struggle' sound too Marxist? asked his *Sarvodaya* friends. JP told them the class struggle that he envisaged had nothing to do with Marxism or violence. 'What Marx had said might be true of industrial societies. An agricultural society like India cannot be seen in terms of classes. Classes were not easy to distinguish between here.' For, JP went on, in India's agricultural society there were labourers and small peasants, but it had not been possible to unite the two against the large landowners, because even the smaller peasants looked on themselves as landowners, and identified themselves with the larger ones.

From what JP had said in his *Samayik Varta* interview, and later in explanation, it was clear that he was using the phrase 'class struggle' in a very limited sense: not as a way to bring about revolution in India. By all accounts, he had in mind those who toiled in the village—wage workers, bond servants and sharecroppers—when he emphasized forming class organizations of the poor: in plain terms, organization of the rural landless. And in doing so, he was drawing much from the Bihar experience. Musahari had taught him that the powerful few in the village will not change, in the absence of pressure from below. And the shocking series of massacres of the land labourers in Bihar in the post-Emergency months made his convictions about this stronger.

Certainly, it was not the industrial working class that JP advocated class organization for. Here, too, he differed from the Marxists: he refused to consider India's factory workers as a proletariat: in his view they had become a part of the *petit-bourgeoisie*. (It is worthwhile to note that the factory workers of Bihar never joined the 18 March Movement, and neither JP nor the youth activists made any serious effort to get them involved. Essentially, therefore, the movement remained an urban movement, with the salariat but minus industrial workers.)

Many in the *Vahini* were excited by JP's new idea of class organization with its promise of something more serious than registering token protest in the towns, where the *Vahini* agreed with JP that the industrial workers were *petit-bourgeois* (though ironically, almost all the *Vahini* volunteers themselves came from the class). With JP's new approach the *Vahini* looked like turning towards the villages. Yet they had no clear idea of how JP, as their commander, actually wanted to go about it. They went to him and asked him to lay down the *Vahini's* role, and he outlined this without assigning them any concrete tasks. The *Vahini* accidentally found a task for itself later in Bodh Gaya.

JP gave them the theory: he expected change in society to come under *duhre dabaw*, 'double pressure'. Upon the powerful few in the village pressure must come from the class organization of the oppressed. This would be pressure from below. The other pressure was to come from above and this would be the pressure of 'mass education', meaning a concerted campaign to persuade the privileged sections to change their attitudes towards the poor. The youths had responsibility for building up both these pressures. They must remain committed to non-violence while they worked for *antima jana*, the lowest person in the community. JP used to say he was opposed to armed revolution not on 'moral' but on 'pragmatic' grounds. First, armed revolution took more time to prepare than a non-violent one: secondly, when it took place it did not bring a stable democracy: it encouraged the gun and post-revolutionary coups. And thirdly, as the experience of Communist states showed, the great basic aims for which the revolution was brought about were never achieved.

Action in Bodh Gaya

Few had thought that, with JP's ideas of class organization, the *Vahini* would ever go into the countryside. Even after several hundreds of its volunteers gathered in Bodh Gaya on 8 April 1978 to join the land labourers for a demonstration outside the old high wooden door of the Sankara *mutt*, the abbey of Sankara, people felt that these tyros from the towns would protest a little, make for home—and then forget about the labourers. Someone like Jayaram Giri, stony-hearted, tough, wily, the chief manager of the abbey property, was not likely to feel a storm blowing up! He was the abbey boss, and in the past had seen all kinds of land-seekers come and go—socialists, the Communist Party of India, the *Sarvodaya*. His boast was that all their plans to damage the abbey had been foiled: no damage was possible as long as he was there.

As the noisy crowd of youths and labourers jammed the main street, on to which the abbey door opened, Jayaram sat inside the huge old white building, with his deputy, Deenadayal Giri, and some monks and abbey employees. The abbey stood at the centre of the small bazaar of the Bodh Gaya town, in the South Bihar district of Gaya, which sustained itself more on tourism than on commerce with the surrounding villages. The chief tourist attraction was the place where, 2,500 years ago, Buddha was believed to have attained his *nirvana* and where, later, the Mahabodhi temple was built. The temple's pyramidal exterior was decorated with horizontal bands of fine engravings of images.

Buddhism today, with scarcely a follower in Bihar, had survived in scattered monasteries in this province until the Turks invaded at the turn of the 13th century, destroying a monastery and killing the Buddhist monks who lived there in their opening offensive, thinking they were Brahmins. For a much longer period in the past, Buddhism had been under attack from the torch-bearers of orthodox Hinduism. The *mutt* in Bodh Gaya was founded in 1590 by a Hindu monk who believed in the monist teachings of the Hindu Sankara scholar and who liked the place for its natural beauty. Several other sects had their monasteries in Bodh Gaya, but none had so much property as had the Sankara *mutt*. No one to this day knows, not even the government, exactly how much land this abbey illegally owns!

After the *Vahini* demonstrators had shouted slogans for a while, the abbey's tall door was opened to admit four of their representatives for a meeting with Jayaram Giri. They were led into the building where the chief manager received them very courteously, heard them attentively, and then calmly said to them: 'As far as I am aware this *mutt* doesn't illegally hold a single piece of land anywhere. But if you happen to discover any, do bring it to my notice. The *mutt* will be pleased to have it speedily released.'

Concurrent with the demonstration, the *Vahini* had planned to revive a campaign (which a prominent *Sarvodaya* leader, J. Jagannathan, and his tender-hearted wife, Krishnamma, had launched in early 1975 and given up after the Emergency) to mount pressure on the Sankara *mutt* to relinquish its estates to the men who tilled them. The Jagannathans had come to Bihar to participate in the 18 March Movement, and had stayed for many months. During this time they came to Bodh Gaya, where the *Sarvodaya* had for 20 years had a well-established *ashram*. As they moved round talking to people, someone happened to mention the conditions thousands of labourers were living in, under the tyranny of the *sannyasis* of the Sankara *mutt*, the biggest landlord in the area. In their home state in South India there had been struggles against several monasteries which had greatly affected them. The land-rich monks in Bodh Gaya gave rotten, unhealthy, coarse grains to their labourers as wages. The Jagannathans were more interested in discussing the Sankara *mutt* with the people in Bodh Gaya than the 18 March Movement. They gathered some internal information from one Pradeep, son of a *mutt* employee and a leading activist of the 18 March Movement in Bodh Gaya.

Jagannathan decided to go straight to the *mahanth*, abbott. From what he had learnt, from various quarters, Jagannathan was now aware that the abbey, to avoid the legal ceiling on agricultural landholdings, had long ceased to 'own' its property singly. It had (in addition to the *mutt* trust existing since 1932) created no fewer than 17 religious trusts, each shown, on paper, to possess an area of land within the limits set by law. It had also placed more land under the names of monks or *mutt* employees or non-existing persons. Inside the monastery the abbot received Jagannathan warmly, and they began to talk. Jagannathan reeled off all he had heard about the abbey's land monopoly, and its exploitation of labour. He also spoke of the 17 fake trusts, in the end appealing to the abbot to surrender the land, about 2,100 acres, held by the trusts, while retaining the *mutt* trust for the upkeep of the abbey. Turning down the appeal, the abbot remarked he would rather have it the other way round should Jagannathan agree to it: retaining 17 trusts he would rather leave one trust whose land the *Sarvodaya* leader would be free to distribute among the poor as he liked.

Jagannathan, disappointed, went to see the district magistrate in Gaya, who told him of the legal obstacles that stood in the way of acquisition of the *mutt's* estates. Jagannathan was now convinced that the monks would not give in unless pressure was brought to bear upon them by the masses. But where were there men in Bodh Gaya whom he could associate with to build up an agitation against the abbey? He had only Krishnamma. In the *ashram* the old *Sarvodaya* set were in a rut; they all had good accommodation and meals with vegetables fresh from a home farm, and wore milk-white homespun *koortas*. Twenty or so years before, as the followers of Bhave, they had gone about begging land around Bodh Gaya for the poor, and not everyone had turned them away. To the some 100 strips of land they got, they had brought several land labourers to settle, largely the untouchable Musahars. Later, they had opened primary schools for their children and started other welfare schemes. As they worked for the Musahars, they also built their *ashram* in Bodh Gaya, not far from the abbey of Sankara. The abbey had been among the landowners who had donated land to the *Sarvodaya* in the villages. And they, the devotees of Bhave, were now fond of comfort and of performing routine duties, and the *ashram* had become just one more monastery in Bodh Gaya.

But there were one or two village workers of *Sarvodaya* who wholeheartedly supported Jagannathan's proposal. Yet before the group started its organizing activities, it needed some more local men. Jagannathan wanted Pradeep to take part in the agitation he was proposing. But when he raised the subject, Pradeep started in surprise, went pale, and said nothing. Could Pradeep even in fantasy dream of joining a campaign against the Sankara *mutt*! He was now 22 and had virtually grown up under the care of the *mutt*: today he had a BA degree, and was studying law but with the *mutt's* support: the *mutt*—and not his father, a farmhouse manager—had met his educational expenses, given him money to supply his wants, and permanent accommodation free of charge (a room in the abbey, from whose kitchen he also got his meals twice a day). He had always considered himself part of the abbey community: and he held the abbey in reverence.

On some occasions he had acted for the abbey in dealing with outside people who had a dispute with the management. All who knew him there knew him as a trusted *mutt* man. Even when he became a leading activist of the 18 March Movement, not many people changed their opinion, but merely thought that the *mutt* had succeeded in 'planting' a 'mole' in the opposition. Although this was not true, for all his sincerity towards the JP movement he never thought of taking the struggle down to the actual villages. So Jagannathan's proposal was a dreadful shock. When he had pulled himself together he told Jagannathan he wanted some time to think it over.

Pradeep left Jagannathan in his room, walked slowly to the *ashram* gate and, shunning company, turned straight into the abbey and shut himself in his room.

He had promised Jagannathan to give him his decision the next morning. He lay on his bed, and pondered over the proposal nervously. He had not known Jagannathan previously. This elderly *Sarvodaya* man and his wife had travelled from as far south as Tamil Nadu to Bodh Gaya, for a short visit. Here, their hearts went out to the poor *mutt* labourers, and they felt an urge to do something to help them. To do this, the couple had decided to stay on indefinitely in Bodh Gaya. But he, who had grown up here and knew all about the living conditions of the labourers, had never thought of doing anything for them. Pradeep felt ashamed. But the next moment, the picture of his father and other members of the family appeared in his mind's eye: he trembled when he thought how vindictive the monks would be towards the farmhouse manager whose son became a traitor. Certainly, Jayaram Giri was not going to take such a betrayal lightly. Jayaram was a monk and the abbey's chief manager, but also a Congress politician, who had even been a minister in the state government for a time, and who had influence with some of the Congress leaders and bureaucrats.

If Pradeep knew about the labourers' conditions he was also fully aware of the devilish powers of the abbey. There was nothing the monks would not resort to in bringing their enemies to heel: they had more than enough money and grain to bribe the local civil and police officials, to inundate the courts with cases in order to harass an enemy, to keep or hire as retainers any number of rough-necks to use against troublemakers. To oppose the monks was to play with fire. That night Pradeep tried in vain to sleep. When day broke, he came out of his room, locked the door, and slipped out of Bodh Gaya into the countryside to hide from Jagannathan. But he had only been out a few days when a message reached him that Jagannathan eagerly awaited him at the *ashram* in Bodh Gaya. Pradeep hadn't been able to put out of his mind Jagannathan's words and good intentions as well as the frightening images they evoked. After very long consideration, he was beginning to feel he ought to support Jagannathan come what may. He ought to work for the people. Having made this decision he might be able some day to fulfil a desire that he had been nursing for some time: to embark on a career in politics.

When Pradeep left the abbey for good and set out with Jagannathan and Krishnamma and a few *Sarvodaya* workers to tell the villagers how to set about agitating in order to put an end to the Sankara *mutt*'s monopoly of land, it caused a minor sensation. People felt as though a pillar of the abbey had crumbled. His father thought it disastrous. The monks tried through him to get Pradeep back to the abbey: they tried several other ways; they felt the trouble would die down if only Pradeep would pull out. For quite some time, even after the *Vahini* came on the scene in 1978, the monks would not change their opinion, which was that this whole nuisance was of one man's making—Pradeep's!

Jagannathan's team moved from village, holding discussions both with the peasants and the labourers. A few peasants came forward to help. When visiting a village, the campaign group would ask people to gather for a meeting somewhere roomy—on the verandah of a peasant's house, a classroom in a primary school, an open space—where the audience were reminded how the Sankara *mutt* had been exploiting them, and made to realize the compelling need for a movement to liberate the large amount of land the abbey illegally held. The land thus freed, said the campaigners, should be shared out among the poor. Jagannathan never forgot to add one more thing: the movement they were proposing must be absolutely non-violent.

Every village overwhelmingly endorsed the campaigners' views about the *mutt* and its oppression, but very few people were willing to participate in planned agitation against it; they feared the *mutt* would be quick to strike back. The labourers of some villages, notably Gosain Pesra, were, however, prepared to join in. And when the first protest—a continuous group fasting for three days—gathered in front of the Sankara *mutt*, it was these labourers who thronged there to participate. This was in April 1975. On one of the days of fasting JP came to Bodh Gaya to address the protesters. A big crowd gathered to hear him. In the crowd there were also a hundred or more workers of the Communist Party of India, which had opposed the 'right reactionary' movement led by JP. They were determined to create a disturbance during JP's speech. He began to speak, but his words were drowned in the mad chant of the CPI men: 'CIA agent, out! out! out!' The policemen on duty to keep peace at the meeting place ran towards the CPI demonstrators, and made a baton charge, sending everybody in the audience scurrying for shelter. JP was whisked away to the *Sarvodaya ashram* where, some time later, he made the speech he had come to make. It carried an appeal to the trustees of the Sankara *mutt* to give up voluntarily the land they held illegally.

Shortly afterwards, Jagannathan went again to see the abbot. But the abbot hadn't changed his mind: he was ready to release just one of the 18 land-owning trusts and no more. Jagannathan and other campaigners returned to their organizing activities in the countryside. Towards the end of June the same year, a five-day sit in was planned opposite the *mutt* entrance, but the five days had not ended before Indira Gandhi imposed the Emergency on the nation. The police quickly moved in to dismantle the protesters' tents and arrested many. Soon Jagannathan and Pradeep too were put in jail. About 400 labourers who had taken part in the campaign remained in prison throughout the whole Emergency. While they were detained, their wives and children sank deeper into poverty; they sometimes went without food; their huts fell apart lacking their annual repair.

After the end of the Emergency in April 1977 Jagannathan and Krishnamma did not return to Bodh Gaya. This came as a shock to the labourers, who were newly out of prison, many still committed to the campaign. They had, the labourers felt, undergone suffering for no purpose. There wasn't even any help from the *Sarvodaya*, Jagannathan's organization for repairing their shacks or paying back loans. The *Sarvodaya* leader from Tamil Nadu and his wife had gone away leaving them in difficulties. Why? It was surmised that they now felt their campaign to be futile, that the monks would never give away the estates; that no government or court could find anything untoward because the monks had made all their property documents conform perfectly to the law. Or, perhaps the two, after Jagannathan's arrest and all the trouble, had been unwilling to undergo possible suffering in the future, if they stayed on in Bodh Gaya.

This campaign had ended with no results. Yet it had done one positive thing by creating an atmosphere which was to prove to the *Vahini*'s advantage when its volunteers arrived a year later to work in the area. Here, due to that brief agitation, the scene for struggle was set, and the participation of quite a few of the labourers assured from the outset. Pradeep was already in the *Vahini*, as its Gaya district convener, and ready to work for the resumption of the campaign. Besides, the *Vahini* volunteers from Patna or other districts of Bihar did not have to go here and there in search of a place in Bodh Gaya where they could stay and get a meal before they set out for, or returned from the organizing work in the villages: the *Sarvodaya ashram* from where Jagannathan had operated, was also ideal for *Vahini* volunteers. When they were in the rural areas they found the *Sarvodaya* village office at Shekhwara the best place to stay.

But meanwhile, within the *Vahini* organization, the chasm between the volunteers who had come from a *Sarvodaya* background and the independent youths widened. Shortly after the Bodh Gaya campaign started, it became unbridgeable. With the *Sarvodaya* volunteers withdrawing themselves from the *Vahini*, the independent youths came to regard the *Sarvodaya* hospitality in Bodh Gaya as improper to enjoy. After a time, they stopped going to the *ashram*, whose men in any case had never liked their place being used as a centre for agitation. Latterly the independent youths' relations with the *Sarvodaya* men were to deteriorate to the point of acrimony.

The struggle in Sankara

Inside the white-painted Sankara *mutt* another struggle was taking place. Every corner of the rectangular-shaped old three-storeyed abbey smelled of plots and counter-plots. The outside world knew nothing of it: pilgrims and devotees continued to visit the abbey. But anyone wishing to see the abbot was met with suspicion and many questions: often, callers were turned away. The abbot had several monks and employees who spied on people coming to meet Jayaram, the chief manager, or his deputy, Deenadayal. The strife seemed unlikely to end until it was decided who was the real boss, Jayaram or the abbot.

There were no fewer than 500 monks attached to the abbey. Some of them had been sent to the villages as heads of the abbey's more than 50 known farmhouses, and the others were living in the monastery. Entering the monastery from the street, through a high door on the left, was the shorter side of the rectangle; in the centre, on the longer side, was another high door. Here the watchmen stood and here you had to take off your shoes; this door opened into a very large inner courtyard, above which on each floor of the building were the rooms, 100 in all, where the monks or employees or the employees' dependants (in exceptional cases like Pradeep) lived. A number of monks slept on the long verandah. For the abbot, there was a corner suite on the top floor. Some of the bigger rooms on the ground floor served as small temples where priests chanted morning prayers to the image of one or other Hindu deity, either in the centre of the room or against the back or side wall. A small part of the courtyard was a raised platform made with slabs of marble, and on it was a metal emblem of a lion's head. This platform served as a rostrum from which the abbot or itinerant Hindu sages gave sermons to an audience of monks and pilgrims.

The abbey admitted no women. And, though in theory caste was no bar, it admitted only upper-caste Hindus, the monks were mainly from different districts of Bihar and Uttar Pradesh. A man who wanted to become a monk had to fulfil certain conditions before the abbot could accept him—as a disciple. In theory, the requirements were no less important than those of a proper novitiate, but in actuality, all sorts of people had become monks: the rules retained their form only. All the monks, for instance, observed the rule of tonsure (which was why every monk at the Sankara *mutt* was called *mudia*, the one who shaves the top of his head). But, almost all other customs were ignored. For example, one condition was that before being admitted to the order a man must leave his family and have no home. But it was an open secret that several monks maintained relations with their families; some were even said to take frequent trips home to spend a few days with their wives and children.

It was also said that some of the monks were obtaining money, or whatever they could lay their hands on, from the monastery for the use of their families. There were a thousand ways one could 'earn' such money. The abbey was a huge establishment; its kitchen alone catered for several hundred people twice a day; its grain godown regularly received and released too much grain; and then there were donations made to the abbey, and money when the bags of grain from the farmhouses were sold; and also their imbursements of various accounts. The monks supervised or carried out these tasks and fell into a habit of pilfering. Pilfering was equally common in the farmhouses. The property was too huge to keep a close watch on at harvest time.

Though the quest for further evidence about the way in which the Sankara *mutt* acquired so much land goes on, researchers suggest that the abbey had no property until the Mughals settled in Delhi and, through their provincial governor in Bihar, made a rent-free grant to the abbey of two villages nearby, Mastipur and Taridih, for its maintenance. Later, the Mughals gave it more rent-free villages. Under the Raj, the abbey's rent-free estates were initially confiscated as illegal, but were restored after inquiries. The British later even made the abbey a *zamindar*, a position in which it kept on acquiring more estates. From the villages, the abbey collected its rents, through its offices or *kutcheries*, by which name its farmhouses continued to be called even after the abolition of the Permanent Settlement. The abbots of the monastery during the colonial period remained loyal to the Raj; supported them in 1857 at the time of the rebellion of sepoys and *zamindars*, and had even provided shelter in the abbey to a body of British troops beleaguered by rebels of the Gaya district.

Like most *zamindars*, the abbey flouted laws in order to retain a huge property after the end of the *zamindari*. After that the land was cultivated via the *kutcheries*-turned-farmhouses under two arrangements; where the size of the abbey holdings was small it was leased out to sharecroppers who handed back half the harvest; where the estates were large, the cultivation was done by *kamias*, cottagers, as bondmen, each of whom might be given a parcel of land to grow coarse grains for themselves. These *kamias* worked under atrocious conditions of supervision by the abbey's men. At each farmhouse, there was a hierarchy; the top ranks went, as a rule, to the upper castes: and the order was *godaits* (peons), *barahils* (labour overseers), *dewan* (book-keeper) and *gumasta* (manager), headed by a *mudia*, one of the abbey's monks. There was a kitchen in the farmhouse where meals were cooked for all the staff, but the monthly salary of the kitchen staff was abysmal—two, ten, twenty rupees—and even the fixed quantities of grain given them at the end of the year for their families were painfully inadequate. On these grounds employees, from the manager downwards, secretly justified their pilfering and dishonesty.

Not all that was produced under the farmhouse system went to the abbey. Often the monk, the most trusted man of the abbey far afield in the farmhouse, turned a blind eye to the selling of unrecorded grain, and was given his due share. Money and power made the monks seek comforts at the farmhouse, like those they contrived for themselves in the abbey. Some had built good houses for themselves in other parts of Bihar and Uttar Pradesh; Jayaram had seized the abbey's estates in certain villages of Muzaffarpur and Vaishali districts of North Bihar. Some became interested in women, and even kept women from the *kamia* families.

In his room, Dhansukh Giri, the abbot, clad in a double-breasted saffron tunic, sat on his foam bed. He was in his early thirties, wore glasses, and had sparkling, mischievous eyes set in a round, fair face. A fan whirred by the wall below the window looking out on to the abbey's inner entrance door, where the watchmen stood. The advantage of occupying this room seemed to be that you could, sitting on your bed, keep a watch through the open window on the people or things coming into or going out of the abbey. At the time our interview began, bags of grain were being unloaded from tractors at the entrance door. We sat down on a mat on the floor which the abbot, tonsured and clean-shaven, had pointed us to.

There was a litter of small, thin books on the bed where the abbot sat simpering. A great deal of the literature surrounding him was that put out by numerous Indian publishers specializing in books about the Hindu faith. They were freely available at the railway bookstalls, and from wayside vendors; there was no bookcase. The abbot seemed more interested in talking about the rivalry and intrigues against him than the issue of the abbey's land or the *Vahini* campaign. He dismissed the land campaign in a few words: 'We all—I, you, the *Vahini* youths—agree—don't we?—that this *mutt* is a religious institution, a very old one. Why should any of us do something to its detriment? Aren't the *Vahini* boys Hindus, too? Are they or not? I say that if the *Vahini* wants the *mutt* to look after its people properly we can discuss proposals about opening schools and medical dispensaries in the village. *Kya sochte hain*—What d'you think? All right or not?'

But outsiders, the abbot went on his peculiar manner, were not to be blamed for the crisis. It was his opponents in the abbey (the abbot avoided mention of any names, but nodded quickly, 'The same', when Jayaram's name came up in one of the questions put to him) who were the wicked venal lot who had created the crisis. And they, he said, needed putting down if the abbey was to be salvaged. The Sankara *mutt* was nobody's personal property, he said; it was a trust, and it should be run like a trust, 'All right or not?' The monks must live like monks—'mustn't they?' Abruptly, the abbot broke off and glanced quickly round the bed and, rummaging about among the books littering it, picked out one with the title *Bharat ke patan ke sat karan* (Seven causes of the decline of India), written by a Swami Jagdishwaranand Saraswati. He quickly found the page he wanted to read to us. 'Of the decline of India', the abbot began to read, 'there is another cause: and that is the good-for-nothing multitude of six million "monks". . . . The place of monks today has been taken over by money-seekers, selfish and vain elements and those who seek positions of power and authority, and who are hoaxers and hypocrites. . . . '

Dropping the book back into the litter, the abbot said, 'What do you think? All right or not?' He went on, 'These people want to become the masters of the Sankara *mutt* while I remain the abbot in name only, content just with the title.' There, the abbot, it seemed to us, had disclosed the crucial point of the abbey's inner conflict.

News and gossip about the monastery ordinarily took a long time to reach the villages. The confrontation between the abbot and Jayaram Giri was, however, too sensational to travel along the old slow route. Very few people believed it to be true, however: outside the abbey, nothing showed; its work in the villages did not seem to have been in any way affected. For the thousands of *kamias* who worked the abbey's fields, the institution remained as intact and as oppressive as before. Should a *kamia* try acting as if inner conflict had incapacitated the abbey, he would tread a dangerous path, for every labourer believed that the abbey still had the power to grind him down. Work continued, therefore, in the old servile way.

Most of the *kamias* were Bhuyans, an untouchable caste, whom the abbey's agents had brought by deception from distant villages or the edges of the outlying jungles, long ago. Some were slaving for other masters, and others, almost like tribals, scratching a living out of the soil about the woods, when the abbey's agents had found them and told them stories of a great benevolent master in Bodh Gaya in whose villages workers enjoyed marvellous meals daily, and a far better life than elsewhere. Should they wish to go to live here, the master would be willing to take them on, the agents said. The temptation was impossible to resist. On the day they arrived, the Bhuyans were actually served very good food; *aloodam*, curried potatoes, and *poorie*, small fried discs of bread, with countless glasses of local brew. For the rest of their lives they starved.

There were reasons for the abbey to choose Bhuyans rather than other labourers. They were semi-tribal, guileless and hard-working, and prone to drowning their woes in pots of liquor. They were the kind of people who could be made to work longer hours, and used in breaking fresh ground. They were to be tied to the abbey's farmhouses; and to shackle them securely the farmhouse staff were helped by the *sirdars*, community heads, of the Bhuyans in every village, corrupted by the staff with petty bribes or just an occasional good meal and drinks. The children of the *kamias* would never go to school, and whole families, whole generations of Bhuyans would thus be condemned to work for the Sankara *mutt*.

Seldom were the *kamias* allowed a day off. Their movement was severely restricted. Kosambi, a 40-year-old woman labourer of Jairampur village, said no one could go out of the village even to visit a close relative in another village. If you had guests to attend to in your hut, that was no excuse to get leave from the farmhouse manager. Huts were empty by day, for the wife, too, deemed to be bonded if her man was, had to slave for the abbey. Kosambi said she returned with her husband late in the evening after collecting her wage of one and a quarter kilos of paddy (paddy was an improvement brought about by the agitation; until recently they had been given rotten coarse grains). Then she would squat, her body aching from the day's overwork, monotonously to turn the hand millstone to husk the paddy. That task done, she would make a fire and put the rice on to boil. She ate her food after her husband and children had finished their meals; and then she arranged things in the hut, and by the time they went to bed it was past ten o'clock or, quite often, close to midnight.

Before sunrise they had to be in the fields again, where the farmhouse overseers distributed to each of them breakfast of a handful of *mahua* fruits or parched coarse grain. No break was permitted before noon. That meant Kosambi could have no time to feed her children. The young ones would be crying near the family shack or on the ridge bounding the field where she worked with others, watched by the overseers and peons. They had hearts of stone, the *mutt's* men. Kosambi remembered how they had turned a small bunch of children away when they were found standing on one or two occasions in front of the farmhouse, hoping to be given something to eat, while their fathers and mothers were working in the fields. Hungry children were only able at midday to share the meals their fathers and mothers were given. The farmhouse kept the women occupied even when there was no work for them in the fields; they could be asked to follow the trail of the buffaloes and cows through the village, to collect their droppings in baskets; or directed to carry things on their heads from and to the farmhouse. And yet when the hard work for the day was over the women and the men were not always sure of getting their daily wages. 'Come tomorrow,' some employer might say, waving them away as they gathered outside the farmhouse after dark to collect their wages. The reason given might be that there was 'no electricity' in the farmhouse. Sometimes no reasons were given. There was one more problem: the grain wage a labourer received was always less than it should be because the farmhouse used no standard weights, but only kilos and grams, made of brick pieces that were partly rubbed away through constant use.

At Mastipur, a few miles away from Kosambi's Jairampur, the *kamias* lived in no better conditions. And rebellion stood less of a chance here, for Mastipur (one of the two first rent-free villages the *mutt* had been given by the Mughals) was located on the edge of Bodh Gaya, some minutes from the abbey. There was little response here to the exhortations of the *Vahini* volunteers in the initial organizing days. The *kamias* dissolved, to hide themselves away when the volunteers arrived in the village from the *Sarvodaya ashram*. If they had to attend any meeting, they would all listen silently but pay no attention to the visitors' persuasion. The volunteers would say to them, 'You cleared the jungles and the wasteland, but you get a wage that doesn't even fill your stomachs. You must fight to get the land that belongs to you.' But the *kamias* of Mastipur had not joined the Jagannathan campaign, but because they lived so near the abbey, they had watched the group fast and the sit-in outside the *mutt*, and were aware of what the protest was all about. Some of them came forward to support the *Vahini* volunteers and showed interest in holding discussions with them in the village. But then there arose a new problem. Reports of these activities reached the abbey's authorities, through their peons at Mastipur. The *kamias* were summoned to the abbey; the morning became one of gloom, fear and guilt. They had heard, indeed some had actually seen, disloyal servants being flogged and tortured. At the end the man would slump to the ground, his body cut and scarred all over, his mouth pouring blood; sometimes red chilli powder was put into his eyes and as he screamed, he was hit with clubs.

The terrified Mastipur bondmen, as soon as they appeared at the door of the abbey, were directed upstairs to the abbot's court hall, next to his suite. There the abbot sat with Jayaram and his deputy, Deenadayal. The *kamias* bowed to each of them, and were motioned to sit on the floor, a few yards away. As they squatted, pale, speechless and shivering, and avoiding the eyes of the masters, Jayaram snarled at them: 'Who's the instigator turning you against the *mutt*?' Shivers ran through to wooden bodies. The chief manager's words echoed in the silence of the court hall; no answer came. The abbot remained quiet, his face taut and wrinkled. Jayaram thundered: 'Listen, you will all be betrayed. They will vanish as they have come, no one will suffer but you idiots who will be in the street, starving.' The wooden bodies did not stir; they were incapable of speech. Finally, Jayaram ordered them to take a pledge, and they all recited emphatically: 'We shall never act on the instigation of outsiders. From tomorrow we will not let them in.'

As a token of the *kamias'* reiterated fealty, Deenadayal instructed the *mutt* godown-keeper to issue a seer (900 grams) of rice to each of them. They bowed to the masters as they left, and ran back home, feeling light-headed. But the next day the *Vahini* volunteers, whom the *kamias* called *bhaji* (brothers) were in the village again, rebuking the *kamias* for going to the abbey at the abbot's bidding. 'Once you mind to join the struggle against the masters, why should any of you be afraid of them?' asked the volunteers. In the next few days meetings were held in Mastipur and, after a great deal of effort, the volunteers succeeded in bringing the *kamias* back and committed to the struggle. The abbot sent for them again. Panic gripped them. This time they had no doubt they would be carried back home with broken bones and bleeding wounds; yet they could not refuse to go. Once more they sat facing the abbot, Jayaram and Deenadayal. This time, it was the abbot who spoke to them. 'My sons,' he said, coating his anger with a transparent layer of softness, 'what, after all, is your problem? Tell me.' A dead silence followed. After a few minutes, one of the *kamias* stuttered, faintly and prayerfully, 'Baba, my Guru, the thing is. . . the thing is that with two kilos

of paddy, that does not suffice Baba. If the wage is raised a little it would, ... '
'I see,' the abbot snapped, nodding his head in a slow and stern way. 'Then listen, sons. The wage will not be raised, even if the sun begins to rise in the west. All right? Any other problem?' There was complete silence again. When none of them would say a word, Jayaram got into a rage, and shouted that he was giving them a last warning. 'Remember the warning. Now go.' The *kamias* silently walked out of the abbey building and, in a cold sweat again, went home.

Land for the landless

Bodh Gaya was chosen by the *Vahini* as a *saghan Kshetra* (intensive area of struggle) at a meeting of its main activists held in Patna City, an old town east of Patna, in February 1978. Several considerations went into the making of this choice: JP had given up his idea of 'peaceful class struggle', and had urged the youth to integrate themselves with society's *antima jana* (lowest person): and Bodh Gaya was a region where already the Jagannathans, aided by some local activists now in the *Vahini*, had, in a way, set things going. This spadework offered promise to the *Vahini* for the practising of JP's ideas. At the meeting the possibility of taking up work in another area (Panchamania in Madhubani district in North Bihar for example) was ultimately rejected in favour of Bodh Gaya, because it was a much bigger area with but a single big landlord to contend with.

Actual work in Bodh Gaya, however, made slow progress: the urban youths of the *Vahini* were occupied with urban protests. To the first demonstration in Bodh Gaya town, staged a couple of months after the Patna City meeting, up to 500 *Vahini* men and women had come from all parts of Bihar. It was announced at the end of the rally that three or four activists would be staying on to work full time for mobilization in the villages: and there would also be a team of five coming by turn from other districts in the state.

But no activist arrived in Bodh Gaya for over two months: then one turned up, but he left in less than two weeks. Another, shortly after his arrival became ill and he, too, went back. Later, a third one, Narendra, a senior volunteer, would visit for ten days every month. A meeting was held in August at a village in the Bodh Gaya area to discuss the state of volunteer deployment, at which the *Vahini*'s state convener promised to deploy at least six activists for full-time work. Not one arrived. At another meeting held in Patna, where the agenda related to something else, the *Vahini* convener again made a promise to direct at least five volunteers to go to stay for a month in Bodh Gaya. Only one made an appearance, Prabhat; and he came from Patna not because the convener had asked him to or because he was eager to participate in a land struggle; he had insisted on coming to Bodh Gaya because he was bored by his monotonous duties as office secretary at the *Vahini*'s state office and badly needed a change. The absence of activists, and the short visits of the few who did turn up, angered the local cadres in Bodh Gaya. One of the cadres wrote to the state office:'If flying visits like the politicians' were a solution, then the face of our nation would have changed long ago.'

It was left to the few, Narendra, Prabhat, Karu, a *Sarvodaya* youth rebel, Karujira, a local youth active since Jagannathan's campaign, and Pradeep and others, who were prepared to live rough, to do the organizing work. They ate irregularly; the meal was usually a coarse one, or bread or rice without vegetables; and they seldom had money to buy themselves food. They moved about the villages on foot. They never asked the people to give them any money, which helped to remove initial doubts that might arise among the people that the *Vahini* volunteers were just another bunch of touts promising to buy titles or plots of land with bribes in the government's land offices. But doubts were not so easy to set at rest. The volunteers of the *Vahini* had made it a point to approach only the *kamias* and other land labourers, deciding that they alone fell into the category of *antima jana*, lowest persons, whom JP had called upon them to integrate with. But the *kamias* would not come out to welcome a volunteer on his arrival in the village; they shunned him. The volunteer insisted on talking to them; he waited a long time for the people to gather, and if no one came, made his shoulder bag into a pillow and went hungry to sleep on a pallet outside.

Once the *kamias* were convinced that they were not touts, and that they belonged to an organization of youths living in large towns like Patna and led by JP, they accepted them. For one thing, the hunger for land was there; the agitation organized in the past by the socialists, the CPI, Jagannathan and his team, and the begging and redistribution of land by Hoodan's men, had created this longing. Apart from some *kamias*, mostly the older ones, who were resigned to fate, all the Bhuyans were interested in getting land out of the abbey's possession. The feeling that they would be able to gain a plot with the aid of the city youths, who, as they were led by JP, would stand firm against the Sankara *mutt*, made the Bhuyans agree to form a *mazdoor kisan samiti* (Committee of Labourers and Peasants) in every village. The name, though, was misleading, for there were hardly any peasants on these committees; the members mostly owned small slices of land in the villages where much of the agricultural land was held by the abbey; they cultivated their plots with family labour, sometimes hiring a hand to assist and felt no bitterness against the abbey. In several villages the abbey customarily demanded a few days' free labour from these independent peasants during the cultivation of its land, in ploughing for instance. Punishment, like a fine, was meted out to the peasant not reporting to the abbey's fields with his bullock and plough. The community never took decisions in village affairs without the consent of the *mutt's* men.

Yet the peasants did not join the *mazdoor kisan samiti*. They probably stayed out because land for the landless became the principal issue of the campaign; and also because the *Vahini* volunteers made only a half-hearted attempt to involve them. A third reason was that the peasants themselves were reluctant to be on a committee where the untouchable *kamias* would be equal to, if not above, them. Like the *kamias* the peasants wanted land to add to the small parcels they already owned. Yet in one or two villages where they joined together, the peasants pulled out, for the *Vahini* volunteers insisted that the labourers must have an opportunity to attend and decide matters at the *samiti* meetings. The *samiti* in every village came thus to be filled with labourers, especially the Bhuyan *kamias*. The identification of the organization with the Bhuyans was so strong that in certain villages the Bhuyans resisted taking landless labourers from other untouchable or lower castes on to the *samitis*. Behind the reluctance was the notion among the Bhuyans that the *Vahini* was trying to help them build up a caste organization to fight for land!

After a few months' work, the *Vahini* found its whole campaign becoming concentrated in one village, Gosain Pesra. It was a village with an old *mutt kutchery*, a spacious brick building of *zamindari* days, now used as the farm-house where the monks and staff of the abbey lived to look after the cultivation done by 80 *kamias*, 70 of them Bhuyans. Independent middle peasants made up one-third of the Gosain Pesra's population; there were also several landless labourers other than the Bhuyans who worked for the peasants of the village or employers outside. One immediate reason why Gosain Pesra became, initially, the *Vahini's* campaign centre was the involvement of the *kamias* of this village in the pre-Emergency protest led by Jagannathan. Even before the Jagannathan campaign began, the *kamias* nursed a desire for land. Not very long ago the *mukhiya*, the head of the village council, had assured them he could get titles to plots of land if they would raise a small fund with which to bribe the officers and clerks. He had twice taken them along to Patna, to the secretariat; outside there he would stop, telling them he would go inside to see what progress their 'files' had made; he would then take them to the legislative assembly building, and repeat the charade. The *kamias* never received any title deeds through him. After this, the *kamias* had pinned their hopes on Jagannathan and Pradeep and had participated with enthusiasm in the fast and sit-in in front of the abbey. During the Emergency no fewer than 26 of the *kamias* were jailed.

The *kamias* of Gosain Pesra were in the forefront when the *Vahini* organized its demonstration in April 1978. At the meeting after the demonstration the leader of the Gosain Pesra's *kamias*, Janaki Das, sat on the dais with the *Vahini* leaders as one of the two representatives of the labourers. They were also the first to take action: after the demonstration they quickly scythed up wheat from the small parcels of land they had taken that year from the abbey for sharecrop-ping; they gave the farmhouse none of it. After that, events in the village were to follow one another rapidly: the farmhouse men wanted to stop the *kamias*; the two sides clashed and the *kamias* faced the farmhouse men with stones, clubs and fisticuffs, leaving several *mutt* men wounded, the *dewan* with two or three fewer teeth and two *barahils* (labour overseers) with bleeding heads.

Jayaram, the chief manager, ordered a change in the arrangement at the Gosain Pesra farmhouse as the situation there seemed to be getting out of hand. He decided that the abbey would no longer undertake direct cultivation, but get it done through a private contractor from whom it would receive a fixed share of each harvest. The contractor, shortly after he moved into the farmhouse, announced his decision to fire 60 of the 80 *kamias*, on the grounds of redun-dancy. This was disturbing for the Bhuyan segment of the village. At once the sacked *kamias* signalled a general boycott of farmwork for the monastery: several of the 20 *kamias* still employed also joined the boycott. Yet the boycott had not been well thought out as later events proved. The *Vahini* had not been consulted: neither did the Bhuyans call the peasants or the day labourers to a meeting for discussion before they decided to face this new challenge by a boycott. But once it had been called, the boycott had to continue indefinitely, until the 60 *kamias* were reinstated. The abbey then leased out its land in small parcels to the village for sharecropping, an arrangement the peasants gladly accepted. The *kamias*, determined but isolated, offered no resistance at the time of ploughing the abbey's fields by the peasants, nor when the peasants did the sowing, and, after the crops ripened, took half the harvest as agreed, into the abbey's farmhouse.

After the boycott started the *kamias* were forced to look elsewhere for daily work. Sometimes they found work in another village or with a road or building contractor, sometimes not. Meanwhile, the *mazdoor kisan samiti* of Gosain Pesra passed into a state of inactivity. 'Have we borne so much to end like this?' The *kamias* could not help some self-recrimination. They had, they felt, toiled hard enough for the *mutt* to be entitled to its land. They, not the abbey of Sankara, must be deemed to be the real owners. After all they were not ordinary labourers who could be taken on or thrown out at will: the ground bore witness to their blood and slavery. Regaining their spirit with these thoughts, the *kamias*, after consultation among themselves and with the *Vahini* volunteers, were back again to claim their rights.

Winter crops such as wheat and pulses must not be sown, it was decided. The *kamias* therefore went to the peasants, the smallholders, to dissuade them, but they would not listen and went ahead with sowing. As the time for harvesting drew near the *kamias* again approached the peasants, this time with a plea that they should carry out their harvesting as they wished, taking half the yield to their homes, but giving the other half of the yield to them, the *kamias*, the real owners of the land, and not to the *mutt* as they had wrongly done in the case of rice paddies the previous summer. Not a single grain should reach the farmhouse. Again, the peasants declined: they refused even a reduced demand of a quarter share by the *kamias*. The *kamias* then announced that they would hold demonstrations during the harvesting and would themselves cut and take the crops away. Watching everything from behind a screen, the *mutt* authorities got police posted in the village to provide protection to both peasants and crops. They also had some thugs lodged in the farmhouse to do the same job. It appeared impossible now for the *kamias* to harvest the crops forcibly. Still, they gathered at the fields and did succeed in harvesting lentils from about ten acres.

It was greatly worrying to the *Vahini* and the Bodh Gaya area *mazdoor kisan samiti* to see the struggle localized in one place. For the movement to survive the monastery's onslaught, the struggle must expand rapidly. At a conference of the area *samiti*, held a little before the ploughing for paddy was due to begin towards the end of summer in 1979, a decision was taken to call a general boycott of the abbey work which, essentially, would mean repeating the Gosain Pesra situation in every village. The decision had manifestly been made without much groundwork in other villages. But the boycott in Gosain Pesra was already on and the younger *kamias* from some other villages like Katorwa near Bodh Gaya had supported the general boycott proposal, which was called 'non-cooperation'.

Throughout the months of non-cooperation, Gosain Pesra was repeated in other ways. The monastery quickly leased its land to the smallholders, arranged to have police camps established in larger villages, and installed roughnecks in the village farmhouses to see the ploughing was done everywhere without hindrance. Non-cooperation meant that the *kamias* would not stop at boycott; they would prevent anyone from trying to cultivate the abbey's land. Since Bodh Gaya was the ground for realizing JP's ideas of peaceful class struggle, the *Vahini* and the *kamias* had vowed to do no violence. But they would prevent cultivation, fearlessly and firmly.

In Katorwa, the *kamias* stormed into the fields as the ploughmen, guarded by some of the abbey's thugs, arrived, scaring away the ploughing party by their number and their mood. But a few days later some labourers, despatched by the *mutt* authorities, came and, under the thugs' protection, hurriedly scattered lentil seeds over the unploughed ground, probably to prove, symbolically, that non-cooperation had failed, at least in Katorwa, for lentil had been 'sown' there. The *kamias*, like a flock of hungry birds, descended on the field and, hopping from place to place, bent down and picked up all the lentil seeds between their fingers and ate them. Thereafter, they turned their attention to the rice stocks in the *mutt* farmhouse and, in a swift raid, carried the bags away.

Such brave acts by the *kamias* of Katorwa, together with the courageous and aggressive initiative of Gosain Pesra's *kamias*, inspired the abbey's farm servants in about 20 villages of the Bodh Gaya administrative area to come out during the non-cooperation programme. These were the first examples that showed the Sankara *mutt* was not as impregnable as it had looked. If they were united the *kamias* could deflate the *mutt*'s men, frighten them away from the farmhouses, strike fear in the hearts of even the thugs, and remove bags of rice, rightfully theirs, from the farmhouse stores. A great deal of encouragement during the non-cooperation came from the presence of a much larger number of *Vahini* volunteers in their area than was usual. In the months to come, the *kamias* were to carry out a programme within the programme: to go in large numbers in every village to demolish the farmhouses and take with them the bricks, wood, doors and fitments the fleeing staff had left behind in those old buildings. The aim of this was to destroy the abbey's local centres.

At Mastipur in disregard of warnings delivered twice at the abbot's court hall, there was also a boycott. No fresh summons came from the monastery. But the morning of 8 August 1979 brought the Mastipur *kamias* disconcerting news: an army of hired workers and armed bullies had gathered at the farmhouse with bullocks and ploughs. The farmhouse was separated from the *kamia* segment by wide fields bordered by a metalled road: the *mutt* appeared about to move in, in order to plough. At once the *kamias* called an emergency meeting to discuss what to do. That morning two *Vahini* volunteers also happened to be there. On the evening before, some men and women volunteers had stayed overnight at the village. All but two had left for other villages earlier in the morning, before the gang was seen at the farmhouse. At the emergency meeting opinions differed on the advisability of going out to stop the ploughing: but finally, those supporting swift action won. Messengers were rushed out to call back the *Vahini* volunteers who had left earlier.

It was midday when about 200 labourers, empty handed, filed out of the village accompanied by two *Vahini* volunteers who had stayed on: the other volunteers had not arrived. The slogan-chanting *kamias* were spotted across the fields, where, at the farmhouse end, the ploughmen were beginning to work. Just as the head of the *kamias* procession reached the metalled road and was about to cross it into the fields, there were deafening explosions all around them. So many home-made grenades came flying in quick succession from the other side, so thick were the clouds of smoke, that it became impossible for any of the *kamias* to see beyond one or two feet. Then tearing the blinded sky, as the grenades continued to explode, a cry reached everyone's ears: one of the *kamias* had fallen beside the road, hit by a bullet in his foot. As others rushed in the direction of the screams more gunshots struck another *kamia*, young Ramdeo, in the thigh and in the foot. He stumbled and in the next instant was dead.

The fatal attack stunned the *Vahini* volunteers. Ramdeo's father sat by the side of his son's body screaming crazily. Suddenly the old man got up and yelling 'I'll kill them; I'll kill them!' he ran empty-handed across the fields towards the farmhouse. By then the wind had carried off much of the smoke. A young *kamia*, Panchu, ran after Ramdeo's father, shouting to others that the old man must not be left alone to face the thugs. But Panchu had run hardly a few yards when a grenade hit him in the stomach leaving a large hole through which his intestines spilled out. Coming to after a short stupor, one of the *Vahini* volunteers rushed off to find a telephone to call the police. The other one ran a few yards into the fields and, once there, jumped about hysterically, his hands slicing through the smoke as though he were swimming. (He later explained that he felt so ashamed and guilty: they, the *Vahini* volunteers, had persuaded the *kamias* to fight the *mutt*, and as a consequence they were dying through no fault of their own—that he wished that a grenade or a bullet would hit him.)

Meanwhile some of the processionists had swung back to their village, and returned with axes, hatchets, clubs, whatever they could find. They were going like the wind towards the farmhouse, where Ramdeo's father was now receiving blows from the roughnecks. Having probably exhausted their grenades and cartridges, the roughnecks, as they saw the armed *kamias* running towards them, let go of the old man, and turned to rush into the farmhouse building and, when all were in, to bolt its doors. Only one man from their side failed to do this, Ramadhar Singh, the manager of the *mutt* farmhouse at the adjoining village, Tikabigha. He tried to escape towards the town but the avengers chased and grabbed him, and killed him with a shower of blows. Later it became known that the murdered farmhouse manager was an uncle of Pradeep's.

There was a public outcry over the brutality of the Sankara *mutt's* thugs. Political parties condemned it in press statements: it was reported in all the papers. Severe punishment was demanded by the *Vahini* against the thugs and the abbey's authorities. Yet, even as the *Vahini* leaders called for action, thoughts of the murder of the farmhouse manager by the *kamias* gnawed at their hearts. The murder threatened to impair the Bodh Gaya movement's reputation as a unique experience in 'peaceful' class struggle. If the truth were publicized the foundations of the JP's theory would be shaken. Already, some violence had taken place in Gosain Pesra. The two volunteers who led the Mastipur *kamias* that morning had difficulty in explaining to the *Vahini's* central committee in Patna that they had done all they could that day to dissuade the armed *kamias* from rushing to repulse the *mutt* attack, but that no attention had been paid to their appeal.

Several meetings of the *Vahini* were held in Patna to discuss the subject. Meanwhile, JP set up a committee of three *Sarvodaya* men to conduct a detailed inquiry into the incidents at Mastipur. The committee went to Bodh Gaya, talked to the people, and returned to write a report which told how cruelly the *mutt* thugs had attacked and killed two landless labourers and how an infuriated mob of labourers had, in a swift revenge, taken the manager's life. Before the report was released to the press, JP went through it: he deleted the parts relating to the manager's murder, and the adverse comments of the *Sarvodaya* investigations. Soon the *Vahini* also blotted out from its minute book the proceedings of the meetings it had held on the Mastipur issue. The matter was never reported in the papers; even periodicals run by *Vahini* volunteers or people sympathetic to the *Vahini* censored the killings. JP, the *Vahini* leaders, and the sympathizers were satisfied that the murder was an 'aberration' in the experiment of peaceful class struggle. Had Mahatma Gandhi been alive and leading the Bodh Gaya struggle he would certainly have called it off, condemning the *kamias'* violence. JP was a Gandhian, but he saw the pragmatic side too—at least in the case of Bodh Gaya. He did not want the movement to stop for one single incident of murder. The movement must continue, but of course with the greatest possible precaution so that no violence took place in future.

The death of JP

On the other side, following the Mastipur incidents, the dogfight within the monastery took a serious turn. Police had registered cases of murder on both sides; the public outcry over the thugs' cruelties refused to die down. Accusations were made against the abbot, and more directly against Jayaram. The chief manager was trying to wriggle out of the situation. He was, he would say, merely a servant of the monastery; it was the abbot who gave orders; he only obeyed them. Jayaram and his trusted deputy, Deendayal, had been listed as the main accused in the murders of the two *kamias*. The abbot was reluctant to be dragged into such infamy; so he, very cleverly, started using the opportunity to get rid of Jayaram, thinking probably that once the chief manager was gone, the monastery could disown its involvement in Mastipur. Quickly he stripped Jayaram and Deendayal of all their powers, an act that stunned the monks living in the monastery. He also circulated a public notice in the form of printed leaflets, which warned that no one should deal with the chief manager or his deputy in any kind of cash transaction or transactions relating to the sale and purchase of *mutt* land. Tigers were transformed into a pair of mice. Going a step further, the abbot had them both arrested.

To the *kamias*, the arrest of Jayaram was the event of the year. It was difficult at first for many to believe it. Most people felt relieved and much bolder as they celebrated Jayaram's 'downfall' in every village. In their eyes, the Sankara *mutt* had fallen apart; the process had begun with the defection of Pradeep, continued with the flight of the *mutt* employees from the farmhouse and the losses in agriculture and reached its end when the terror was handed over to the police. It was noteworthy that a number of *kamias* did not see the abbot as their enemy; Jayaram was the man believed to have taken all the decisions which perpetrated the atrocities. The perception was not totally wrong, but the fact that the abbot was as determined not to give up land as Jayaram had been was not realized. Somehow a rumour had spread around that the abbot was a compassionate, holy man, concerned for the welfare of the *kamias* and did not object to the idea of distributing parcels of land among them. Those who believed this felt that, with the ousting of Jayaram, the chances of their receiving land had improved.

But about the same time, after a prolonged illness due to kidney failure, JP died in Patna. The *Vahini* lost its ideologue; and feelings, spurred by rumours, ran deep in the villages of Bodh Gaya that the *Vahini* was finished as an organization; that it would cease to be active in the region; that its crowd of volunteers would quickly melt away. The prospect of JP's death had, no doubt, worried the *Vahini* leaders for a time. Towering over other public figures in India, he was always a source of strength for the *Vahini*, even on his sick bed. It was worrying that JP had not much elaborated on the ideas he had formed in the last years of his life, especially the one of peaceful class struggle. He had never fully explained how peaceful class struggle was to be linked to the *total revolution* of his dream. After JP's death the *Vahini* lost some members; they left the organization for lack of inspiration. Yet, despite the odds, the *Vahini* maintained its presence in Bodh Gaya, and the struggle was carried on into the 1980s.

The sowing and the harvest

The non-cooperation of 1979 had been a great success. Upwards of 3,000 acres of the abbey's land, spread over 30 villages in four administrative blocks, had remained unploughed. The peasants who had leased plots for sharecropping failed to cultivate them. It was, of course, true that the success of non-cooperation was due in part to the failure of the rains that year which brought the *kamias* acute distress, for while they had boycotted the *mutt* work, there were no jobs for them, even with other landowners.

Some went in search of uncertain employment outside the drought-hit region. As the drought was prolonged, others found it increasingly difficult to earn a meal; at least four of them died from hunger, the *mazdoor kisan samiti* reported. Starvation now became the main issue for the landowners; only daily work with a wage could ward it off.

The *samiti* decided to stage an insistent protest at the administrative block offices to force the government to start crash employment schemes, such as constructing beaten earth roads connecting the villages, building canal embankments, digging wells. Announcements had already been made by the government about the sanctioning of such schemes for the drought-affected areas, yet local officials, the agitators suspected, were holding them up, partly because they were inefficient and partly because they wanted fatter bribes from the contractors vying to carry out the schemes than they were prepared to give. After the protests, however, the officials cleared a few of the schemes for some villages, which still left a large number of the labourers unemployed. On the other side, the monastery, too, faced a crisis due to the *kamias'* non-cooperation and to the drought. Very few bullock carts, tractors or trucks now arrived with bags of grain at the *mutt's* entrance door visible from the abbot's top-floor room: and dwindling stocks in the inner godowns led to a heavy reduction in the amount of food cooked in the *mutt's* kitchen, and consequently to noticeable desertion by the monks.

After five long painful months of non-cooperation, a proposal was mooted by some of the *kamias* that next year the boycotters ought to cultivate the *mutt* land themselves, so as to put a stamp upon the plots that belonged to them. But doubts were expressed by others: where would they obtain ploughs, bullocks, seeds—possessions they had never had? These doubts were resolved in the coming months. The Bodh Gaya area *mazdoor kisan samiti*, when it endorsed the proposal at a conference, decided that the *kamias* should get ox ploughs on hire and borrow seeds from the peasants in their villages: they could also buy, or take on credit, seeds from grain traders. The interest on the seed loans was likely to be 50 per cent for the season. Many of the *kamias* raised their own money by selling goats and chickens, and any household article that would fetch a price. There would still be a huge shortfall: so the *Vahini* state convener placed an urgent request with the Association of Voluntary Agencies for Rural Development (AVARD), with which JP had for some time been connected, for at least 40 quintals of seeds.

Paddy, maize and lentils were sown in 1,700 acres, or over half the land left fallow due to non-cooperation the previous year. There were stray cases of resistance by the peasant lessees of the *mutt* land in certain villages. At some places the police in the camps also tried to stop the *kamias*, but the sowing went off without bloodshed or serious trouble. Yet the growing divide between *kamias* and smallholders worried the *Vahini* volunteers. The *Vahini*, it was true, wanted to work in the region primarily for the landless labourers, yet they must tactfully keep the peasants out of the battlefield if they were ever to win the battle against the *mutt*. From the outset the *mazdoor kisan samiti* had become restricted to the Bhuyans, and that was the movement's strength as well as its weakness. At the start of sowing, the *Vahini* and the *samiti* made a great effort to persuade the peasants to stay neutral. There was prolific leafletting on the subject. A *samiti* conference was held in June 1980 to find ways of tackling the peasants. Probably thinking that the issue of untouchability prevented them from sympathizing with the labourers, the delegates passed a resolution which said:

'God did not create caste. It is artful men who have separated society into castes, in their own interests. This division is proving an obstacle to its progress. In reality we all belong to one single community—the Human Community.'

A curious, but significant, resolution also passed at the conference was related to *samuhik kheti*, collective cultivation, by which the labourers who had started sowing were to be bound. It demonstrated that the *Vahini* volunteers wanted at once to put into practice the vision they had, through JP, of a communitarian society where labour and its fruits would be equally and justly shared. The central committee of the *Vahini* had never discussed the practice of collective cultivation in Bodh Gaya; it seemed to have been brought up at the conference by the *Vahini* volunteers stationed there, and passed by the *samiti* delegates without much thought or argument. It was to prove yet another romantic idea, probably stemming from the urban youths of the *Vahini*; it was too early to start making dreams real. Neither had there been any efforts made to educate the *kamias* about it. It was not surprising, therefore, that in several villages the *kamias* cultivated individually, with family labour; the same happened even in Gosain Pesra, the core of the movement, where the largest single area, 300 acres, was put under the plough. At some villages, the *kamias* were found to have tilled and sowed jointly, but such an arrangement arose more out of necessity (for there were fewer ploughs and bullocks) than from a commitment to collective cultivation. As the idea seemed in practice to be failing, the volunteers stationed in the region were worried and dejected; every progress report on the cultivation programme that they wrote for circulation in the area and for the information of the central committee lamented and deplored it.

Dormant at the time the *kamias* sowed the fields, the monastery became active against them during the harvesting. Armed policemen again moved in; they were deliberately directed into villages where the crop promised to be excellent. A complaint was handed by the *mazdoor kisan samiti* to the district magistrate of Gaya, asking him to order the withdrawal of the police from the villages. But the district magistrate said angrily to the *samiti* deputation, 'The sowing by labourers is illegal, for the land belongs to the *mutt*. The police are there to protect the *mutt*'s harvest, and have standing orders to shoot anyone getting in the way.'

It started at Katorwa village. A gang of harvest labourers, brought by *mutt* men from outside, entered under police escort into the green cropfields: stalks of unripe rice fell rapidly to the blades of their sickles. Then, in the same way, unripe rice was cut in several other villages, a swift pre-emptive move to ruin the rice crops if the *kamias* did not want the *mutt* to take them. The stunned *kamias* crowded round trying to offer resistance to the destruction, but the police stopped them and chased them away: they arrested several of them and sent them to jail, and in certain villages, went to the extent of plundering and pulling down *kamia* shacks. There were a few villages where the *kamias* succeeded in collecting the harvest: though, once again, the *Vahini* appeal to the collective spirit went unheeded, as the harvest was not stored at a common place: every *kamia* family, men, women and children, carried home as much as they could cut with their sickles and carry on their shoulders.

At Gosain Pesra, the police stationed there made no move until the paddy was ripe. Then one day, while the men of the Bhuyan segment were away working on a project at another village about 30 policemen, along with the *mutt's* 50 harvesters, trooped into the fields. The Bhuyan women had seen them coming; they ran to the fields, trying to stop them, but were chased away by club-brandishing police. That day rice from three acres was harvested by the *mutt's* labourers and carried away to the farmhouse. The same evening two *Vahini* volunteers, walking towards a village by way of Gosain Pesra, were stopped by the policemen and severely clubbed. 'No troublemakers allowed here,' the police officer shouted. The volunteers were dragged into the farmhouse and detained in one of its rooms. There, as the villagers slept, they were again beaten up: in the stillness of the night their screams could be heard in the village. As the news spread next morning, the *mazdoor kisan samiti* brought about 1,000 labourers from other villages to a demonstration at Gosain Pesra. The *mutt's* harvesters were at work as the demonstrators came on; they saw them heading towards the fields and took to their heels. As the demonstrators passed by the farmhouse, police suddenly came out to charge them; insane hitting with clubs and rifles sent most demonstrators scurrying. But two woman volunteers, who were spared the blows, stood fast, shaming the police officer who was shouting abuse and yelling to encourage his constables. The police officer hurled obscenities at the women, and was stoutly, though not obscenely, answered back. More enraged, he now called some of his men away from other demonstrators. 'Hit them!' he shouted, pointing a shaking finger at the women. 'Hit them in front of everybody!' No opportunity could be better for the officer to show the *kamias* how frail and impotent were these urban youths who were their leaders.

The tillers of Gosain Pesra lost the crops they had sown. So did the *kamias* in most villages; on a rough estimate, two-thirds of the area where they had sown crops had either been damaged or harvested by the *mutt*. It was a great setback for the organization; the *kamias* started drifting away, the *samiti's* village meetings became rarer, and poorly attended if held. The number of *Vahini* volunteers also fell. Those among the volunteers and *samiti* members who felt it their duty to restore the movement called a conference of the 223 of them who had already suffered imprisonment for the cause; the idea was to strengthen the resolve of those who had made sacrifices. At the conference, in June 1981, 160 turned up. A resolution was passed to continue the programme of sowing that year. It was easier said than done. The idea of re-sowing quickly petered out because the *kamias* were no longer prepared to take chances. The loss of one season's crops had been severe enough. Those who had already sold their animals and goods were drowned in sorrow: those who had borrowed knew not how to pay back.

As few showed an inclination to sow again, the *mazdoor kisan samiti* had to reconsider its call. After discussion, non-cooperation was made the programme for 1981: the *kamias* would, it was decided, prevent sowing as in 1979. It shocked the organizers to see that the demoralized *kamias* had no enthusiasm even for the changed programme; the *mutt* encountered little resistance during the sowing. It was then decided not to prevent the *mutt* from harvesting. Once again, the men would not come forward, though in some villages, defying the police and the thugs, *kamias* rallied in large numbers to carry off the harvest.

'The woman question'

In 1979 a short time after the villagers' demand for land, a new element had been introduced: the 'woman question', which was raised by a few women volunteers of the *Vahini* from Patna. These women, like the men of the *Vahini* from Patna, were of middle-class background, mostly from the families of government officials, living reasonably well, but not much Westernized; educated but not speaking English at home. There were few women in the *Vahini*; Patna, among the district units, had the largest number, a dozen or so. Those women who had joined the 18 March Movement or the *Vahini* had done so because, like the men, they were deeply worried about unemployment, rising prices and corruption. But quite a few of them had joined because they were equally worried about the status of women. All of them had direct experience of unequal treatment within their families, and had seen other women in the same, sometimes worse, condition. Such women, who wanted to change that condition, led the *Vahini* on to feminism.

It was the same desire that brought some of them to Bodh Gaya and to investigate the lives of the women in *kamia* families. What they found astonished and angered them. The *kamia* might be a servant of the abbey, but to his wife he was the master. It was she who gathered fuel, cooked and washed up, looked after the children and cared for the sick. In addition, she worked outside the home, for a wage less than the man's; the *kamia's* wife was the slave of a slave. Taking issue with the male *Vahini* volunteers in Bodh Gaya, the women activists argued that the *antima jana* was being wrongly identified; the male volunteers were trying to fit the male *kamia* into JP's concept of the lowest person: it was the *kamia's* wife who was the *antima jana*. They also criticized the male volunteers for excluding *kamia* women on the *samiti*, which meant that the women had no role in the decision-making process in so far as the struggle was concerned. Sometimes, such arguments at meetings irritated the male volunteers, some of whom perhaps felt that concern with feminism prevented a serious concern with the land struggle.

Gradually, however, the men in the *Vahini* began to appreciate the questions confronting the womenfolk: today they admit they owe it to the zealous spirit of such volunteers as Manimala and Kanak.* In Bodh Gaya, once feminist

---

* Manimala left the organization in in 1980 to join a small feminist group in Patna after she was heckled by men at two meetings of the state committee of the *Vahini* called to give judgement on her complaint that a male volunteer attempted to take liberties with her. She said she was bewildered to find the members of the accused male volunteer's group expressing doubts about her evidence which, she felt, ought to have been accepted as true. Even in law courts, she said, the victim's evidence was believed in cases relating

consciousness was raised the whole culture of the Bhuyans came under attack.

The *kamia* was addicted to home brew, and in drink he often quarrelled with and beat his wife. The *kamia*'s wife accepted this; she never complained: few of them even acknowledged it for a long time although the *Vahini*'s volunteers began to educate them and constantly urge them to speak of it. It was as though the husband's cruelties were part of the Bhuyan culture, a private grief deserving no social thought. The Bhuyan women did speak out at last, and then the female volunteers had a warning circulated that any *kamia* found guilty of beating his wife would cease to be a member of the *mazdoor kisan samiti*. In October 1979, a three-day camp of *kamia* women was held, sponsored by the female volunteers; the first resolution to be passed declared that women would no longer tolerate wife-beating. Then a campaign to stop the brewing and drinking of liquor began. In the Bhuyan segment of almost every village, four or five families distilled strong drink out of *mahua* fruits, and the campaigners who came from all sections, all concentrated on these brewing centres. Identified houses were ransacked; the earthen pots and jars used for brewing and as containers were taken away, and after the liquor had been poured away, were either broken or 'confiscated' by the *samiti* and 'auctioned' for better uses in the village.

At the same time, an attack was made on certain Bhuyan beliefs. The Bhuyans continued to believe in spirits, ghosts and witches. The sick were still not taken to medical doctors; never took capsules or had injections. But neither did they have the reliable systems of cure handed down from generation to generation, of which some communities could boast. They had their own way of dealing with illness; they waited for the disease to abate naturally. If it was prolonged, the sick person's family was sure it was due to a curse of evil spirits. They would go to *ojha*, the sorcerer, of the local Bhuyan community, and he would invoke his magic powers to direct the evil spirits to go away (on that day the *ojha* enjoyed a square meal). The *Vahini* volunteers tried to wean the Bhuyans away from this kind of belief.

There was a deeper issue awaiting the attention of the *Vahini* feminists: the issue of titles to land for the *kamia* women. The idea had not come from the feminists, but arose accidentally. While the struggle for land continued, the government, waking up to the existence of illegal landholdings in the region, had detected such holdings of the *mutt* at a village called Bija and had distributed them among the landless there. The distribution had taken place in two phases. In the first, all adult male labourers were given plots of land. No one was left landless. Yet there was more land to distribute in the village; and at the next distribution the male labourers had the names of their wives, daughters and daughters-in-law listed as allotees. When this fact became known, some of the

---

to atrocities on women. Later, however, the male volunteer was suspended as a member of *Vahini* but was soon reinstated. Kanak who, like several other women volunteers, married a male volunteer lived for a time in 1984-85 in a village in the Bodh Gaya region and ran a school in a hut there with her husband. She later gave up, and left to live with her parents at Ranchi.

male *Vahini* volunteers, especially Pradeep, began to ask why the *kamia* women of other villages should not also be given pieces of land. With one or two volunteers, he went to Piparghatti village where the government officials were also going to distribute land. Pradeep's suggestion sounded strange and absurd to the *kamias*.

Pradeep quoted the example of Bija. But he wanted Piparghatti to go further. At Bija, the women had received the titles only after all the men had received theirs. In Piparghatti, Pradeep said, the women must get the land first, but the *kamias* were very reluctant. What difference did it make? What did a woman know about husbandry? Did not a neat social division of labour between man and woman already exist? Pradeep and the others told them that it was wrong to justify the old division of labour if they were really participating in a struggle for revolution. The *kamias* were reminded that the women of their families contributed as much to the land movement as they did; the women joined all the *samiti'*s programme in large numbers, and had therefore every right to claim land ownership. After several long discussions the *kamias* agreed.

The day approached for the government officials to arrive at the village to distribute the allotment papers. The officials had already made their own list after inquiries about who were the landless in the village; their list bore the names of men only. As the officials, on their arrival in the village, waited for the listed men to come to receive their allotment papers they found a large crowd of men and women gathering round. They were bewildered to hear several voices demanding titles for the women, but not for the men. The officials declared that they had a list, and they were going to distribute the papers accordingly. Finally, in disgust, the officials drove out of the village, shouting that if the listed men wanted their papers they could come and collect them from the block office. 'There are no laws or orders or conventions,' they cried, 'which allow women to have titles to land from the government.'

For a long time there was no land distribution in Piparghatti. Some weeks after the officials had left, some of the *kamias* had gone to the block office to ask the officials to give the allotments to the women; Pradeep himself met the officials twice, but they turned down all the pleas. After a time, murmurings began in the village which soon grew into a bigger grievance against the feminists. Because of them, it was felt, land remained so near and yet so far from their possession. They retired to discuss the matter with *Vahini* volunteers. A senior volunteer who visited the village was received very coldly, and left to complain to the area *samiti*. The *samiti* decided to isolate Piparghatti's *kamias* from the movement: no activist would go to the village until an apology was received. The *kamias* went instead to the government officials and received their land allotment papers in accordance with the government list.

Meanwhile, ironically, the *Vahini'*s women activists made 'Land to Women' a key issue. Their arguments added a new force. The *kamia*, the feminists said, was a man without property, yet he still oppressed his wife: what would he not do when he owned a piece of land? He was too fond of drink; in order to buy drink, he might one day sell his plot. On the other hand, the wife would be responsible, the best person to run family affairs, and in so doing she could also be saved from the ill-treatment that was inflicted on her at home.

Though the feminists' case was strong they failed to appreciate the complexities. If the *kamia*'s wife owned a piece of land, what would happen when she died? Would the land go to her daughter or to her son? If the daughter inherited, what would happen when after marriage she left for her husband's home which, observing the code of village exogamy, would be elsewhere, at an uncertain distance from her mother's home? Would she not become just another absentee landowner, if the cultivation was done through a sharecropper while she lived with her in-laws? Would it be possible for a daughter to sell the strip she inherited from her mother and buy a new one in her in-laws' village? Was it possible for a husband to live with his wife's parents rather than the other way round? Could society be brought to accept it? The feminists had no answer to these questions. Yet they kept chanting their slogan—Land to Women—trying to force the idea upon the *kamias*. They campaigned at Piparghatti, and ended up with nothing. And Bija was not the right example to cite: when women had received land allotments there it was without thinking to establish women's equality or right to property; instead the *kamias*, after receiving land themselves, had submitted the names of the women in order to have more land for themselves. In reality, the male head of the family owned all the land, the women none.

About 1,000 acres of the abbey's illegal landholdings, spread over a dozen or more villages of the region, were distributed by the government. Nowhere, however, did the women receive any titles to land despite the fact that Indian law, both Hindu and Muslim, gives rights to women to hold property through inheritance or purchase. The government officials in Bodh Gaya had no legal justification to deny the women's right to titles to land. In Gosain Pesra, the heart of the movement, the issue was not even considered. The village *samiti* there was too preoccupied trying to retain unity in the face of quarrels over the distribution lists. The *samiti* became redundant in the competition for land. The feminists also soon left Bodh Gaya, and went back to the city whence they had come, leaving the matter unresolved. Pradeep also withdrew.*

Nevertheless, women's issues did not fade. When the feminists left, Promod, Karu and Priyadarshi, essentially all that were left of the *Vahini* in Bodh Gaya by 1983, kept them alive. They never ceased to speak against the evils of drink, cruelty to wives, primitive attitudes to illness; their views on these issues appeared in all the speeches, resolutions and circulars, with the constant affirmation of their opinions on women's right to land. At the 1983 annual conference

---

* By 1983, Pradeep had drawn back from the movement, partly due to his anxieties about the murder of his uncle, the farmhouse manager at Mastipur. His name, even though he was not present that day, stood at the top of the list of the accused persons named by the *mutt*. He quietly waited until he was over 30 years of age, when, according to the *Vahini's* constitution, one ceased to be a member of the organization. Shortly thereafter, he embarked on a political career by joining the Janata Party. The hearing in the Mastipur murder cases began in the district courts, despite Pradeep's efforts at a settlement between the *mutt* and the *Vahini*, and was still going on when these lines were written.

of the area *samiti* held at Shahpur village (where I watched the open session on the last day) there were no fewer than 1,000 people—largely women, who squatted on the ground in their stained unwashed saris under the trees, listening intently to the *Vahini* and *samiti* leaders.

One leader, towards the end of his speech, wanted all present to declare their affirmation to women's right to land: 'Do we all agree that women ought to have the titles when the next distribution take place?' The speaker waited for a moment for the hands to go up and, satisfied with seemingly unanimous support, was about to move on when a middle-aged *kamia* jumped up and shouted: 'You all want the women to get land, not the men. This is dangerous, no good at all. I don't like this kind of talk. It will destroy the community. Will the women go down to the courts to fight a case?' He could say no more, as others forced him to sit down.

His was a lone voice, allegedly intoxicated and yet, one suspected, one that spoke for many men who either sat with lips compressed or who had not turned up. He had called attention to another potential problem if women became owners of land. The customs of the Bhuyan community, indeed of rural society, forbade women to appear in courts. As owners of land women would have to breach such customs, for they might be involved in agrarian disputes or asked to stand security for bail. Deep down, the women knew the community would never allow them to own or inherit land. They had realized this after seeing land distribution ceremonies in several villages, and from the way their men argued against it in the absence of activists. Confronted by the activists everyone supported it, men and women, because their leaders had made it a principle; and one must show loyalty to a principle until the time came to put it into practice.

The fight with the abbot continues

Today the *kamias* of the villages where land distribution took place have left the movement, even in Gosain Pesra, its original centre. The *kamias* there no longer have the time to attend even to the annual conferences. The *Vahini's* response to this has been bitter and punitive; their volunteers, it was decided, would not go to any of those villages to re-establish contact. If the *kamias* there had any problems they would have to come to the volunteers.

It was never the *Vahini's* intention to confine the aim of the Bodh Gaya movement to redistribution of land. The *kamias* who now possessed a plot of land had, however, drawn the line there: for them that was the end of the movement. But the *Vahini*, with its dream of revolution, took the long view. The *kamias'* longing for land had been the foundation of the movement; yet the volunteers were angered by the attitude of the *kamias*. What about cultural reform? The *kamias* had pretended to participate in the campaigns for women's right to one land, to end brewing and addiction, to stop cruelty to women, against the giving or taking of dowry, against illiteracy, primitive beliefs and superstitions. Partial reform had been achieved even with their half-hearted involvement, but the *kamias* had treated such reforms as tiresome preconditions for the ownership of land. The *Vahini* activists despairingly lamented in their progress reports from Bodh Gaya: 'The struggle is now restricted to pieces of land'; 'The struggle is losing its revolutionary perspective.'

There lay the irony of the situation. No matter what the *Vahini* volunteers might do, it was impossible to rouse the bondmen to action in Bodh Gaya without making land the principal issue from the outset. The volunteers became reconciled to the situation. A *people's movement,* they concluded, derived its initial strength from the people's avarice. They would, therefore, despite the limitations, keep land as the focus of the struggle. Today the struggle is on the wane in Barachatti and Bodh Gaya, two of the four areas involved. The abbey land is either distributed or hopelessly tied up in court cases. In the other areas it continues with some force, for in certain villages the *kamias* have, without waiting for distribution by government, gone ahead to occupy and till the abbey land, and they need *Vahini* support in order to hold on to it.

But if land was a priority, great obstacles stood in the *Vahini*'s way. The monks were too clever to let anyone, even an organization, take their estates away. They had studied Bihar's land laws more deeply than JP's young followers, and knew how best to circumvent them. They had long known ways of dealing with politicians and state bureaucrats. No one outside the small circle of the monks had any idea how big the Sankara *mutt*'s estates were, and the government had a miserably insufficient record of their extent. Investigations by officials in the past had either been given up or perfunctorily dragged on in the files.

Following the *mutt* violence at Mastipur in August 1979 JP had written to the chief minister of Bihar, urging him to set up a committee to investigate the property held by the abbey. The committee of inquiry, too, headed by the chairman of the Bihar Bhoodan Yajna Committee, came up against a blank wall. For reasons best known to the chief minister or his officials, the state government seemed to have lost interest in the inquiry once it had notified the committee. It made K.B. Saxena, an Indian Administrative Officer then in Ranchi as the Tribal Welfare Commissioner, the secretary, but would not release him from duty even for a short while to work for the committee. The chairman and most of the members lived in Patna, the secretary stayed in Ranchi, and the subject of inquiry was in Bodh Gaya! The government also forgot the small temporary bureau it had promised to open in the Gaya collectorate for the committee to operate from, helped by a team of specially assigned officers and clerks. Neither did the committee's requests for information receive proper attention. Whether it was pressure from the monks or bureaucratic inefficiency, it came to the same thing, so far as the bondmen's interests were concerned.

After months of intermittent work, the committee did submit a short report to the state government, listing no fewer than 17 recommendations for further action. The committee of ten (three from Sarvodaya, four members of the Bihar legislature, the Additional Advocate-General, a youth leader of the 18 March Movement and a senior IAS officer) in its report had briefly put together what was already on record in dusty government files. The committee called for a more detailed inquiry. It had been unable, it admitted, to discover anything about the abbey's presumably illegal estates in several other districts of the state (Patna, Bhojpur, Rohtas, Nalanda, Aurangabad, Nawada, Hazaribagh, Muzaffarpur, Munger, East Champaran and West Champaran). Even in Gaya inquires had not got very far, thanks to the former manipulations of the monks.

According to the committee, in 1932, the then abbot established a trust to safeguard and manage the property, most of which the abbey held as a *zamindar* under the Raj. When the *zamindari* ended, in the early 1950s, the abbot put forward a claim to the government that the land within the trust had been under his 'personal cultivation'. The Bihar Land Reforms Act (1950) exempted from acquisition by the government 'private lands, the privileged lands, and the lands used for agricultural and horticultural purposes (which were) in *khas* (self) possession of the proprietor (*zamindar*)'. The abbot thus claimed exemption. The government rejected his claims; and the abbot appealed against the decision. He lost in the lower courts, moved to the Patna High Court, and lost again. He then appealed to the Supreme Court; but while the case was going on, the abbot achieved an amazing feat in the corridors of power in the form of a settlement between him, the State of Bihar and the Bihar State Religious Trust Board (an autonomous board established by government to oversee the affairs of the state's numerous religious trusts). The Supreme Court allowed this settlement, and the appeal was dropped. 'This settlement (of September 1957) went against the public interest,' observed the 1979 committee of inquiry. For by this compromise the abbey retained an estate including no fewer than 534 villages in various districts, 488 of them in Gaya district alone. The committee failed to discover how much land there was in those villages, and how much of it was believed to have been under the abbot's 'self-possession'.

In 1961, the Bihar Land Reforms (fixation of ceiling areas and acquisition of surplus land) Act laid down that an agriculturist could own no more than 20 acres of canal-irrigated land or 60 acres of hilly, sandy and surplus homestead land. The abbot divided his property (technically, on paper) into small parcels, bringing each below the legal ceilings, and placing it under a different name, in addition to creating new religious trusts, as we have seen. The Bihar government had ordered an inquiry. But inquiring into the Sankara *mutt*'s estates was a 'can of worms': frustrated, the officials gave up after they had covered 108 of the 400 villages in Gaya district where the abbey allegedly had its land. Official inquiries have never gone beyond this.

Records from these 108 villages show that there are 9,576 acres held piecemeal under three types of owner: trusts, the abbot and individuals. The trusts together held 2,096 acres (and were found to be illegal because fictitious) but the abbot has challenged this in the courts and the case drags on. The abbot owned 1,712 acres. The remainder, 5,768 acres, was divided among no fewer than 680 'individuals'. No action was taken on the abbot's holding, which puzzled the committee. The 680 'individuals' were suspected to be none other than monks and associates of the abbey, 122 of whom produced evidence to show that half the land had been 'purchased' from the abbot but at such low rates as to raise doubts about the legitimacy of the 'purchase'. It was not known how the remaining 2,940 acres had been transferred. After these official findings, proceedings had been started according to the 1961 land ceiling law, and notices served upon the 680 individuals: 253 of them (most probably non-existent) never materialized. The other 427 responded, and hearings had been completed in the cases of the judgements given, and other action by the court were now known to the committee.

The committee's inadequate findings contained one interesting thing. The committee interviewed Dhansukh Giri, on 29 July 1980 (at a time when the *kamias* were sowing the land left unploughed from the previous year through 'non-cooperation') in the *dak* bungalow in Bodh Gaya. The abbot admitted quite openly that all the lands held in the names of trusts, the monks and so on belonged to the abbey. Asked about the transfers made by 'sale' by him, the abbot admitted them to be spurious too, though in a roundabout way. He said: 'The property is *sold* to the monk-disciples because they are trusted people of the *mutt*. They will look after it well, as if they are cultivating their own land. But, as I told you, all monk-disciples comprise one family. Transfers by sale to them don't meant the land becomes their private property. The land *purchased* in their names belongs to the *mutt*.' Cultivation everywhere, the abbot went on, was done under the central control of the abbey through its farmhouses. The abbey sent the seeds, the fertilizers and pesticides to the farmhouses for every crop and, after the harvest, received the entire produce from the land.

Some of the illegal land was acquired by the government and distributed in Gosain Pesra and other villages. Among its important recommendations the committee asked that the government launch a drive to enquire into the abbey's illegal property simultaneously in all the districts; there should be a time limit and officials should be specially assigned to work under a monitoring cell in the government secretariat in Patna. When the investigation was complete, steps should be taken urgently to acquire the illegal estates. The committee urged the government to secure the co-operation of the abbot to a settlement of the pending Patna High Court case pertaining to the land belonging to the religious trusts. The abbot had admitted that the land belonged to the abbey and had also unequivocally stated that he had 'no interest' in the High Court proceedings.

The state government, as was its wont, approached the matter lackadaisically. The committee report remained in some corner of the secretariat, unpublished, unimplemented. Since the committee was notified, the ministry had changed parties several times: Congress followed Janata and the Lok Dal, and three different men from Congress were chief ministers in five years. New chief ministers are notoriously uninterested in pursuing something that a past minister has been much concerned with, such as setting up a committee to investigate the Sankara *mutt's* illegal property. And that could be the end of the affair.

Should the *Vahini* fail to mount a campaign to force the government to publish the committee's report and act on it, the Bodh Gaya struggle would stagnate. For unless urgent steps were taken to distribute the abbey estates the *kamias* might drift away from the *Vahini* moorings. The greatest issue of all for the *Vahini* is, therefore, the publication and implementation of the committee report. There were no signs of the government becoming in any way less indifferent (or through its politicians and bureaucrats, involved with the *mutt*) than in the past. But the *Vahini* continues to try to build up pressure through demonstrations and seminars.

In August 1985 the *Vahini* was split. A section of it left the organization to join the *Sampoorna Kranti Manch,* the Total Revolution Forum, formed by some dozen small groups which owed allegiance to JP's thought, though without knowing how to build on his vague ideology. A few of the *Vahini* volunteers and *samiti* activists in Bodh Gaya, and some of the former *samiti* men in the villages lying dormant after the land distribution, joined the *Manch.* Confusion, so usual after a split in any organization, reigned for some time. Both the *Manch* and the *Vahini* worked in Bodh Gaya under the old name of *mazdoor kisan samiti;* but the confusion ended after a brief trial of strength through local rallies. The *Vahini* continues in Bodh Gaya, inevitably weakened by the split and by the manipulating geniuses in the Sankara *mutt,* blocking land reforms.

9. The Battle of the Sharecroppers

Background to the Communist Party of India (CPI)

In India, as elsewhere, the October Revolution influenced many young people, intellectuals and labour leaders. But they knew little about it, or the ideology behind it, except vaguely that a new, egalitarian and exemplary political structure was being established in Russia, under Lenin. The 1920s was also the period when Gandhi was transforming the Indian National Congress from intellectuals' talking-shop into a mass movement. Nevertheless, in Bombay, Calcutta and other cities, there were men who thought Congress, even with Gandhi, was 'too soft' towards the British; Gandhi's almost religious attitude to non-violence 'proved' the lack of thrust. For some of these men the Soviet revolution offered a powerful resolute way to liberate India and establish socialism in the country. But as they were unfamiliar with Soviet ideology no progress was made. Under these conditions, it is not surprising that the Communist Party of India (CPI) was founded (in 1920) by Indian intellectuals abroad. The centre of the CPI was Tashkent, but later shifted to Berlin and other cities in Europe, from where the writings of Marx and Lenin were mailed to interested intellectuals in India.

The Comintern, by which the small CPI group was guided, considered it imperative for communists to lead 'national liberation movements' in the colonies, in unity with the Soviet socialist movement. As for the 'bourgeois liberation movements' in the colonies, the Comintern laid down that the Communists could support them provided they did not oppose the revolutionizing work of the communists. The CPI accordingly supported the Indian National Congress, while going ahead to establish its own organization in India.

The CPI saw Congress as a party of India's propertied classes, a banner under which native capital was fighting foreign capital. In the Congress programme of Indian nationalism, said the communists, there was no place for the interests of the workers and the peasantry, precisely the classes that the communists should organize along revolutionary lines. 'Our programme,' noted the founder of the Tashkent CPI, M.N. Roy, 'places the national movement, not on the basis of racial issue nor of capitalist antagonism, but on the wider basis of the economic interest and social emancipation of the masses of the population.'[1] But for a long time, the communists would have no real base in the peasant masses. Their initial strength lay in a section of the industrial working class which, though still very small in proportion to the agricultural workforce, had arrived in India; the conversion to Marxism in the mills and factories began with the leaders of the trade unions, and flowed downwards. In those days, there was too much injustice to fight against: dreadful working conditions, very low wages, no fixed working hours, living in hovels, torture and punishment, whether just or unjust. Militancy was easily encouraged.

The Raj wanted no communist activities, no 'Bolshevik agents' operating in the colony. Mail was intercepted to cut off channels through which Bolshevik literature flowed into India; leading communists were watched; and a series of 'conspiracy cases' instituted in order to arrest and punish leading communities on charges of subversion against the British Crown. Nevertheless, the communists, though dropping the name CPI and reappearing as Workers, and Peasants' Parties in different regions of the country, persisted.

Gandhi's Congress was not prepared to do more than demand Dominion status for India in the early 1920s, but the communists pressed for full independence. Congress thought this demand naive and ill-advised at that period in India's history. The communist called this compromise and surrender. A number of 'revolutionary' groups, apart from the communists, were formed in different provinces, despairing of Congress politics, believing in armed action: these groups were led and run mainly by students and young people. If the communists were 'Bolshevik agents' to the colonial authorities, the armed youth groups were 'terrorists'. Many of their members had also been inspired by the Soviet revolution and by Marx and Lenin, and several of them were to join the CPI in the 1930s and 1940s.

During World War II, after the Hitler-Stalin pact, the CPI opposed the British war effort (military supplies by Indian businessmen and recruitment of Indians in the army and their deployment abroad) and the colonial authorities quickly banned the party and threw several communists into indefinite detention. But when Hitler's troops attacked the USSR the CPI came out in support of the war. The ban on the party ended, and most of its men were released. Throughout the war, however, the party remained committed to its goal of full independence for India.

During the 1930s and 1940s, the communists were trying to elicit support among the peasants through Swami Sahajanand's Kisan Sabha. They were competing with other leftist groups within the Sabha—the Socialists and Forward Bloc, the group founded by Subash Chandra Bose, after he left Congress in disgust over its soft approach to independence. Sahajanand was, basically, a 'peasantist' by ideology, but sometimes made common cause with the communists. He was in prison when the Nazis invaded the USSR, and the CPI changed its policy to help the Allies. In the meantime, the Kisan Sabha was being pulled in opposite directions by two groups; the communists wanted the Sabha to support the war effort, but like the Congressmen the Socialists remained opposed to them.[2] (The Forward Bloc leader, Bose, was leading at the time his 'Indian National Army' against the Allies in Asia.)

Ultimately, however, the communists succeeded in persuading the Sabha to come out in favour of the war effort. The Sabha decided to suspend all anti-war activities 'as anti-war propaganda would merely assist the Nazis who were attacking Russia'. A 'Soviet Day' was observed: and the Sabha decided to organize a Soviet Relief Committee in every district to collect funds for Russia's assistance.[3] Sahajanand, whom the British released before he completed his prison term, endorsed the Sabha's pro-war line when he was released. The students' body, the All-India Students' Federation where, too, the communist had their members, also passed a resolution of 'unconditional support to war'.

Soon after the war, the efforts of the communists to organize the peasants in the Telangana region of what was then Hyderabad state in South India had borne fruit. The struggle was against the Nizam, the prince of Hyderabad. The peasants fought his troops and mercenaries with firearms. With extraordinary mass support, the communists were winning for the first two years and had practically ended the Nizam rule in a large part of his state, and had carried out, in the 'liberated' territory, their own land reforms, but the coming of independence in 1947 failed to end the Nizam rule: the Nizam was at first given freedom to choose whether he wanted his state to be integrated with India or Pakistan or to remain sovereign, independent of both. Towards the end of that year, the CPI-M was split three ways: one section wanted to support Congress; another, led by then general-secretary of the party, B.T. Ranadive (later to join the CPI, after the split in 1964) considered Congress to be pro-imperialist and called for armed liberation, headed by the working class in the cities; and the third supported the way of Chinese revolution (then taking place), starting with peasant war and agrarian revolution in the villages. Liberation might have been their genuine desire, but the situation barely warranted it. The country had just become free; there was no reason why the people should not want to give Congress a chance. The CPI had an organization, but one irrelevant to nationwide revolution. The Telangana communists carried out their war of liberation even after the Indian Army had taken over Hyderabad from the Nizam. They had to give themselves up (but not before 2,000 people had been sacrificed, for most peasants believed everything had been achieved after the Nizam had gone).

Then came the new Soviet world view which divided the world into two camps: Western imperialism, and socialism; freed colonies like India must go along different paths to achieve revolution. That path was the gradual elimination of Western capital, by Soviet aid; freed colonies like India would have to depend more and more on Soviet aid to build a non-capitalist regime. In 1956, Khrushhchev put forward the theory of 'peaceful transition to socialism'. The CPI adopted these Soviet policies which it continues to follow.

Today the CPI refuses to put the existing form of Indian agriculture into neat categories of feudal or capitalist. It believes that, despite the legal abolition of intermediaries such as *zamindari*, 'strong survivals' of feudalism persist in the countryside. But amidst these survivals, capitalism has entered agriculture. The 'interpenetration of the strong survivals of feudalism and growing capitalist relations of production is the dominant character of the socio-economic life in India's countryside.'

In the party's view, the national bourgeoisie, which led the freedom movement, led the nation down the capitalist path of development. While, trying to take measures to curb 'some of the worst forms of feudal exploitation' (for instance, integration soon after Independence of the princely states into the

Indian Union and the abolition of the Permanent Settlements) the national bourgeoisie gradually transformed the feudal landlords into capitalist landlords as well as helping the rich peasants to flourish. This process served a double purpose: to increase agricultural production and to create a stable class base for its rule in the countryside. The party called this process of agrarian development the 'landlord bourgeois path', and pointed out that it proved 'extremely costly' to the nation and 'extremely painful' to the peasantry and landless labourers.

The party's analysis holds that the landlord bourgeois path has caused slow agricultural growth and shortages of food-grains and agricultural raw materials, making the nation dependent on food imports. At the same time it has made the masses poorer, and hampered expansion of the home market for Indian industries, ultimately giving imperialist financial agencies like the IMF and World Bank an opportunity to pressure India to 'gradually tilt towards a policy of export-led growth, thereby tying the Indian economy still more firmly to the international capitalist division of labour'.

To the peasants these policies have brought only loss and suffering. The party, subscribing to the orthodox Marxist view, believes that the small peasant will be ultimately squeezed out so that capitalist relations can emerge in their true form. But the landless labourers and poor peasants (like sharecroppers) are in the most tragic situation. They had no class organization of their own, so the party formed the Bharatiya Khet Mazdoor Union (BKMU, All-India Agricultural Labourers' Union) in 1968. The issues before the BKMU were, and still are, fair wages, land and freedom from debt-slavery, caste and social oppression.

The party, however, believes landless labourers cannot achieve these aims without 'unity' with the working peasantry (and without the support of the working class and other democratic classes and strata). 'There are several issues which are of common interest to the agricultural labourers and the working peasants. Implementation of land reforms and distribution of land held above the ceiling (by the landlords) among the landless and the poor peasants are matters for which the Kisan Sabha and the BKMU can fight jointly.' The labourers should support the peasants in the matter of good prices for their produce; and the peasants should support the labourers in their struggle for wages and land and against oppression.

The CPI's 'main tactic', then, 'is to rely firmly on agricultural labourers and poor peasants, unite solidly with small and middle peasants and try to win over or neutralise the rich peasants in order to isolate and defeat the landlords, the usurers, the monopolists and the multinationals in alliance with the industrial working class and other democratic classes and strata'.[4]

The 'main tactic' in action

Towards the close of the 1930s, the first Congress ministry of Bihar took certain steps to restrain the *zamindars*. The *zamindars* had in the recent past raised their demands extraordinarily, thus provoking rural unrest. The government's new measures did not take away all the hated powers of the *zamindars* such as the one of distraining; yet, because of the checks put upon the imposition of arbitrary levies, the tenants had some relief. It was about this time that the CPI established its unit in Bihar province. Its provincial founders were mostly youths and students just released from months of detention as 'terrorists'. They were influenced by the tenant agitations under the leadership of the Kisan Sabha. Soon, a few prominent associates of Swami Sahajanand also joined the CPI; with the 'revolutionary' youths, they set about radicalizing the Sabha.

With Congress refusing to demand full independence, these youths, in various districts of Bihar, had been attracted to Bolshevik ideology. In what is now Madhubani district, in North Bihar, the first to join the party were a couple of students. Both were from the Brahman caste: Bhogendra Jha was doing his Intermediate at college, and Srimohan Jha was in his final year at school. After the Nazi invasion of the USSR, the two went round towns and villages distributing pamphlets which explained the party's pro-war stance and sought the people's involvement. During the Quit India movement of 1942, the tiny Madhubani district unit of the party, led by these two young men, became very active, and this first gave the party a foothold in Madhubani.

The young Brahmans came from ordinary tenant families, and in becoming educated had not lost their village roots. They had seen at first hand the distress caused by the *zamindars* to their families and others; they were embittered. So, while participating in the programmes to throw out the British, they took up peasant mobilization under the flag of the Kisan Sabha. This set them apart from the Congressmen, and made them appear radical in the eyes of the tenants.

They held meetings, at first small because the tenants were frightened and hesitant, in the villages they toured; the leaders of the Kisan Sabha came to speak to the tenants too. At the meetings, the importance of organization was emphasized; the tenants were asked to resist the excesses of the men of the *zamindars*. The young communists went to tenants of all castes. They had abandoned the Brahman insignia; they wore no sacred thread or pigtails, and ate meals with the lower-caste tenants, even the untouchables. But this, of course, was not something they could do easily or unflinchingly. 'When our low caste hosts offered us cooked rice on pieces of soiled and shabby cloth—hardly anything was clean—several times I came close to throwing up. But there was no going back,' recalled Srimohan Jha, now 60, and an assistant secretary of the Bihar state council of the CPI.

The Brahmans at large were scandalized by acts that drew the low-caste tenants closer to the young communists; they had polluted themselves and were to be shunned. But soon events that would dramatically alter the situation occurred. In the course of their organizational activities, the young communists encountered a Brahman *zamindar* in a village called Andhari. The *zamindar* was also the head monk of a village monastery. In Andhari, which was close to Srimohan Jha's native village, were over 1,000 people, mostly from the lower castes. Previously, most of them had been tenants paying rent to *zamindars*, but they were unable to meet his extraordinarily increased demands and the *zamindar*, using his powers, had seized the land from them for default. Other tenants had to give up their plots because they had failed to repay his loans—the head monk also was a considerable lender of money and grain. In such ways he had acquired about 500 acres of land, and the former tenants had become his sharecroppers and labourers. As sharecroppers, too, they were deprived: the *zamindar* first took half the produce as his share, and then he took from the sharecroppers' half levies of many different sorts, leaving little for them to live on.

When the Kisan Sabha became active in the village, the head monk was alarmed. His men brought news of how some peasants called his demands 'unfair' and illegal, and he was very upset when some of his former tenants lodged suits in the court for the recovery of their plots under amended laws. He decided he would contest the cases in the court, but knowing where the claimants' strength actually flowed from, he began to propagate the view that what had been started by the tenants at Andhari was not his personal battle. 'It is a battle', he declared, 'in which the lower castes seek to triumph over the Brahmans.'

This propaganda did not win him caste support, probably for two reasons. First, the Brahman *zamindars* had never been known to treat the Brahman tenants fraternally; they would no more allow their caste brethren to sit with them than they would allow the lower castes. So, the Brahmans were not disposed to regard the Andhari *zamindar* as a Brahman. Secondly, and no less important, the young communists who led the peasants were Brahmans too. Quite a few of the Brahman tenants had revised their opinion of the young 'caste rebels'. They had no doubt violated the caste rules, but they were fighting for a right cause; they were taking risks, making sacrifices; they had no self-interest; they were real monks.

The head monk had to seek solidarity elsewhere. He shifted his appeal to other landlords in the area: 'If I lose, the tide will swallow all of you up!' He found some support here, but meanwhile the judgement on the tenant suits went against him. He was ordered to restore 60 acres to the tenants, a ruling that endangered all his property, as other tenants were likely to follow in the footsteps of the winning tenants. This happened as 1946 was drawing to a close. There was jubilation not only among the tenants of Andhari, but also among those in other villages who had been closely watching the conflict. But within a few days of the judgement the head monk made it known that he proposed to ignore the court decision, and would occupy the plots, come what may. In view of the threat to breach the peace, the administration posted a section of police to the village.

Following the usual practice, the police became the guests of the *zamindar*, staying in and eating at his home. So the presence of the 'peacekeeping' force helped the head monk ward off any possible attack from the Sabha men. And from his side, no doubt with the knowledge of the police, he hired a *hanseri*, a squad of rural mercenaries, to deal with the rebels. It was later learnt that the mercenaries had collected at his place on the night of 3 January 1947. The following morning they entered the peasant houses, assaulting the occupants and looking for the 'leaders'. As soon as they saw Bhogendra Jha and Srimohan Jha, they attacked them with clubs and iron rods. Bhogendra fell to the ground with serious injuries. They continued to assault him, but Paltu Yadav, a peasant, broke through their ranks and covered Bhogendra's bleeding body with his own. The unceasing blows cut into his flesh, breaking his bones, but Paltu accepted death rather than that his leader, his redeemer, should be unprotected. He died within minutes. Then the mercenaries ran off. Paltu became the first of 39 peasant martyrs of the CPI in Madhubani district over a period of 40 years. Their roll of honour hangs in the tile-roofed office of the party's district council in Madhubani town.

On the following day, more than 10,000 extremely agitated peasants from other villages flocked to Andhari; many of them wanted to attack the head monk's house and avenge Paltu. But the leaders stopped them, telling them that this might bring more repression. (The head monk, Ramdeo Das, is still alive, now in his eighties, with ten acres or so left in his possession.) In a few weeks, the leaders were detained by the administration, to avert, they said, more incidents in Andhari. The detention resulted in separation from the peasants, a separation much prolonged by the banning of the CPI by the new nationalist government of India. Using the lull, the head monk hurriedly sold off almost all the land he had illegally acquired, and several tenants of adjoining villages— some even of Andhari—leapt at the chance, for the plots were being offered at very low rates. In a genuine distribution, the plots would have gone only to the tenants who had previously owned or tilled them. With the leaders in prison, however, moral sense was lost; the peasants, in or out of the Kisan Sabha, who could afford to pay rushed to buy. The buyers had a good bargain, but the head monk was finished as a landlord. The CPI considers Andhari as its 'victory' in Madhubani district.

The case of Korahia

Numerically, the CPI has its largest state organization in Bihar, and among all the districts, and its largest organization is in Madhubani, and its largest organization among all villages there is in Korahia, where there are about 300 party members. Korahia is a very large village, 27 kilometres north of Madhubani town. The slow, narrow-gauge trains running from Madhubani to Jainagar, on the Nepal border and back, pass through it several times in the day. Men with large barrels of milk, and women with headloads of vegetables or cow-dung fuel cakes, stand in readiness on the platform as the smoke from the train is sighted, and then shout and push their way into the compartments already swarming with people. People travel to Madhubani or Jainagar to sell their home produce or to buy things they need. A village of 6,000 people, Korahia has half a dozen shops lining the unshaded platform; a small pharmaceutical store run by a semi-educated young man of Rajput caste, who is also a member of the executive committee of the party's village unit; and ramshackle stalls selling tea and snacks, betel and tobacco.

There are about 1,300 families in the village, drawn from 15 or so different castes and living on either side of the railway line. People live in caste clusters, though there are exceptions. Most of the castes consist of poor men, without land or with little parcels of land: in certain castes such as the Rajputs, Yadavas and Koeris, both rich and poor can be found. The Yadavas are the dominant caste, making up half the village population. Two of the Yadava families are ex-*zamindars*, and the high school in the village is named after them. It was opened in 1955 and though it was constructed on public land, the then-*zamindars* claimed the credit for 'pioneering the spread of modern education' in the village. None the less, Pyarelal-Ramswarup High School (though still with only one man from the village on its teaching staff) has made its contribution to the growth of literacy in Korahia; over 20 per cent of the population have been to school, a few even going on to higher education and, then, to jobs outside. Of late, girls, mostly from upper-class families in the village, have also started attending the school, and lower-class parents, too, have started to send their daughters. But one or two inter-caste romances and marriages have taken place between schoolmates, and shocked and 'disgraced' parents declared that if education meant abandoning one's religion, their daughters must leave the school.

There was no school at Korahia at the time of the tenant upsurge, triggered by Andhari and accelerated by the departure of the British. Two or three young men in the village were drawn towards the communist cause. In the years of proscription they would arrange shelter and food for leaders on the run from the police, and hold secret discussions with them. One of the young men was Ramlakhan Yadav, whose father had been a petty *zamindar* and his elder brother the president of the local Congress committee. As a child, Ramlakhan had seen his father brought to ruin by the Maharaja of Darbhanga. His father was self-respecting, courageous and stubborn, and it was over tenurial rights that he fought the maharaja. His *zamindari* was not seized; after his death, Ramlakhan's elder Congressman brother assumed it. Like numerous other petty *zamindars* of Bihar, the heir was patriotic and avowedly anti-communist; he died in 1949. His son, Rajendra Yadav, the secretary of the CPI's village committee for a long time, was then about 14 years old and was taken from his studies by his uncle Ramlakhan and his mother. The family fell on bad times.

The renting of farms in Korahia was not a monopoly. There were over a dozen *zamindars*, great and small, who held the village in portions. Barring the two who named the high school after themselves, they were all non-resident, living in various villages of Madhubani district, in Darbhanga town, or as far away as in Rajasthan. Even the Maharaja of Darbhanga had a stretch of 165 acres here. The *zamindars* had appointed men from the village or outside to look after their interests, they themselves visiting once or twice a year. The village had 4,000 acres of land, of which *zamindars* together owned more than 3,000 acres; the remainder was legally held by the tenants who paid them rent and levies.

For the cultivation of their lands, the *zamindars* kept sharecroppers and tied labourers. Having carved up the land of Korahia among themselves, they ('Rare visitors in the finest and most expensive dhotis', the peasants recalled) had made an apportionment of the tiller hamlets too; each had a set of 'my men'. The families of *Mallahs* (boatmen) were shared out, for instance, between three *zamindars*, Zaki Ahmed of Sukhi village, Madhubani district; Mahadeo Jayasawal of Darbhanga; and Bijnath Singh of Cnaora. Each had seized all the rights of 'my men'. No one could fish in the tank unless he arranged to send the biggest fish of the catch to the master or his agent. Nobody could leave the village, or think of marrying off his sons or arranging the *gauna* (the ceremonial home-leaving of the bride) of daughters without the master's clearance.

The abolition of *zamindari* by law brought no immediate significant change to the village, except that the legal tenants were no longer to pay rents to the *zamindars*. Anticipating the blow, the Maharaja of Darbhanga quickly sold the 165 acres he owned in Korahia. The other *zamindars*, rewriting the land records, as did most others in the state at the time of the *zamindari* abolition, seemed to carry on as though nothing had changed, as did their servants.

Yet the tiny communist group in the village was growing, very slowly, with young men joining who had some education and who usually came from families with medium landholdings, families neither very rich nor very poor. Bhogendra Jha and other district leaders continued to visit Korahia: it was often Ramlakhan who, apart from doing other work for the party, organized such matters as where the leaders and members would stay and which family should send meals for them, which he had been doing since the days of proscription. Rajendra Yadav, the present secretary, had in those days on several occasions seen his uncle come to ask his mother for extra meals. It was a hush-hush arrangement between his uncle and mother; his Congressman father never knew that his brother was lodging and dining communists. Out of curiosity Rajendra, as soon as he saw his uncle whispering to his mother, would follow him out to have a look at the communist lodgers.

At first the communists did not inspire him. What he had regularly heard about them in his father's sitting-room had made him rather hostile to the communists. On one occasion he went to where Bhogendra was lodging, and asked him, after sitting there for a few minutes: 'Isn't it true that what you people really want is to hand over India into the clutches of Soviet Russia as soon as we get rid of the British?' Friends of his father, when they gathered in his sitting-room, would tell each other such things as: 'Nobody is allowed to live without working in Soviet Russia'; 'All the old men are killed there'; 'Every woman is *nationalized* there'; 'There is no sister, no wife, no mother'. On another occasion the young anti-communist asked Bhogendra: 'Aren't you just interested in making all Indian women prostitutes?' It was long after he joined the party in 1958 that, said Rajendra, 'I came to realize that the things that my friends spoke of were all part of the Roosevelt plan of anti-communist propaganda!'

The struggle in Korahia began in the late 1960s, two decades after Independence, and more than two decades after Andhari. In 1967, in the first coalition government replacing Congress, a CPI man became Bihar's revenue and land reform minister. This boosted the morale of the communists everywhere in the state, and thus in Korahia. The minister gave speeches inside and outside the Assembly strongly in favour of the rural poor. At meetings of the party's state council and other bodies in Patna he spoke of the possibilities that policies and laws, such as those relating to the occupancy rights of the sharecroppers or the distribution of the *gairmazarua khas* lands (the lands held privately by the *zamindars* which had been vested in the government after the abolition of *zamindari*) held for the rural poor. The party wanted its grassroots activists to have a full understanding of these laws so that they could make local officials act on them. Other state leaders of the Party were sent on tours of the districts to explain the scope of the laws.

Before their party joined the coalition government, the communists in Korahia had organized some minor protests. The law now accorded the share-cropper more than three-quarters of the produce: the communists had sat on relay fasts at the barns of the landlords to force its implementation. The landlords, according to the customs long set by themselves, were actually taking as much as a three-quarters share, two-thirds as rent and the remainder in the form of a variety of levies. The government officials called both the parties together after the dispute: the landlords told downright lies; they said they had been leaving three-quarters of the harvest to the sharecroppers as the law required. A few sharecroppers challenged this, most did not. (The major reason for the sharecroppers not pressing enough was that they hoped the landlord would give them plots of his own accord. If they remained docile and quiet and servile the master, they hoped, might, some day in the future, give land gratis or at a nominal price, partly as a token of their generations of service, partly to avoid the plots getting into the hands of rebellious sharecroppers.)

The party organization, not only in Korahia but in the whole of Jainagar administrative circle of which the village was a part, was still confined to educated men from small and medium landowning families. The landless and the illiterate had not joined: they were not yet ready for a confrontation. A few of them as a kind of individual protest, individual escape, gave up tilling and migrated to other districts of Bihar or to Calcutta and Assam, or opened a shop in the village.

The departure of the few tillers, though by no means unsettling, did make the landlords think. After the coming to power in 1967 of new, non-Congress politicians they grew even more suspicious. Legislation clamping a ceiling upon landholdings had already been passed in 1962; and the new government was planning to reduce the ceiling further, and also talked of acting strictly to identify land above the fixed ceiling. Also, the sharecroppers must have secure tenure and the landless labourers a parcel of homestead land. The sharecroppers and labourers in Korahia, too, heard this through the communists and were begin-ning to find it attractive. The new ministry soon fell, but the momentum gained from participation in it was not completely lost by the CPI. The party was soon trying to speed up the implementation of laws by making a conditional alliance, in mid-1969, with Indira Gandhi's Congress government in New Delhi, as well as her party's ministry in the state.

At the time the state was being run by a loose coalition headed by a Congressman. The minister was surviving with the support both of the CPI, which had 25 members in the Assembly (although the party had not joined the ministry), and of the Praja Socialist Party which had 18 members. The two parties were to join together to start in (1969-70) a 'land liberation movement' whose aim was to put land into the hands of its rightful owners. The Coalition government tried to meet the demands of the situation: it enacted the homestead laws to allow landless labourers the right to possess the pieces of land upon which their tiny huts stood. The government also ordered that claims by the sharecroppers for occupancy of their plots would be settled at tripartite boards, each consisting of the sharecroppers' representative, the landlords' representative and government officials.

Amid such 'state-fostered confusion', the ex-*zamindars* of Korahia thought it better to eliminate the sharecroppers: at the same time the sharecroppers took their cases to the government officials. It was necessary for the CPI men leading the sharecroppers to be resourceful. The landlords had never given any documents or receipts to the sharecroppers: and the laws demanded evidence of twelve years of continuous tilling for a sharecropper to be eligible for occupancy rights. How was the sharecropper to prove his bona fides? The problem was not new to the CPI in Madhubani. It had been present when the movement started in Andhari, where the tenants also had no papers. At Andhari, the district leaders had found a way: they started forging papers and receipts, credibly 'stamped' and backdated. In the absence of landlords' receipts, fabricated receipts would prove that a person had been an established tenant or sharecropper.

There might sometimes have been an error. In the suit that the sharecropper filed, he had to give the measurements of the plot that he claimed to have been tilling for an unbroken period of 12 years or more; he had also to put in the number of the plot, recorded by the state revenue department during the last survey and settlement of land. Sometimes the measurement and the number would be wrongly stated, or the measurements might be of one plot while the number was of another. In Korahia quite a few sharecroppers lost their claims because of such errors; but after making the correction they would claim again. At the new tripartite boards, however, the settlement of disputes did not depend only on papers and receipts, but also on witnesses.

It was usually the party men (even the leaders) who represented the sharecroppers at the tripartite boards. The progress of the hearing was undoubtedly slow because CPI leaders were occupied elsewhere and the board's work had to be postponed as a result. Nevertheless, the landlords at Korahia, as elsewhere, were losing cases at the boards, and panicking. They did have their own fabricated mass of land records, but they could not rely only on them, so they began to sell off the land cheaply to other peasants in Korahia. The CPI campaign, then, in Korahia would follow a set pattern, which had been set at Andhari: the tenants filed suits, the landlord sold plots to other peasants and many legitimate tenants ended up with nothing. The CPI campaign in Madhubani had the effect of depressing land prices, to the benefit of peasants with a little money. At any rate, the campaign seemed to benefit peasants no less than the sharecroppers, and created a crisis for the Party. On one side were the sharecroppers whose cause it had made its own, on the other were buyer-peasants who, political strategy demanded, should not be alienated, and were therefore left undisturbed, even if the sharecroppers felt strongly about it.

But the sharecroppers had themselves set up a positive process, which was not confined to plots of land. It began the destruction of the landlord regime, much more devastatingly than protest through individual outmigration could do. Backed by the CPI organization, the sharecroppers saw the landlord as the snatcher rather than the giver of bread. The rights they had lost to the landlord must be firmly regained, even the cultural rights. They stopped the presents of fish, the best portions of goat meat, the pots and water-fruits; they stopped doing unpaid labour. And they began to arrange marriages of their sons and daughters without asking the landlord. In other villages of Madhubani district, the land claimants were involved in confrontation with the landlords' men at the time. At Korahia, the 'rare visitors in the finest and most expensive dhotis' ceased to put in an appearance.

And the land was not lost by all the sharecroppers. A few hundred (today, about 300) had taken their claims to the tripartite boards where the landlords' representatives had won on 'facts' and 'technical grounds', but they never gave up the plots. In the same way, over 100 landless labourers occupied a large area of land illegally held by landlords. During the 'Land Liberation Movement' led by the CPI and other parties in 1969-70, the landless labourers, all of them *Mallahs* (the party organization in Korahia was confined to the *Mallahs*, giving it an unfortunate caste identity), were led by the party on to the landlords' illegal land. At all four corners they hoisted red flags (in the form of red rags tied on the top of small sticks). In the days following, they built rows of mud-walled huts, and the families of the occupiers hurriedly moved in and then put in applications to the Circle Officer (who had powers to 'regularise' occupation of the homestead by the homeless) which he turned down. But the *Mallahs* did not leave. During the state revenue department's land survey and settlement operations in 1971, landlords manipulated the records to keep the occupied land as their own, within their holdings, under the legal ceiling. It made no difference to the squatters: they are living there even today. Within this squatter colony is the large brick-built office of the party's village committee—two rooms, set apart by an ample hall, are for the use of office bearers and for the files of papers and documents; the hall is for party meetings.

In other parts of Madhubani district the battle was becoming more intense. The landlords' hired squads were attacking and murdering sharecroppers. It gave its 'militia' the name of *Jana Seva Dal*, the People's Service Corps. The militia in Madhubani district was more loosely organized than, for instance, the one the party had built up in Begusarai district, on the other side of the Ganga, to match the mercenary power of the landlords there. But it did recruit fighters from the party and trained the men, and women, in villages in the tactics of guarding the hamlets and repulsing assaults. Bows and arrows, and *rasai-dhela* (a weapon in which a small piece of rock was tied at the end of a short rope) were made to use as missiles and along with other common village weapons, such as hatchets and axes, were collected and kept in readiness. Firearms were very rare: for one reason, in Madhubani, unlike some southern Bihar districts, even the landlords' men did not have or frequently use firearms. But that was not to say the *Jana Seva Dal* would not kill the landlords' men; several killings and counter-killings took place. 'We might not have killed as many people as the landlords did but the tally on our side was certainly not short,' said a district party leader.

The landlords had formed their own fronts, such as the Madhubani Kisan Mazdoor Congress, Madhubani Peasants and Labourers Congress. It was their last attempt to liquidate the peasant movement with arms: after that they fell quiet. In November 1972, in Selibeli, a village five kilometres west of Korahia, they succeeded in inflicting the greatest tragedy upon the CPI. There, for over a year before the tragedy, sharecroppers and other peasants had been fighting legal battles with a monk-landlord, who would neither recognize the rights of the sharecroppers nor give up public land and properties—such as a fishpond— he had acquired by force. The sharecroppers had been assaulted and falsely accused of stealing the precious metal crown of the god from the monastery: the loot of paddy from the peasant fields had followed. Then, as the sharecroppers and peasants did not yield, the monk organized a gun-squad raid, to slaughter seven communists, among them a most respected and active peasant leader, Santu Mahato, aged 30, who had left schoolmastering to become a full-time party worker.

The former *zamindars* despatched no hired squads to Korahia; instead they sent proposals for a compromise. Neither the leaders nor the sharecroppers were averse to agreements; and the continued possession of land by many of the 300 sharecroppers who had lost their claims but held on to their plots, could be a possible result. It was partly a reading of the signs, a grudging recognition of the CPI power, a pragmatic acknowledgement by non-resident landlords that things now had better be done with the CPI's consent. The landlords wanted only their owner's share from the harvest, and were sometimes more liberal, as long as nobody claimed their land. A good example was that of the heir of a landlord who had not more than ten acres left in the village. A senior government engineer, he one day journeyed to the village and asked to see Rajendra, the secretary, and told him he wanted to make a personal deal. He would, he said, leave his land in the leader's charge, but wanted no sharecroppers' claims to be lodged for his ten acres. 'Get the land cultivated and do whatever you like with the harvest, for as long as you want,' the engineer said, handing over the keys of his farmhouse. Today Rajendra continues to handle his charge personally; no claims have been filed for that land. The party members talk about the deal stealthily; no one knows where the money from selling the harvest goes. But if Rajendra does receive it, argue some party members, he sometimes puts it to good use too, as when, for instance, some years ago, some young and semi-educated *Mallahs* were selected for technical training in Bombay and as they did not have enough money, Rajendra gave them about 1,200 rupees.

Internal clashes

By the late 1970s, a decade of claims, confusion and land capture, the former *zamindars* had sold half of their land in Korahia, selling it even as they tried to meet the communists halfway, and still the buyers and the claimants had not come to the point of collision. Korahia looked on with dismay when the first collision over land took place between none other than party men. A landlord in far away Vaishali, who had in the *zamindari* days been a revenue collector, sold four acres of his land in the village to six people, registering the sale at the local court. It was a piece of land on which a father and son (the family had a little land of its own) had successfully filed occupancy claims as sharecroppers. Five of the six buyers were members of the party, and so was the younger 'sharecropper'; they were threatening to occupy the land since they had paid money for it; but he was determined to keep them away since he and his father had secured legal occupancy rights. This happened in the first half of the 1980s.

The son, Kapildeo Singh, had never been a sharecropper, but his father was. A family of Rajputs, they were the poorest of the 20 or so families of his higher caste in the village, which was why they had to work in the fields. Kapildeo, aged 29, had had some schooling; he had gone to Assam in search of work, then returned to run an allopathic store a few yards from the railway platform. The land on which he built his shop, and later added a room, belonged to the Maharaja's former revenue collector. The young Rajput had obtained a 'landless person' certificate from the Block officials, then applied for a homestead as an adult, claiming the land of the former revenue collector, and had got it. A *Mallah* and an untouchable were also staking claim to the same piece of land (its value was due to its central location) but Kapildeo was the successful one.

His shop was a small room almost fully occupied by two wooden cupboards, a very large one facing the door, a smaller one on the left, both stacked with bottles of cough syrups, packets of capsules, tablets and other drugs: with a wooden chair and a table, there was hardly any space. Kapildeo had no training as a pharmacist but, with his knowledge of the drugs he stocked, had made himself into the nearest physician the villagers could think of rushing to in sickness. He made no charge for consultation and people could take home drugs on credit; such acts of kindness made him influential. After he joined the party in 1977 he had added to his influence by making a meticulous study of the land reform laws and related official circulars, and developing a skill in drafting claims petitions and in arrangements at the sharecroppers' tripartite boards, even courts. From his little, cluttered shop he operated like a clerk and broker for the party. And the nature of the party's campaign in Madhubani or Korahia was such that it could not do without men like Kapildeo.

His own case was most demanding of his skills. Murmurings were heard among the party members even while his own and his father's claims petitions were being argued at the tripartite board. Kapildeo did not feel he was trying to gain something to which he was not entitled. Half the land father and son were asking rights to had, he said, 'actually' belonged to his family. Nearly half a century before the former revenue collector had bought it from Kapildeo's distressed grandfather and leased it out to him again for sharecropping. His grandfather had still owned a few acres which, along with the sharecropped land, was shared between Kapildeo's father and uncle after the old man's death. In 1980 the family had heard that the landlord was putting the sharecropped land up for sale and made haste to submit a claim to a tripartite board. In the following months other members of the CPI had raised objections and a meeting was called. 'Why should one family get as much as four acres?' was the general feeling. Even Jagdish Singh, the only other Rajput in the party, said it was not proper, since other sharecroppers had not got such large pieces.

Before Kapildeo and his father won titles to the land only 50 or so sharecroppers had succeeded in their claims to land. (The 300 others had no legal titles.) These 50 sharecroppers had received between them roughly 50 acres, all from a single landlord, a monk living in Basuara village. But their suits and their titles did not have the impact they should have had, because the sharecroppers involved lived at the far end of the big village, from where reports did not easily reach the centre. Kapildeo lived near the railway station and the shops; and this, apart from the intraparty quarrel, made his case a subject of discussion in the village.

In the meeting few spoke in Kapildeo's favour; but Rajendra, the secretary, supported him. It ended in a compromise; Kapildeo was instructed by the party committee to give three-quarters of an acre from his four acres for the use of the party. In agreeing, Kapildeo had privately made his plans. One of the plots he and his father had won was located far away, almost at the edge of the village and was worthless. He earmarked that for the party. But shortly afterwards, the six purchasers jumped in, waving their documents of purchase for the four acres, creating a new controversy within the village party committee.

Another meeting of the executive committee was held. The new dispute troubled them because the six people not only belonged to the party but they also belonged to the caste of *Mallahs* who formed the largest segment of party organization in village. The party office was in the *Mallah* squatter colony; and the party was identified with the *Mallahs*. Others saw it that way too. When a group of *Mallahs*, going to fish in a village pond, were assaulted by a group of Yadava peasants whose fields were close by, the word flashed around the village: 'Did you hear? The Communist Party got beaten today!' The next day, the *Mallahs* again went to the pond, and the Yadava peasants yelled.' 'You here again? Want a fresh lesson, do you?' Without saying a word, the *Mallahs* pounced upon the peasants, belaboured them harshly and came back with a triumphant air. The prestige of the Communist Party had been restored.

No decision could be made at the meeting. Very soon the air became thick with pejoratives. Kapildeo was blamed for 'capitalistic tendencies'. He, in turn, branded his opponents as 'stooges of the anti-communist camp' bent upon destroying the village party. His rivals felt certain about his being a clever high-caste man, a go-getter; certain that he had joined the CPI simply because he had concluded that he could achieve nothing through 'casteism' since the Rajputs were a minor segment of the village population, only 20 families. Sometimes, in private, he himself admitted this.

His rivals said he was getting the freedom fighter's pension for his father on a forged jail certificate. They talked about his legal manipulations to procure the prize plot for his shop. Another episode mentioned was related to the auction of the best fishing-pond in the village by its non-resident owner. Kapildeo wanted it but as the day of auction drew nearer he became certain of losing the bid to one or two *Mallahs*. One *Mallah* was the same man who had competed with him for the shop plot; lingering animosity prevented him from becoming reconciled to the loss of a pond, whose fish were large and plentiful. Kapildeo pressed for a meeting of the executive committee. At the meeting, he proposed that a co-operative, supervised by the party, be formed for the bidding. It was not proper, he argued, for this or that individual to take over the pond, and in the co-operative, resources could be pooled. The suggestion was carried overwhelmingly. Kapildeo had once again beaten his rivals.

Eventually, in the quarrel with the six purchasers, Rajendra threw his weight behind Kapildeo, who had become desperate; he secretly petitioned the district officials in Madhubani town and the local police officer, on the grounds of 'breach of peace', saying that he and his father, as the rightful sharecroppers, needed protection. Rajendra was unaware of these moves; but Kapildeo was relying upon his support. After all, he said in private, he did not work hard for nothing during Rajendra's election as the *mukhiya* of the village, as he had even been to the doors of such people opposed to the Communist Party as the Rajput families where there were about 100 voters. The election for the *mukhiya* post in Korahia was usually decided by a slender margin of about 75 votes. In a close contest like this it was pragmatic of Rajendra or anyone coveting the most important post of the village to be interested in drawing on whatever support was possible from the non- and anti-communist camps. That Rajendra knew his politics well was evident from the way he ran his own nominee, against the party candidate, for the vice-chairmanship of the Jainagar agricultural markets committee and succeeded in getting him elected. The party had suspended Rajendra for six months for that.

The quarrel between Kapildeo and the six buyers was still unresolved when this report was being written.

Conclusion

The landless made up more than 40 per cent of Korahia's population. Some had gone elsewhere in search of work, some were combining other work with land labour in the village. In 1968 the CPI at the national level formed the BKMU, its 'class organization' of the landless labourers. But the BKMU could not prove very active in Korahia: most of the landless remained outside it. So until the mid 1970s many of them remained debt-bonded to the former *zamindars* and the landowners of the village. The CPI in Korahia never made debt-bondage an issue: it was left to Indira Gandhi's propaganda machine during the Emergency to do so. Many of the bondmen became free during the Emergency.

Their freedom from bondage came through the intervention of the state. During the Emergency, the state was tough to the landlords. In Korahia, it had even had one or two of them booked under the Bonded Labour Act; even these isolated punitive measures immensely emboldened the former bondmen who would never have registered cases against their masters in the past. In the post-Emergency years these labourers began to demand higher wages: they were then getting two kilos of coarse grain or paddy; they wanted five. The party intervened to bring about a compromise at three-and-a-half kilos. In Korahia as elsewhere, the party faced the difficult task of keeping the peasants and the labourers united; they seemed always to clash on questions related to land. In a bid to keep the conflict between the peasants and the labourers at the lowest level, the party decided to take the struggle of the landless outside the village. They led the labourers to government offices to demand old-age pensions and fair wages by the contractors for the small rural employment schemes.

The landless in the village have not emerged as party leaders, although some of them are members of the 31-member executive committee of Korahia including even untouchables. But comradeship does not seem to be forging ahead: the party is afflicted by caste feelings. Some years ago, the executive committee decided that each time it met a communal dinner would be held. The dinners were to be hosted, in turn, in the hamlets (or streets) where the members lived. This went on happily until the turn of the Chamar (leatherworker members). Only Rajendra, the secretary, and Ramdeo, the office secretary, attended that dinner: all the others invented excuses for not coming, and thus ended the party custom.

10. How the Thakurs Were Contained

The rise of the CPI-M

In 1964, the Communist Party of India (CPI) split, and the dissenters formed the Communist Party of India-Marxist (CPI-M) which was to grow stronger than the CPI. It was a major split with one main cause: the 'leftism' of the Congress Party.

Some years after independence, Congress and Prime Minister Nehru began to talk of establishing a 'socialist pattern of society' in India. (Nehru, even within pre-independence Congress, was seen as a leftist; he had progressive cultural ideas, and advocated agrarian reforms.) Then Nehru said that India would have a mixed economy, with both public and private sectors; and in this economy the public sector would have an important, a 'commanding' place, and include heavy industry (the core industry). It would not be a free enterprise economy; there would be controls on trade and industry.

Nehru devised these policies through a 'contingent' of planning advisers from socialist countries, and Indian experts who had 'a slight orientation towards leftist political-economic thinking'.[1] 'When, in the mid-1950s, the policies were published, they were welcomed by leftist circles within and outside the Congress Party. Within the CPI these policies sowed dissension. Namboodiripad, a senior leader of the CPI-M, in his book *Conflicts and Crisis: Political India: 1974* remembers how, after Nehru's new policies, the character of the Congress Party changed in the eyes of many, who now started saying that Congress should no longer be considered a party of landlords and represented a basic shift in the party's political complexion. They wanted the CPI to ally with the Congress for the sake of 'unity of all progressive democratic forces' in order to defeat the Right. Namboodiripad writes: 'A furious inner-party battle was waged before and at the fourth congress of the Party (CPI) held at Palghat (Kerala) in 1956. This line was of course, rejected at the Congress, but it received the support of as many as one-third of the delegates attending it.[2]

Giving the reasons why the other section within the CPI (which was to evolve as the CPI-M) opposed the line, Namboodiripad says Nehru's new policies had only a leftist *appearance*. They had come in the wake of Congress losses and the leftist parties' gains, in the first general elections in free India in 1952; the Congress wanted to show that it, too, was leftist. In reality, Congress was leading the country down the capitalist path, but thought it essential to give the impression of ushering in socialism. Such a stance would take the wind out of the leftist parties' sails, and strengthen Congress.

Clearly, the future CPI-M men held the aims of the new policies were capitalist. For instance, if they gave heavy industries to the public sector there was an underlying motive. India's major capitalists wanted it so. They were not prepared to invest in heavy industries because this would require a massive investment which would give returns only after a very long time. Likewise, state controls on trade and industry did not 'unduly' worry the major capitalists. As a matter of fact, says Namboodiripad, such capitalists were themselves among 'the most ardent champions' of a planned economy; and Nehru's new policies were essentially 'modelled' on the famous Bombay Plan that top Indian industrialists had themselves presented during World War II. Therefore, the new policies were 'a consummation of the innermost desires of the top monopoly capitalists'.

As this conflict was growing within the CPI, relations between India and China became strained and eventually, in 1962, there was war. Inner-party conflict became sharper. For the future CPI-M men refused to term China as the 'aggressor' in the war, as did Nehru's Congress and all other parties. And, said the dissenters, India's standpoint in the border dispute was wrong as it relied on old and illegitimate British maps and records: India, they said, must have a peaceful settlement with China. The pro-Congress section within the CPI was opposed to such views; they saw themselves as 'patriots' and the other section as 'traitors'. The inner-party conflict becoming very serious, a split became inevitable. When it finally occurred in 1964, Nehru's government ordered mass detention of the new party's leaders and cadres, condemning them as traitors.

The new party, while denouncing the pro-Congress policy of the CPI, also rejected the old party's Soviet-given theory of a non-capitalist path of development and peaceful transition to socialism in India. But neither was it taking up arms for an armed revolution. The CPI-M's strategy would be to try to attain revolution through peaceful means by 'combining' the parliamentary and extra-parliamentary forms of struggle. Soon the CPI-M was recognized by the Communist Party of China as the only communist party in India.

The CPI-M's goal was to be a people's democratic revolution, whose 'axis' was an agrarian revolution in the countryside. Very soon, political work was devoted to building up a Left and Democratic Front (LDF) to fight the forces of authoritarianism represented by Congress, major capitalists and landlords, and the increasing influence of foreign capital. The LDF was to be an alternative to Congress and other bourgeois-landlord parties; it was to end a situation in which, during elections, people had only the limited choice of voting for bourgeois-landlord parties.

But the LDF, according to the party's strategy, was not only an alliance serving elections or the forming of ministries: it was part of the CPI-M's endeavour to bring about a 'change in the correlation of class forces', to isolate the reactionary classes that kept their grip on the economy. It was to be a fighting alliance for the 'immediate advance' of the revolution. It held that, 'The struggle to realise the aims of the people's democratic forces with the worker-peasant alliance as its core is a complicated and protracted one. It is to be waged in varying conditions in various phases.'

The LDF was not, then, for elections but for struggle. In theory, the elections would serve the struggle, but in practice the struggle seemed to serve the elections. In West Bengal, Kerala and Tripura, the LDF came to power; it continues to be in power in West Bengal and Tripura. As a combination of left and democratic parties, it has proved an alternative to the Congress in these states. In 1966–67, the CPI briefly joined the front with the CPI-M, but then returned to their alliance with Congress. For a long time the Congress-CPI alliance continued: then in the 1980s, the CPI broke away and drew closer to the LDF.

On the peasant front, the CPI-M worked through its Kisan Sabha. But later, as the Sabha became dominated by the middling and rich peasants, the party came to regret this. The Sabha failed to build up the peasant movement during the prevailing discussions (within the party) in the period 1972–73. Basic questions relating to the total abolition of landlordism and the out-and-out agrarian revolution were raised, but little attention was paid to the working out of slogans, demands and tactics relevant to the current situation and the state of the Kisan movement. Except for the stray, local movements (one of which is examined in the section below) no momentum on the peasant front was gained in Bihar, where the party remained very small and peripheral. In order to make the Sabha strong, the party felt it must work among the landless labourers and poor peasants.

Thakia and the two 'trends'

Tall, and in his early fifties. Umashankar Shukla was a Brahman and a lawyer of moderate income. He was the CPI-M secretary for the East Champaran district, in North Bihar: he had been the secretary for many years. He lived in Motihari, the district town, in his own large house with a room set apart for his consultations. From there he went to the district courts every day. Obviously, he had no time for revolutionary work in the villages, and seemed to have continued as party secretary perhaps because the party was seeking respectability in the district through respectable middle-class leadership.

As a lawyer Shukla proved to be of help to the party. To earn his living Shukla had a free-earning practice, but represented his party free. The cases in which party workers became involved were many; after all, if Shukla could not, others at the village level, however isolated, carried out agrarian mobilization.

Shukla was at times worried about 'peasant movements'. As the local party secretary he surveyed the recent history of the peasant movement in the East Champaran district and summarized his experiences. The 'trends' he noted disappointed and disturbed him, he told me, two especially. First, the involvement of peasants in court cases. Shukla had reached the conclusion that the landlord found court cases the best way to punish his non-conforming peasants. He was not interested in having them sentenced, his aim was to harass them to breaking point. Court cases were the peasants' greatest trial: if they could 'endure' them, they had succeeded. This was because the cases went on for eight, ten, even twelve or more years, and the peasant had to appear on each day of hearing. 'He must not miss one day, otherwise he would be in jail, forfeiting his bail,' Shukla said.

The second 'trend' that troubled Shukla was the 'exclusivistic tendencies' among the untouchables. It was becoming more and more difficult to carry the untouchables along with the landless. Shukla blamed Congress government propaganda: day in and day out politicians and ministers spoke of discrimination against the untouchables and the need to make giving them uplift a 'top priority'; embedded in their minds was the notion that 'only they are entitled to land, whatever distributed, and wherever—and no one else!'

In Shukla's view both 'trends' were impediments to the growth of the peasant movement, but were of advantage to the landlord. Either the peasants stopped resisting because of harassment through the courts or they failed to unite because of the sectarianism of the untouchables. Talking to Shukla in Motihari, one might begin to feel that prospects for a peasant movement in East Champaran district were bleak. But Shukla, perhaps because he spent most of his time reading briefs and law books in Motihari, seemed unaware of what was actually happening in the rural parts of the district. For, only seven kilometres north of the town in which he lived, in the village of Jhakia, neither of his two 'trends' was visible. There, not only had the peasants 'endured' court cases but there was no 'exclusivism' among the village untouchables.

Jhakia was no ordinary village for the CPI-M, but the one famed for the strongest party organization in the whole of East Champaran district. Many district party members considered Jhakia to be the campaign that kept the party flag flying during the crises of those few years following its split with the CPI. The party had but few villages of East Champaran district in its fold; even today it remains confined to isolated villages. But it was Jhakia that gave the party its small foothold in the district. But rivalries within the district party led to different views. Shukla, for example, without belittling the Jhakia campaign, pointed out that the origins of the CPI-M's agrarian movement in the district lay elsewhere. According to Shukla, they could be traced to the 'land occupation movement'— that he led, and which had existed for a year or more before Jhakia 'received prominence'. The centre of that movement was a village called Laukaria, located in what is now West Champaran district. In 1967 nearly 5,000 landless peasants had seized more than 10,000 acres around the forests near Laukaria. The occupation was so momentous that, Shukla remembered, 'Even Radio Beijing hailed Laukaria as a "liberated area", probably thinking that it was the work of the Naxalites, not ours.'

A few days after the 10,000 acres had been 'occupied', the police forces moved in: high-ranking officials, even the commissioner, arrived: there were police shootings, killings, injuries; the 'occupation' was broken. Shukla said he was there, in the area of struggle, the day that the police began shooting at the peasants: 'But I was in a different village, and didn't know anything about it until later in the evening. "What happened after the police dispersed the 'occupiers'?" Shukla fumbled here: obviously the 'movement' petered out; the peasants didn't return to reoccupy the land. But Shukla was happy to note that the government was forced to distribute 6,000 of the 10,000 acres in the area, which was an 'achievement' for the movement he led. But he was unhappy with the way the distribution had taken place: it had caused disputes among the landless. Here again, the government wanted to apply its policy of giving priority to the untouchables, but there were not many untouchables among the landless in that area, so, Shukla had learned, the officials in charge of distribution sought out untouchables from other areas and took them there and settled them with a piece of land: thus, Shukla said, denying land to several of the landless of other castes living in the area.

Jhakia belied Shukla's theories. There was no arrogance among the untouchables, for one thing they were few: from Jhakia's streets the landlords took no more than 30 bond-servants. The bulk of the population of the village was made up of the *Mallahs* (boatmen), but not all depended on fishing or the boat ferry; most had joined the ranks of the daily farm labourers. The *Mallahs* comprise almost two-thirds of the village's population of 4,000. In the struggle against the landlords, the untouchables were at one with the *Mallahs* and others. They neither made any show of self-importance, nor demanded any 'privileged' treatment for themselves. On the contrary, they still continue to suffer indignities, even within the CPI-M's peasant organization. This is how one untouchable member puts it:

> We all may be going together from the village to rallies and demonstrations held in Patna or elsewhere. But before or after the rally, when we sit down to open our packets of food brought from home, we don't do it together. Others, particularly (but not only) the peasants, sit and eat separately. And if there are circumstances in which there is no other way but to eat with us every one of them will start saying his stomach is upset, or that he doesn't feel like eating at the moment.

Jhakia's *Mallahs* were the most numerous but not the 'dominant caste' of the village; it was a village of *Mallahs*, not a *Mallah* village. They had no land; land and power lay elsewhere. Jhakia showed the common characteristics of rural autocracy. The labourers sweated all day; unlike in other villages, they were given no breakfast. The income was practically nothing; the labourers were generally very thin and emaciated. (If, rarely, a labourer had a good physique, the masters would brand him as a dacoit. 'How can a labourer have a sound build with honest labour?' they would say.)

There were day labourers, there were bondmen. Then bondmen, who after working in the fields had to work also in the master's household until long after sunset, were given a smaller wage. If the day labourer received two-and-a-half kilos of coarse grain or paddy, the bondman was given only one-and-a-half. Loans were offered on thumb impressions, on plain paper, and 'the masters went on adding zeroes'. Captivity was accompanied by high-handed taking of liberties with the women, bans on wearing clean clothes, having combed hair, or shoes and wooden slippers, and on sending children to school; and never-ending intrigues designed to sow and aggravate quarrels among the captives.

The three or four families of the top landlords, who held much of the village's land, were all Thakurs, and lived in the village. They were not among its original residents, but had settled in Jhakia at about the turn of the twentieth century. It was said that they had originally been living south of East Champaran, some-where in Muzaffarpur district, where, for some reason, their ancestors lost their landholdings; they had left the ancestral place and migrated to Gobari, a village three kilometres from Jhakia, and from there, moved to Jhakia. In Jhakia they bought some land out of their savings and started living like other cultivators. But unlike other cultivators, the Thakurs were ambitious and clever. They wanted more and more land; they bought land, and took it against outstanding loans. Even after Independence their estates continued to expand. Landowners, cultivators, tenants, all came to them to pawn pieces of their land in exchange for loans to meet the expenses of a marriage or a funeral or during festivals; for loans of food, when the crops failed, which was not infrequently since the soil in Jhakia was of only average fertility and there was no irrigation. The Thakurs had diesel pumps for their fields, food stocks, and money from the sale of agricultural surpluses (and as interest for cash loans). They lived well, and gave their children a good education. Some of educated Thakurs secured well-paid jobs in the cities.

As money or grain lenders the Thakurs had proved their cunning. The rates of interest they charged were high and arbitrarily fixed. Many of these transac-tions were oral. But when someone came to pawn part of his land they made him sign the mortgage, or give his thumb impression. They knew the man would never be able to pay off the mortgage; on the contrary, the loan would swell with the interest. His signature or thumb impression would stand as proof of the mortgage; with the 'details'—the 'date' of mortgage, the 'amount' of loan, the 'size' and 'description' of the pawned plot and so forth—filled in the blank space above the signature or thumb impression, the paper was a perfect legal document which would satisfy the courts. In court the man would have no alternative but to sign away the plot to his debtor, towards repayment. Many of the *Mallahs*, the *Bhumihars*, even the once rich small population of high-caste Dewan Muslims, had lost a part or the whole of their landholdings to the Thakurs in this way.

People hated the Thakurs, but were impotent against them; they relied on the gods for revenge. When Singaldeep Thakur, the cleverest of all the land-grab-bers, lay incurably ill for two long years ('rotting, twitching, unattended') before dying in 1978, the peasants said, 'He is reaping as he has sown.' The peasants noted that during his long illness members of his family took no care of him, not even his sons and daughters. Some hours before he died, Yamuna Singh, the president of Jhakia Kisan Sabha, the CPI-M's peasant organization, had visited him. On seeing him, Thakur burst out sobbing: he clasped Yamuna's hand and asked for his forgiveness: 'Pardon me, Yamuna,' he said, 'I was the cause of the ruin of you all.'

Yamuna had gone to see Thakur on his deathbed only out of courtesy; like the others, he hated him. Like others, he had lost land to the Thakurs; no less than 100 acres over the years. Yamuna, aged 55, was an elder cousin of Ramashray Singh, who led the CPI-M campaign in Jhakia and was twice elected to the Bihar Assembly from the area. The Singhs and the Thakurs were both of the same *Bhumihar* caste, but there was a dividing line. The Singhs thought themselves superior to the Thakurs on the grounds that they, the Singhs, were among the original inhabitants of the village while the Thakurs were new and rootless. The dividing line became more sharply drawn as the Thakurs, the newcomers, became more and more wealthy in a very short time; wealthier at the expense of everybody, including Ramashray's family.

From his mother, Ramashray had learnt why his father had become poorer and, finally, was left with only six acres, because of the longstanding Thakur designs. Ramashray's ancestors, before his father, were revenue collectors for the Maharaja of Bettiah who until the end of *zamindari* had vast estates in what is now East Champaran district. Independence had not yet come. The Thakurs had already been in Jhakia for a couple of decades. Cleverly they maintained a good relationship with Ramashray's father. For a rent collector, they found him a simple soul, and started telling him that he was too honest; he was not cheating the Maharaja as he so easily could. 'Why don't you keep part of the collection for yourself? You only have to show less money in the books.' Ramashray's father, tempting though the suggestion was, hesitated: 'I might get into trouble'.

The Thakurs said, 'The Maharaja's estates are too vast for his high-up officials ever to know or bother about one employee in a village not sending them every penny that he gets.' Finally, the rent collector decided to cheat. He stopped sending to the Maharaja's treasury the rents he was collecting from the local periodic market and fishpond, but continued to send rent collections for agricultural land. This went on undetected for three years. And then, Ramashray's mother told him those same Thakurs informed on him to the Maharaja's officers. Ramashray's father was horrified when the officers sent him a notice to pay three-year arrears of rents from the market and fishpond. He had no money to pay, so the officers confiscated about 100 acres of his land and put it up for auction. The Thakurs bought the whole of it.

Since then the Thakurs and the Singhs had been enemies. But there were no battles; the Singhs would have their revenge with the growth of the CPI-M in Jhakia. The young Ramashray was drawn to Marxist ideology in off-and-on encounters with some relatives who were in the CPI and then, after the split, in the CPI-M. Among them was Lakshmi Narayan Singh, Yamuna's younger brother, and Vishawanath Singh, whose in-laws lived in Jhakia. Ramashray's ageing father was against his eldest son—due to take on the family responsibilities—dabbling in anything like politics. He had learnt from some of Ramashray's schoolteachers and also from close friends who watched him grow that he was a promising boy; he was ecstatic when Ramashray became one of the only two boys to leave his school with a First Division. Having high hopes of him, the old man took every care never to say a harsh word to him and even sold a piece of land to finance his studying.

But his Marxist relatives had politicized him. Ramashray left college in 1966 at the Intermediate stage, and never went back. His father stopped speaking to him: the two men lived at home like mute strangers for two years, at the end of which the old man died of cancer. His mother, however, supported and still supports Ramashray, travelling as far as Patna for the CPI-M rallies, unmindful of her failing health. From the outset she seemed determined to make her own contribution to the force that would turn the tables upon the rapacious Thakurs. Her resolve was further steeled by two factors: first, plain adoration by a mother of her child no matter what; and secondly, her own experience during the CPI-M struggle when Ramashray's wealthier kin virtually treated her family as outcasts because Ramashray was working for the lower castes, not even letting her take water from the government-installed handpump.

To his landed kinsmen Ramashray deserved as much contempt for becoming a communist as he did for mingling and eating with lower castes. But the response of the poorer classes in the village was just the opposite. To them all the *Bhumihars*, the Singhs and the more newly-settled Thakurs alike, were *babu sahibs*, gentry, lofty, unapproachable, noble by birth. For a *babu sahib* to give up such a status and brush aside social barriers was to them a great but incredible event. Ramashray's influence as a leader owed much to the impact of his 'condescension', an element that leadership by someone from the lower classes would obviously have lacked.

Before the CPI-M movement started, some landless labourers had adopted their own way of protest and had migrated eastwards to Assam and Bengal, doing all kinds of work involving physical labour. Some of the *Mallahs* among the migrants also put their traditional caste skill to use: where they worked the fields or built roads, they also started leasing fishponds from the local Bengali or Assamese owners: selling the fish, and saving money.

On the face of it, this was escape, the result of a weakening resolve to fight the landlords within the village. But with the new strength of the CPI-M organization, weaknesses were turned into advantages, even a tendency to migrate. Once the peasants came together, the migrants (who spent part of the year outside and part of it in the village) played a special role. In distancing themselves from the Jhakia masters, and by having to grapple with the outside world, they had acquired a courage which the locally-rooted labourers lacked. Some of them may have been influenced by the prevailing rural turbulence in Bengal, sparked off by Naxalbari. Also the migrants could, in periods of severe repression, easily be away for months; their wives and children were accustomed to the periodic absences of a breadwinner.

Shortly after it began, for a brief period in 1969-70, the organization at Jhakia fell under the influence of the Naxalite movement. Naxalite propagandists visited the village. It was difficult to pinpoint precisely how this influence came about for the people who know hesitate to speak about it, including the CPI-M leaders. At that time the Naxalite movement was springing up at odd, unexpected places across the country, and though the lines between the CPI–M and the dissenters of the party who became Naxalites appeared to have been drawn, it was by no means uncommon for the activists and cadres of the parent party to nurse a sympathy for their radical ex-comrades. Ramashray denies ever having joined the Naxalites but admits that in those days (when he was put in jail) he privately supported them, appreciating their activities. 'I felt they were doing the right thing,' he says, Mao's famous Hunan Report had had a great influence on Ramashray: it provoked his thoughts and made him fight for the peasants. A Hindi translation had fallen into his hands by chance: 'I was astonished to find striking similarities between the conditions of the peasants of my village and those of pre-revolutionary China,' he said.

As the organization in Jhakia grew militant it considered 'action' against the local landlords. For this, 'defence squads' had to be raised from among the peasants and the labourers. The training was to continue for some months in a small wood at the edge of the village; this was not undertaken every day, and never in the daytime. The recruits, men of various ages, would gather in the wood on moonlight nights, with bows and arrows, spears and clubs.

The combat skills thus acquired led not to the killing of any landlord, but to a few raids on the landlords' fields to seize the harvest, and some clashes with the landlords' strong-arm men. 'Action' was also taken against a Brahman landowner of the adjoining village who had beaten up a young untouchable boy. The boy, a member of the defence squad, had gone out to relieve himself, and the landlord punished him. An untouchable daring to shit on a Brahman's sanctified patch of earth! It had never happened before! But the landowner did not publicly give that reason; the provocation for the beating came, he said, from the boy's attempt to steal his paddy. To the defence squads, the assault was provocation enough: what had provoked the Brahman was immaterial. An emergency meeting was called by the squad leaders and, ignoring the fact that Ramashray was out of the village on some business at the time, they decided to raid the Brahman's crop fields the following morning. According to plan, the next morning they came back with rice-paddy reaped from as much as two acres.

In the police crackdown that followed the series of 'extremist incidents' the organization suffered a setback. The police came to the village to arrest and beat up people in large numbers. Operations to flush out the Naxalites were going on everywhere at the time; it was hardly surprising that propagandists of the Naxalite movement had stopped visiting Jhakia. There was one propagandist, though, who stayed for over a year and a half in the village. He came from Kerala and was on the run from the police; the people in the Jhakia organization gave him shelter even though the landlords, after a while, began to suspect (a suspicion they quickly passed on to the police) the presence of 'some outsider' whom the people were refusing to give away. But the direct police assault was unnerving, and the leaders from outside did not reappear, so the organization in the village began to rethink its tactics; there were arguments with the men from Kerala about armed action as central to the struggle. Views now seemed to differ widely, and very soon finding it difficult to cope with the reversal the Naxalite left the village. Though the defence squads were neither condemned nor disbanded, Jhakia slowly returned to the CPI-M fold.

About three years of the movement in the village, including the Naxalite interlude, had nevertheless brought about a few changes. The labourers no longer did unpaid work; payment was asked for any extra work. They no longer adopted reverential, passive expressions when a landlord appeared but talked to him and his men boldly, looking straight into their faces; sometimes now they even shouted at them, if they were passing through the village.

The landlords, the Thakurs, stopped their lending activities. Partly it was punitive, partly due to the fear that the people would not repay or accept the giving of thumb impressions on plain paper. But then, the people themselves no longer went to the Thakurs for loans. The Kisan Sabha instructed its members to arrange credit among themselves; if a member needed money, other members would raise it; in this task of mutual help, small landowners and migrant *Mallahs* with their savings out of fishing could play a leading role. This deprived the landlords of their key source of income; they had been getting profit margins unimaginable from agriculture. One kilo of food, when loaned, became two-and-a-half kilos at the end of the year; one rupee during the same period became four rupees. According to rough peasant estimates, one rupee of investment in agriculture in Jhakia was likely to yield produce valued at less than one-and-a-quarter rupees.

There was also agitation for higher wages. For a long time, the labourers had been paid only 12 annas (that is three-quarters of a rupee) or three-and-a-half kilos of coarse grain; tied labourers were given half that amount. The labourers now asked for five rupees in cash or, alternatively, three-and-a-half kilos of grain 'which the labourer concerned produced in the fields', meaning that those working in the rice fields should be given rice and those working in fields of wheat or maize be given wheat or maize. Having been used to paying in certain varieties of coarse grains, like *khesari*, grown separately, and exclusively for the payment of wage labour, the landlords immediately refused the demands.

But none the less, the labourers started getting the demanded wage, eventually. It was the small landowners, like the families of Ramashray and Yamuna, who were in the CPI-M, who started paying the increased rates, and soon it became difficult for the landlords to get hands to work in their fields, for they all wanted to work for the employers, big or small, who paid them a higher wage. But all the labourers could not be absorbed and migration increased. Finally, the landlords, too, began to pay the new rates.

But the Thakurs of Jhakia were not the only ones facing a breakdown of authority as landlords. At the initiative of the CPI-M, and sometimes also the CPI, the peasants' relationship with the landlord was undergoing changes in other such villages in the area as Semra, Singhia, Ajgari, and Siswania. With a view to fighting peasant militancy jointly, the landlords of the area formed a front called *Kirshak Sangh* (the Argiculturists' Association), selecting a landlord, a Hindu fanatic, to head it. (This landlord left the *Jana Sangh*, the pro-Hindu party, to join Indira Gandhi's Congress and, on its nomination, became a member of the Bihar Assembly between 1980 and 1985.)

The *Kirshak Sangh*, like every other brigade of rural reaction, gave itself a green flag, and an open manifesto that it would use any means to put every village out of bounds for the 'red flag'. 'Stop the red flag from entering our villages' was one of the slogans of the *Sangh* processions. And the *Sangh* spared no effort; with contributions raised from its members, bullies from other areas were hired. The peasants recall with horror how these bullies, with weapons and clubs, prowled the roads, and the village tracks. They caught and assaulted several activists, particularly those found alone. One day in 1975, not far from Jhakia, Ramashray fell into their hands. After doing the job required of them they slipped away, leaving him unconscious for hours some distance from the road, in the grass. The peasants of Jhakia at first took him for dead, for he was very badly injured.

Some months later there was an episode that made the landlords eventually draw back; since then there have been no paid squads. It happened over the question of the lease for a fishpond. Under the regulations the pond was leased out by the government department, which owned it, to a co-operative society of *Mallahs*. But for some years the office bearers of the co-operative had been secretly sub-leasing the pond to non-fishermen, often rich landowners, who saw the pond as a very profitable business. Now the *Mallahs* of Jhakia, led by the Kisan Sabha, were raising objections.

That year the co-operative had, by its underhand sub-lease, given the pond over to a partnership of two landlords. They were not from the Thakurs of Jhakia. One belonged to Siswania village, the other to Makhlispur. The co-operative's office bearers, realizing that the Jhakia *Mallahs*, being members of the co-operative society, had every right to the sub-lease, opened talks for a compromise. The *Mallahs* finally agreed to have the pond on condition that they gave the landlord-contractors half of the share of the fish yield. A 50 per cent share to the lease-holder—and in fact, the landlords were not even leaseholders in the proper legal sense—was an exceptionally high rate to pay; the customary share was only about 12 per cent. Yet the landlords turned the offer down, saying that the *Mallahs* would have nothing to do with it. They wanted to put the *Mallahs* in their place; and they had other landlords, including the Thakurs, behind them.

The landlord-contractors announced they would get the fishing done themselves. A challenge was issued by the *Mallahs* and the Kisan Sabha: the *Mallahs* of Jhakia would be those to haul the fish. A clash seemed inevitable. Jhakia's defence squads made their preparations. From the landlords' side, over two dozen bullies (in fact a *hanseriau*, a squad of rural mercenaries) marched one day towards the pond to launch their fishing without disturbance. They were equipped with guns and grenades. The *Mallahs*, informed of their arrival in advance, rushed to the pond in large numbers, they too carrying all sorts of weapons, even some home-made guns they had collected from adjoining villages for the battle. Grenades exploded; gunshots were exchanged; spears were flung, and eventually, after a couple of hours or more, the bullies took to their heels.

Later, in the jail (the police arrested persons from both sides), Dasai Sahni, now the CPI-M's secretary for Jhakia, chanced to meet one of the landords' hired men, Satyanarain Sahni, a *Mallah* by caste but a robber by profession. 'He told me how he was contacted at his home, miles away in Kesaria, and how others were brought; how much the landlords paid them, and how they secretly lodged them a day before the encounter looked set.' But this was information that came after the occurrence. On that crucial day, had it not been for the women and the children of Jhakia, who first collected the information about the gathering of the bullies at the landlords' place, success would not have come to the Kisan Sabha. 'Without that warning we would surely have gone to the pond not fully armed,' says Dasai Sahni. 'And in that case the edge of the pond where we stood fighting might have been littered with corpses.'

In fact, the women and the children were an enormous help to the struggle in Jhakia throughout. They not only spied, they also often put the police in search of wanted Kisan Sabha men off the scent. When the police set up a camp in the village, the women carried food for the men in hiding in packets concealed in baskets filled with cow-dung or garbage. With these baskets on their heads they would walk past the police camp without ever arousing suspicion.

No longer able to hold out, the Thakurs, who had practically to abandon the moneylending business, agreed to pay the new daily wages to the labourers. Sometimes the wage went up to eight rupees. Their falling income also compelled them to put up pieces of their land for sale: the Kisan Sabha estimates that by the mid-1980s the Thakurs had sold 30 of the 400 acres they had appropriated or bought at cheap rates from the peasants over the years. What is important to note is not the area of the land sold, but the fact that the process of the Thakurs' accumulation had been blocked, and reversed.

It was the peasant families with extra farm incomes who were buying the pieces of Thakurs' land. They could be fishermen, or toddy-tappers or those who in recent years had opened shops on both sides of the Motihari highway which ran through the village. And about 35 sharecroppers, working about another 30 acres of the Thakurs' land, find themselves in a better condition today. For the Thakurs no longer press for the maximum possible share of the harvest. In the past, the landlords' men were present at the harvesting, even at the threshing and pounding; and, as everywhere else, they took away much more than their half share. But after the Kisan Sabha campaign, the sharecroppers operate in a kind of freedom. No landlords' men are present during the harvesting; nobody even comes to see how much the harvest weighs. Now it is left entirely to the sharecropper to send the landlord his half share; this share is usually much less than a half, but the landlord makes no complaint.

The sharecroppers however do not have titles to the plots they till. Yamuna, the Kisan Sabha president, is somewhat vague on this question, sounding as incredulous as Shukla, the district party secretary: 'It's no use chancing your arm with a sharecropper's case. You can never win.' But the Sabha has never chanced its arm; even within the limits of the laws, sharecroppers in other areas of Bihar did get occupancy rights; the Sabha has never really taken up the land question in Jhakia. What did the Sabha do to seize back from the Thakurs the plots of land taken fraudulently from the peasants? The Sabha's response is again negative: it says the peasants could never win back their plots of land because the Thakurs have all the legal documents for the transfer of the plots in their possession. But the Sabha fails to explain how legal documents are an impediment to peasant occupation of their own land.

11. A More Radical Line

The background of the CPI-ML

There is virtually no CPI-ML (Communist Party of India-Marxist Leninist) in India today, in fact, the CPI-ML never really existed. Small breakaway groups from the CPI-M in some states in May 1969 coalesced as the CPI-ML, but it never became a party; together they became only a bigger group, an all-India group. The revolution did not come. They started to break away again, into smaller and smaller groups (about 60 today, on a rough count). In place of one party, India has 60 CPI-MLs; but there are distinctions. For one thing, almost all the factions denounce Charu Mazumdar, the 'supreme leader' of the CPI-ML of 1969, who died in detention in Calcutta in 1972. Only one faction, the Vinod Mishra, has refused to denounce him. This faction sees itself as 'the party', the real CPI-ML of 1969, because the people within it were the revolutionaries who did not desert Charu when others were deserting, to form their own factions; revolutionaries who inherited the 'mainstream' of the CPI-ML from Charu and kept it going. Vinod Mishra remains the largest faction in India today.

Charu had said that the People's Liberation Army would march through West Bengal before 1971, and by 1975 India as a whole would be liberated. At the time, scores of sensitive urban youths did not see this as fantasy, but moved into the countryside, to arouse the landless peasants. Charu had not been a major leader of the CPI-M; outside the Siliguri district, where he was one of the leaders of the district committee of the CPI-M, he was unknown, even in his West Bengal state. He was raw-boned, and old and ill most of the time; illness kept him bound to his home in Siliguri town, but he came from a small landlord family, which also had some shares in the tea estates around, and local party members and peasants respected him for that; he was seen as a man who denied himself comforts, made a sacrifice, to fight for the poor. But more than that, people respected him for his participation as a local leader in the Tebhaga struggle of the 1940s, the struggle which agricultural tenants then had against the landowners for taking two-thirds of the annual harvest from the leased plots.[1] On top of all this—the 'transcending' of his family background and his active role in the Tebhaga struggle—there were his polemical-intellectual credentials: Charu had published his series of Eight Documents, heresy for the CPI-M politburo, as a blueprint for Indian Revolution.

The 'thoughts' of Charu Mazumdar became the ideology of the CPI-ML. Naxalbari was the region in Siliguri in which the first peasant uprising in West Bengal took place in 1967, two years before the formation of the CPI-ML.

Naxalbari and Charu's 'thoughts' became one and inseparable. The uprising was seen in the framework of the strategy for agrarian revolution and, eventually, for the people's revolution led by the working class.

After 'Independence', went the CPI-ML analysis, both the Soviets and the Americans began to exploit India. Soviet capital worked through free India's large public sector, with its emphasis on heavy industries. US capital exploited through the private sector, in business collaborations. Both Soviet 'social imperialism' and US imperialism exploited the cheap labour and the raw materials of the country; but what was unique, the CPI-ML found, was that the two imperialisms had joined hands; they were exploiting jointly. From a British colony India had become a neo-colony (or a semi-colony) of US-USSR, which was why India, corresponding to its semi-colonial status, had tacitly backed Soviet aggression in Czechoslovakia and US aggression in Vietnam.[2]

It was China, according to the CPI-ML, that was now the centre of international communism. So Indian revolutionaries echoed what China was saying. The world was divided into two camps, one headed by US and its 'chief accomplice' the Soviet Union, and another, the revolutionary one, by socialist China. The US-USSR combined global strategy was to 'encircle socialist China', and India was pursuing a foreign policy tailored to the needs of this strategy. 'India', concluded the CPI-ML, 'is a perfect example of the entente into which the US imperialists and Soviet neo-colonialists have entered jointly to establish hegemony over the world.'[3] And, therefore the Indian people should rally behind China; all revolutionaries should 'try to prove ourselves worthy disciples of Comrade Mao Zedong': Comrade Mao had given a great blueprint for world revolution, especially for the revolutions in the countries of Asia, Africa and Latin America; the Thoughts of Comrade Mao was the "Marxism-Leninism of the present era".' The 'foremost task of all the communist revolutionaries is to propagate and spread the Thoughts of Mao Zedong'.[4]

Those were the days when China was going through the Cultural Revolution, to purify its socialist revolution. It has inspired the 'revolutionaries' within the CPI-M to attack the CPI-M party establishment. In West Bengal in 1967 after the general elections, the Congress ministry had been replaced by a United Front of opposition parties, including the CPI-M. To the revolutionaries, the CPI was already a revisionist party, toeing the Soviet line of 'peaceful transition' to socialism; the CPI-M became revisionist too, with its active participation in bourgeois politics. Charu wrote that a war had been declared in China upon 'all kinds of selfishness, group mentality, revisionism of the bourgeoisie and eulogies of bourgeois ideology', and its 'blazing impact' had reached India. It was about a month after the CPI-M's United Front came to power in West Bengal that Charu wrote this in the last of his Eight Documents. It opened with a censure of the CPI-M. The action of the party leadership after the 1967 elections, observed Charu, had proved 'our apprehensions' correct; the politburo 'has directed us to carry on the struggle to defend the non-Congress ministries against reaction [the right-wing parties]', and 'this suggests that the main task of the Marxists is not to intensify the class struggle but to plead on behalf of the [ministerial] cabinet'.[5]

Charu's eighth document was, in fact, a programme of armed revolution. No one should imagine, it said, that the CPI-M could ever bring about revolution, for two reasons: one, the judiciary and the bureaucracy were never going to let the feudal land pass into the hands of the landless, whoever might be in the ministry; and two, even if the landless could get parcels of land, this would thwart, rather than advance, the cause of revolution. For experience of peasant movements showed that once a landless peasant came to possess a land title he dropped out, became a middle peasant, was no longer active in the movement. So, neither state-sponsored land reform nor the peasant movement served any purpose. On the one hand, the state remained all-powerful and on the other, the political consciousness of the peasants was never raised. The situation would continue like this, Charu said, if the revolutionaries did not intervene 'today': 'this moment'; 'this very moment'. The first and the principal task was, therefore, to rouse the peasants politically and to arm them in order to destroy and seize state power; there could be no land reform without first destroying state power.

By talking of the task 'today', 'this moment', 'this very moment', the ideologue of revolution was laying stress on the *ripeness of the situation* for revolution. But nowhere in his eighth document did Charu explain why, nor was it explained in the first declaration of the revolutionaries published six months after Charu's eighth document. In two or three places (in the eighth document read with the First Declaration) there was some vague indication made in passing. The first was fanciful: 'An excellent revolutionary situation prevails now in our country with all its classical symptoms as enunciated by comrade Lenin.' The second was hesitant: 'Comrades must have noted that revolutionary peasant struggles are now breaking out or going to break out in various parts of the country.'[6] At the third place, Charu spoke of armed 'Liberation' struggles in Nagaland, Mizoram and Kashmir, with whom the communist revolutionaries could set up a united front.

Ripeness was believed to be there; it therefore needed no explanation. But as it soon turned out, the situation was not as Charu saw it. The common Indian had never been concerned with the 'nationalists' in the border regions or the liberation of Nagaland, Mizoram or Kashmir. Or if they were, they were hostile to it. Likewise, scattered risings notwithstanding, no one was awaiting a clarion call. No doubt the illusion of the post-colonial Establishment was no more, but the disillusionment had not yet taken its place. The fact that people were still going to vote was just one aspect of the impaired but living illusion. In the elections of 1967 people had voted Congress out in as many as eight of the 17 states. To the people, this in itself showed the strength of the parliamentary system. And they were ready to give the CPI-M and other non-Congress parties time. Not every dissident within the CPI-M was disillusioned; thus while some joined the CPI-M large proportion stayed within the CPI-M, and pursued inner-party struggle.

Also, the power of the state was underrated by Charu and other revolutionaries. The ousting of Congress from power in nearly half of India probably created an impression that the state was not invincible. In order to seize state power, the revolutionaries in China (and Russia) needed the defection of a fair number of soldiers from the ruling-class army; in the India of 1967 the army showed not even remote signs of cracking up; nothing like that has ever happened in the Indian army or seems likely to happen. Yet the revolutionaries were exhorted by Charu:* 'In every state (of India) the peasants are today in a state of unrest. The communists must show them the path'. It was their 'task', their 'imperative revolutionary duty', their 'great responsibility'. But doing this duty, Charu repeatedly reminded them, called for 'sacrifice'. 'Chairman Mao has taught us, where there is struggle, there is sacrifice.'

A ripe situation, arms to peasants, self-sacrifice; these were to become the key words of the CPI-ML revolution, which began with Naxalbari.

The brief struggle of Naxalbari

Armed peasant revolution was not being engineered for the first time. In the last years of the 1940s the communists had tried it in Telangana; they too had followed the Chinese path. They had given up but had a very large base and had survived for five years. In terms of intensity and peasant mobilization Naxalbari could not be compared with Telangana. Naxalbari rose and fell within a short time.

There were both tea planters and major landlords in the Siliguri administrative sub-division, where Naxalbari lay. Tea plantations were omitted from the purview of the West Bengal Estate Acquisition Act, 1953 (which ended the *zamindari*) so as to allow them to 'retain land for the purposes of afforestation and expansion'. In the Siliguri sub-division there were 36 tea estates, and no tea planter allowed the land meant for 'the purposes of afforestation and expansion' to go idle; he hired it out to sharecroppers for rice cultivation—illegally of course. There was no dearth of people to queue for the small plots: the tea plantation workers themselves (both casual and regular) or the local poor peasants.

According to Kanu Sanyal, a principal organizer of Naxalbari, the tea worker and the sharecropper (often one and the same) had lived close to each other and fought a 'united class struggle'.[7] In the 1950s they had gone on strike for a bonus and a struggle to occupy plots on the illegal estates of the tea planter landlords and other landlords. So the Naxalbari of 1967 had a history of struggle behind it. In 1973, Kanu Sanyal wrote his article to destroy the myth that Charu

* While Charu might have seen the liberation struggles in the border regions in the light of Stalin's theories about the right to self-determination for the nationalities the average Indian, living inland, failed to relate to them. Those fighting peoples, the Naga and Mizo-tribesmen, were too distant, too unknown. They had lived separately in the hills on the eastern border for ages; and their lives and those of other Indians had never met. Neither was it certain that these tribesmen themselves had any desire, tactical or cultural, to ally with the communist revolutionaries. They had started their own battle; they were fighting their own wars.

Mazumdar was the 'leader-creator' of the 1967 Naxalbari uprising, and presented the long history of struggle in the area as concrete proof that 1967 was not one individual's creation.

But Sanyal had other proof. He pointed out that the Naxalbari had not based itself on the Eight Documents, the Charu gospel, in 1967. On the contrary, 1967 was a 'living protest' to that gospel. Two years before Naxalbari broke out, Charu had selected half a dozen new cadres and sent them to certain villages of West Dinajpur, the neighbouring district, to test out his theory of armed struggle by secret squads. The test was a failure, according to Sanyal, for the peasant mass refused to follow the squads and the cadres returned. But Charu did not lose his faith; he pressed on: and there was a debate on his formulations of tactics in the Siliguri local committee of the CPI-M. 'The leading cadres of the Siliguri local committee ' (Sanyal himself obviously being one of them) while agreeing on the need for agrarian revolution disagreed with Charu on several points. They said the agrarian revolution would not come with armed struggle, or without mass organization and mass movements. They also thought it necessary to carry on inner-party ideological struggles, while at the same time staying within the CPI-M.

Whatever the truth, at least one thing is certain: Charu was never directly associated with the struggling peasants in Naxalbari (or elsewhere). Ill for most of the time at his home in Siliguri town, he kept in active contact with Sanyal and other leading cadres. He held his faith; he kept urging the cadres to make the struggle militant, and wrote letters asking them to stop such mass activities as meetings and processions, and start immediately to build an underground organization to carry out secret action. In fact, his emphasis seemed to be to attack the landlords' houses, and the police.[8]

The actual struggle in Naxalbari lasted only two or three months. It took place under the banner of the *Krishak Sabha*, the CPI-M's peasant front in Bengal. In the three months following the installation of the CPI-M's United Front ministry on 2 March 1967, the local committees of the *Krishak Sabha* held conventions at Naxalbari and Siliguri at which a decision was taken to seize the illegal estates of the tea planters and other landlords. Seizure started immediately. The peasant campaign put the CPI-M leadership in a great dilemma. The partners in the United Front, and the Congress opposition, protested that Naxalbari revealed the CPI-M's double standards: while participating in parliamentary democracy, the party used it as a cover for insurrection. On the other hand, the Naxalbari revolutionaries, still within the CPI-M, and within the *Krishak Sabha*, were saying that the party had turned 'revisionist, class collaborationist, capitulationist'. The people actually involved in the campaign were landless and poor peasants, many of them tribals. The CPI-M could neither denounce Naxalbari outright nor could it own it, for fear of proving the allegations.

Hurriedly the CPI-M sent Harekrushna Konar, one of its leaders, to Naxalbari. Konar was the West Bengal state secretary of the *Krishak Sabha* and Minister for Land Reforms to the United Front government. Konar talked for two hours with Sanyal and persuaded him to agree that the peasant processions with bows and arrows in order to seize land would stop but instead they would go to the local land reform officials to get quicker legal action to unearth the concealed estates. But Sanyal had reckoned without Charu. When Charu heard of this 'agreement' he contacted Sanyal, asked him to forget it, and to go on. In his 1973 article, Sanyal made no mention of his agreement with Konar and the breaking of it; and this casts doubts on his claim about Charu's lack of influence on the beginnings of Naxalbari.[9]

Even Sanyal admitted that Charu took over the reins decisively after May. He mentioned some reasons why the cadres went with Charu: their extreme hatred of all revisionists, chiefly the CPI-M leadership, on the one hand and the 'absence of a secret and skilful party centre' to lead and carry on the mass struggle after the police onslaught on the other. Sanyal did not explain, however, why he dated the Charu takeover as May. But from the course of events, from March to July, it could be seen that the movement in Naxalbari started to collapse from 24 May, the day of the killing of a police sub-inspector. This was a disastrous event for an unprepared revolution. The sub-inspector, with other policemen, had gone to a village in Naxalbari looking for certain wanted peasants. The day after his death, the police went wild; they gunned down ten people, including two children and seven women, who were in a protesting crowd. After that the revolution collapsed due to a strong reaction to the police brutality on the one hand and dwindling peasant participation on the other. Land became a forgotten subject. Unable to stand up to the police directly, agitated cadres and peasants began to attack random targets. There was an unsuccessful attempt to take a gun from a forest department's building; at another village, a landlord was slain. Some of the attacks were made on richer houses in the villages, and jewellery and other goods carried away.[10]

Naxalbari soon collapsed as a local movement in far-off North Bengal. Naxalbari died in Naxalbari. But, ironically, it grew as the ideology of India's alternative. Peasants rose on the Naxalbari pattern in several pockets in India, including Musahari in the Muzaffarpur district of North Bihar. If Naxalbari offered a lesson it was that armed action without a mass base is bound to fail. Charu seemed to understand this; but he never learnt the lesson. He kept his understanding apart and in his writings, but its expression always remained vague and seemingly unimportant. Just as his writings never explained why he thought the situation was ripe, so they kept the strategy for it indefinite and ambiguous.

In his writings in 1967[11] Charu had said that mass (partial economic) struggles were indispensable to the rousing of the peasant consciousness, but an armed liberation war should be the prime concern. In his eighth document he wrote, 'So the question naturally arises: Is there no need for peasants' mass struggle on partial demands in this era?' (Charu often tried to write as Mao did, addressing himself simply and directly to the common man in question and answer form, but ended up, unlike Mao, as clumsy and unclear; strident without any substance.) And Charu answered his question:

Certainly the need is there and will be there in future also. Because India is a vast country and the peasants are also divided into many classes; so political consciousness cannot be at the same level in all areas and among all classes. . . . What tactics shall we adopt in conducting movements for partial demands and what shall be their objective? The basic point of our tactics is whether the broad peasant class has rallied or not, and our basic objective shall be raising of the class consciousness of the peasants—whether they have advanced along the path of broadbased armed struggle.[12]

If what mattered was armed struggle, the partial economic struggles being simply complementary, how were the two to be combined? No one had any idea; and Charu did not know.

Charu showed his prevarication or rather his preference. He believed that rural India was ready to erupt, and thought of a strategy corresponding to this situation. He had total contempt for what he considered acts of revisionism; and he considered almost all acts revisionist other than what he thought to be revolutionary. Those who held the view that mass struggles were a precondition to the formation of a revolutionary party, a CPI-ML, were railed against for nursing revisionism in their hearts. 'If everyone starts building mass organization,' Charu retorted, 'who is to build up the underground party organization?'

In the resolution on party organization, passed a few days before the CPI-ML was announced in Calcutta in May 1969 came the final note: the party was to be a secret party; it should under no circumstances function in the open; it would not have a mass membership like the revisionist parties. ('It is not the number but the quality [of the members] that is essential and primary for a revolutionary party.) The party's principal task would be to develop guerrilla forms of armed struggle; it would not 'waste time and its energies in holding open mass meetings and forming *Kisan Sabhas* (peasant associations) in the old style'. Amidst these clear-cut statements was a vague and evasive directive. It said, the party should learn to utilise all possible legal opportunities for developing its revolutionary activities'. But how could legal opportunities be utilized by an illegal organization without risking exposure and repression? It sounded excellent in theory, but neither Charu nor the comrades knew how it could be done. Already, from the field, there was clear evidence to the contrary. During its short life Naxalbari went through two phases; the first was of mass movement for land without armed struggle; and the second of armed struggle without mass movement. The two could not be combined.

Srikakulam in Andhra Pradesh was following the same path. There since the late 1950s, the Girijans, the tribals, had through mass organizations led by the communists, been fighting for land, wages and freedom from the moneylenders in the plains below. They won some concessions from the landlords, the moneylenders, and from the government. In the post-Naxalbari months, the state went wild everywhere; it moved its police forces to put down Srikakulam. The Srikakulam revolutionaries asked Charu for advice; Charu told them to start guerrilla war immediately. They did; the hilly terrain seemed perfect for a guerrilla war. The war between the police, the exploiters and the guerrillas continued for some time. When it started large numbers of peasants were joining the guerrillas in retaliatory raids. Then their participation fell off. Previously,

Srikakulam had a mass movement, but no guerrilla war; in the end, only the guerrillas were left. The pattern was the same in Musahari, North Bihar, and elsewhere.

But Charu was undaunted. With the dual policy of armed struggle and mass struggle failing, he made the policy a straight, flat one. Now there was to be no mass struggle, only the building of red bases. Building a red base was to begin with the 'annihilation' of the most hated landlord in a village. The revolutionary comrade (often a city youth) would go to the village and secretly make contacts with those landless and poor peasants who might come forward to form a secret guerrilla unit. From them, and from his own inquiries, the comrade must find out who among the landlords was most hated. That landlord was to be secretly annihilated by the guerrilla unit. In this way, the initiative of the peasants would be released. In order to ensure this, only old weapons should be used in the killing. 'Why am I against taking up firearms now?' Charu, in Mao-like fashion, asked the question and answered it himself, at the first congress of the CPI-ML held in Calcutta in May 1970.

Is it not our dream that the landless and poor peasants will take up rifles on their shoulders and march forward? Yet the use of firearms at this stage, instead of releasing the initiative of the peasant masses to annihilate the class enemy, stifles it. If guerrilla fighters start the battle of annihilation with their conventional weapons the common landless and poor peasants will come forward with bare hands and join the battle of annihilation. A common landless peasant, ground down by age-old oppression, will see the light and avenge himself on the class enemy. His initiative will be released. In this way the peasant masses will join the guerrilla fighters, their revolutionary enthusiasm will know no bounds and a mighty wave of people's upsurge will sweep the country.[13]

The 'battle of annihilation' was thus to make the landless peasant a 'new man'; this new man would 'defy death' and would be free from 'all thought of self-interest'. On the other hand, annihilation would turn the landlords into pussycats. After the one most hated was killed, some would flee, others would show the white flag. The village would thus be freed of the 'eyes and ears' of the state, and in the village it would become impossible for the police to 'know who is a guerrilla and who is not; and who is tilling his own land and who is tilling that of the landlords'. Thus would feudal authority be smashed and replaced by a peasant regime in a red base. As the battle of annihilation proceeded, more villages would fall, leading to the creation of more red bases. From these rural red bases the city would be encircled and overrun, bringing about the victory of the revolution.

The successors to Charu

The inheritors of the Charu's CPI-ML—the men of the Vinod Mishra's group—no longer follow his annihilation line. (The Communist Party of China denounced Charu's formulations, prescriptions and slogans in the early 1970s.) But now, the Mishra group functions as an underground organization; although even now they have their armed units armed action is no longer central. In December 1982, at the Mishra group's third all-India congress, the past was evaluated in this way: 'In many areas annihilation was conducted as a campaign with a lot of indiscriminate and unnecessary killings, and it [the movement] got isolated from the peasants' class struggle so that no resistance could be built up against police repression, and our struggling areas were smashed.'[14]

After Charu's death in 1972, the group's own evaluation went on. Mahadev Mukerjee, the new leader, diminished the party even further 'in the name of safeguarding the purity of every word of Charu'. Then several leading party officials from Bihar, West Bengal and Delhi met and 'reorganized' the party's Central Committee, and in July 1974 made Jobar, a young comrade from West Bengal, its general secretary.[15]

The first half of the 1970 was a period of renewed Naxalite (from Naxalbari) upsurge in certain areas of Bihar, mainly Bhojpur and Patna; areas which had not echoed Naxalbari in the late 1960s. (In the area in East Champaran, North Bihar, too, which we will examine more closely later in this chapter, the Naxalite movement caught on only in the 1970s.) Bhojpur was to acquire a glorious place in the history of the CPI-ML. It was there that the Naxalite movement survived, when it had been put down everywhere else. The Naxalites in Bhojpur were chiefly low-caste landless labourers suffering the cruelest forms of upper-caste oppression; they were joined by a section of the peasants from intermediately-ranked castes who faced similar oppression. The fight was for social dignity. Throughout the first half of the 1970s, killing regularly took place between the Naxalites and landed upper castes who were in collaboration with the police.

Jobar, the new Charuist leader, devoting much of his time to Bhojpur, gave himself the task of developing the annihilation line. His political understanding, as his writings showed, was very low, sometimes ridiculously so. [16] Even the Mishra group said he 'had much of metaphysics',[17] a comment that intellectually put him in a lower category. According to the Mishra group's own evaluation, Jobar went from annihilation to 'mobile warfare' in which revolutionary guerrillas were to attack the 'mobile enemy' (police) forces everywhere; this was, ran the evaluation, a 'mechanical upgradation' of the annihilation line. The evaluation noted that the 'negative effects' of Jobar's wrong ideas 'started manifesting themselves in the shape of serious losses in different areas and the petering out of mass initiative on a broader scale'.[18] Jobar died in 1975, in a police shooting in Bhojpur.

But the new leadership of Mishra did not condemn Charu or Jobar outright (as, for instance, it did Mahadev). In fact, it held many of the things they had said or done as positive contributions to the revolutionary movement. Charu, it asserted, not very convincingly, had always stood for a combination of mass struggle and armed struggle; and Jobar was the one who reorganized the party and organized 'heroic resistance struggles' against the police and the landlords; two valuable contributions without which the Bhojpur movement wouldn't have survived. To the Mishra group, therefore, the annihilation line was both good and bad. It was bad where it failed, that is everywhere else, but it was good in Bhojpur, where it kept the movement alive. It was a curious logic: because local conditions saved the movement from destruction in the district, the annihilation line was thought to be upheld, vindicating Charuism.

Nevertheless, the CPI-ML under Mishra has changed a great deal. A 'rectification campaign' has been going on to draw the organization closer to reality; the orthodox 'annihilationists' within the party are subdued. It continues to believe that the ultimate victory of the revolution depends on armed struggle, on the People's Liberation Army (PLA) but says the seizure of power is not the immediate task. The PLA has to be built up.

For the present, it has set itself two main tasks. One is to continue and expand the areas of peasant resistance; there, the armed units could play their role in meeting the challenge of the despotic landlords and their armed gangs. The other task is to build up the Indian People's Front (IPF), which the party formed four years ago as an anti-autocratic patriotic front. With 'deepening crisis' the 'comparador-monopoly bureaucratic' Indian capitalists had created the 'autocratic clique', led by Indira Gandhi, to keep people down. The Indira autocratic clique had reduced the bourgeois democratic institutions to a mockery.

The Mishra group had not joined the 18 March Movement in Bihar, and regretted the opportunity it had lost for work among the middle classes. It formed the IPF because it wanted to lose no opportunities now. Looking at different areas of the country, it saw a number of organizations, Marxist or non-Marxist, conducting their own local struggles. They were, in the Mishra group's view, 'non-party forces', cut off from the influence of the bourgeois opposition parties and the revisionist parties such as the CPI and CPI-M. These forces were independent and, together, were making the greatest contribution to India's democratic movement; they were fighting for civil rights, remunerative prices for agricultural produce, autonomy for nationalities, better living and working conditions for the agricultural and industrial workers, the rights of the religious minorities and so on.

They were 'intermediate forces'. The Mishra group called them 'intermediate' because they were intermediate between itself, the party of the Proletariat, and the ruling classes. The IPF was to be an alliance with these intermediate forces, a grand move to bring all of them together in one forum, a forum that would depend on the people's struggles for its expansion and consolidation. The party, the Mishra group's CPI-ML, would continue to be underground; but while maintaining its independent areas of struggle it would 'also work within the front'. The IPF, like the party, would remain extra-parliamentary, but might think of using the elections although that would be a question which 'only the party Central Committee and no one else' would decide. Ultimately, the Mishra group believed, the conditions might become favourable for a national insurrection and the insurrection brought about by the IPF from above would be combined with the party-led class struggle from below.

Unfortunately for the Mishra group, most of the non-party intermediate forces with which it had hoped to ally did not join the IPF. Some of them attended the conferences where the IPF was to be founded, but were disappointed to see that the Mishra group had already made up its mind about everything; at the conference, they said, some people, clearly acting under the group's instructions, produced political and other drafts out of their pockets and wanted everybody to accept them. Free discussions were not allowed. In the opinion of those who did not join, this could only mean one thing; the Mishra group was over-cautious about losing its grip on the new Front. Thus from the start the IPF could not become the grand alliance of struggling, non-party forces that was claimed for it. Yet the IPF exists, and through struggles and protest demonstrations, and by participation in the last general elections to the Bihar State Assembly, in which all its candidates lost, continues to grow, helping to broaden the mass base of the Mishra group.

A raid on Darpa

The skinny boy, aged about 12, came running up the dirt lane winding through the hamlet of Darpa. His face was pale with fright; he gasped and screamed as he ran. Many people, in and outside the mud huts, heard him screaming: 'They are here! They are here!' All were taken aback, but no one stopped the boy to ask him anything more; everybody's concern was how to pass on the signal to those who may not have heard him. The women squatting outside their houses with their babies under the early winter sun, or slapping fuelcakes of cow-dung on the outer walls, slipped through the door holes into their mud shelters. The men, young and old, were the first to hide and be hidden, some inside the nearest hut. Huddled and shrunken, everyone froze wherever they believed themselves to be most protected.

On the spur of the moment, the mud walls alone served as a refuge. Most huts had just one room where the whole family slept, often beside bleating goats and dirty bundles, and where the family cooked and ate their meals. Without much improvement over 100 years, the huts had stood and multiplied over generations, one beside the other. Since the need for a door was never felt, there was none. But the families had wanted to give the places where they lived the look of a house: so some had picked out rusty canisters from the garbage and flattening and joining them together had made door frames and hung them across the open doorways; some had doors made of wood.

Darpa, a quarter consisting of some 70 such earth boxes and 400 people, was shut up and mute; the winding lane, filled with the child's cries moments earlier, was completely deserted. The people had hardly any idea from which side the assailants would enter. On the right lay the Kabir *math,* the monastery of the order of the Hindu poet-reformist Kabir, whose abbot was a land-grabber and very oppressive; and to the left, past the rice fields, was the hamlet of Sukhlahia, where lived the ex-*zamindar* Binda Singh, who was even crueller. Ears were strained to catch any sound outside.

When the boy had yelled 'They are here!', everyone understood who 'they' were. The surprise was not in the raid; they had known that a raid would follow. What had stunned them was that it had come so quickly. And here they were, caught within easily overrun walls, unable to offer any resistance. They had no firearms: Charu Mazumdar had said that the weapons to start the revolution were to be the conventional tools of the peasants' everyday life; sickles and choppers were to 'release' the initiative of the landless peasants.

Neither could they expect the police to be of help. For over two months now a dozen or so armed police had been camping at the Kabir monastery, 100 yards from Darpa; the administration had sent them there for peacekeeping. The day the police arrived the abbot gave them a hearty welcome and ordered their beds to be set up in the monastery, and left standing instructions with his disciples and servants to look after them to their utmost satisfaction as long as they stayed. Everything organized, the abbot then sent word to every landlord of consequence in the cluster of half a dozen villages; they gathered to welcome the police and confer with them.

The attackers, some of them now spreading out in groups to surround the hamlet, others entering through the dirt lane, shouting and swearing, had first gathered at the monastery that morning. They were highly agitated when the abbot, through his messengers, had them informed of the death of Ramaji Mahato, one of his most loyal retainers. From the villages around they arrived swiftly but stealthily, with their arms hidden, so that no one would know of their plans. Binda Singh the ex-*zamindar* was there with his strongmen, and so were other landlords. A few hours earlier, Mahato had been seized in the Darpa hamlet, taken aside and hacked to death—'annihilated'—with farming tools. The labourers had been after him for some weeks. He was one of those instrumental in helping the police, shortly after their posting to the monastery, to lay hands upon the man whose life had become most precious to the poor of the area—the young Gambhira Sah. (Another collaborator, Zahur Dewan, the ex-*zamindar* of Gambhira's village Mahuawan, had also been seized about a month earlier; he was stabbed all over his body, no fewer than 50 times, but survived in hospital. Immediately, though, the administration had posted a guard of policemen at Dewan's house.)

Groups of assailants were breaking into every hut, pulling down their rickety doors. They were hurling abuse and striking wildly with their guns and clubs at men, women and children. They stared hard at every male face, and seemed to be looking in the dark rooms for some particular persons. Nobody tried to offer any resistance. Then, suddenly, loud cries were heard at the other side of the hamlet: 'Catch him! Catch him!' A young labourer had tried to escape, and was running through the small grove between the hamlet and the shallow stream that formed its boundary. Some of the armed men who had encircled the hamlet were chasing him. He ran faster; he left them behind, crossed the stream and went on running along the dirt road towards Pipra, the next village, but on that road his pursuers overtook him and shot him down instantly.

Inside the hamlet, they killed another young labourer, and took three captives: Madan, a leading associate of Gambhira Sah; Manmatia, a widow aged 70 whose two sons had committed the greatest crime in the landlords' eyes by becoming 'Naxalites'; and Ramlal, a labourer. Hurriedly, pieces of wood, bamboo, dry twigs and leaves were collected and piled under a tree. They were lit, and the three captives were pushed into the raging flames. The attackers, their guns in readiness, screamed with devilish excitement. As the flames leapt up, the green leaves of the tree were burnt. And it was these scorched leaves that were to bear lone witness of the human bonfire because, after everything was over, the assailants quickly swept away, and removed the ashes and bones.

Until a few years previously the landlords would not have thought of making such a desperate strike upon the labourers' quarters. They considered the labourers to be their own people; an offensive against them would have been totally unwarranted—sheer madness. What had engaged the passions of masters and servants alike was a standing feud between Binda Singh and the abbot. To put it simply, two landlords of the same Chanau caste were competing for local power. The Chanaus, with their small population, confined to Sukhlahia and the adjoining village, Tinkoni, are a caste almost unknown in the rest of Bihar. Like every caste, they are endogamous, but owing to their small population (60 families in Sukhlahia, 350 in Tinkoni, both villages being under the Chhaundadano block of East Champaran district and far apart from other pockets) they have dispensed with the taboos on village endogamy. A Chanau man can marry the girl next door.

In the social hierarchy the Chanaus are placed between the upper and lower castes. They themselves claimed to be Awadhia Kurmis, the highest sub-caste among the Kurmis, a middle-rank caste. They were said to have migrated to Sukhlahia and Tinkoni four generations ago—from where nobody was sure—about the turn of this century. Those were colonial times; they settled as tenants. Binda Singh's grandfather was the only one who later rose to acquire a *zamindari*, which was spread over seven villages, under the Estate of Madhuban. The Kabir Monastery was established much later. Those who founded it were from the Teli (oilman) caste, but after the monastery, endowed with portions of land, became a substantial landholder there was a coup. The Teli abbot was overthrown by a group of Chanaus who had worked their way up in the orders of the monastery. Since then these Chanaus, and latterly their sons and grandsons, had held control, not always without causing discomfort to Binda Singh, the ex-*zamindar*.

Until recently the labourers were divided into two camps. The alignment simply depended upon whom one worked for. To the master, each labourer was his conscript. When the master organized a *saheja* (assault party) for an offensive against his enemy, by hiring mercenaries, his labourers had to join it; they went behind the vanguard of mercenaries with clubs and farm implements. The *sahejas* happened frequently, and sometimes they contained 500 men. As a *saheja* marched towards the enemy the other side rallied its forces; there were clashes, firing, clubbing; deaths and injuries.

There was no victor in this eight-year-long war, which drew to a close only in 1977; but by then, in spite of certain setbacks, Binda Singh was able to prove his superiority over the abbot. He had a head start; he had a much larger number of labourers, and the bulk of the Chanau peasants behind him. He had more money and grain with which to advance credit. He had a vast stretch of land which encircled and overshadowed the plots of many smallholders who could reach their plots only by crossing his vast fields. If they offended him, the first thing he could do was to forbid them taking ploughs or bullocks over his land, as he had indeed done on some occasions.

Binda Singh took pride in his authority. Though his *zamindari* had long lapsed and he was no longer a collector of rents, he did not want the people to feel that he had given up his charge. He still saw himself as superior to everyone in the village, in the administration, the tribunal, the local regime. It was he who constituted every *panchayati,* arbitration panel (*panch;* five, council of five men) to settle disputes between villagers, and nominated himself as its head. Even a minor quarrel between two brothers went as a case to Binda's *panchayati*. Both the parties had to pay a fee, preferably several rupees in cash, to the panel head before the hearings could start. The punishment also often meant fines in terms of money, grain or goats.

The *panchayati* was not limited only to disputes. The ex-*zamindar* used it against anyone he found acting against him, or disobeying his standing instructions, or committing a crime (such as not keeping goats on a leash so that, leaving the roadside weeds, they went instead into the landlord's fields and nibbled his crops). Such offenders also had to pay fines in cash or kind.

But the *panchayati* was not something peculiar to Binda Singh or Sukhlahia. The landlord of every village in that cluster—and in several others in East Champaran district—ruled in the same way: to remind the peasants and labourers every morning of the pervasiveness of his power. This had turned Gambhira Sah against the landlords at a very early age; he had twice fallen into the *panchayati* grip. The first time was when he was 13 or 14 years of age, an Eighth Class student at the High School at Chhaundadano, the town in the centre of the village cluster, with its Block Development Office and a small bazaar. The people of his village, long having felt the need for a primary school, had got together to start building one with their own labour.

They selected a ditch, which was part of the village common land, as the site and were filling it with baskets of earth. But the work came to an abrupt halt as the Rajput landlord, whose one plot began just at the boundary of the site, appeared shouting and threatening. Some of the earth-filling had unintentionally fallen beyond the ditch and on to the edge of his plot. 'Your school or whatever it is going to be is making an encroachment upon my land, you can see that,' the landlord warned. 'Stop it! If you persist, then keep your ears open. For every basket of earth thrown on my soil, one body is going to fall on your side.' Dead silence reigned; people fidgeted, didn't know what to do. Gambhira stood a little way off from the crowd of volunteers, watching. Suddenly, he violently flung a metal jug at the landlord. A *panchayati* followed and the boy was fined.

He was hauled up on another occasion for beating four women of a Rajput family in his village. This family had a smallholding and was hard up because the four brothers of the family, grown-up and married, were all idlers. They did not even work properly and regularly on the land they had, and would not try to make a living by working for others in the village—for that would have been demeaning to their high-caste status—or by migrating to the town. They spent their days lying about, chatting or roaming around. So, to get food became the responsibility of their wives who fell into the habit of stealing. That particular day, when Gambhira and his father were away, the women had tiptoed with small baskets into their grain store and were just sneaking off when Gambhira's sister had spotted them. When he returned, Gambhira dashed round to the Rajputs' house and beat up the women. Within a few minutes the word had spread; 'Oh my God! He raised his hand to the women!'

Zahur Dewan the *ex-zamindar* immediately set up a *panchayati* with the Rajput landlords and summoned Gambhira. Gambhira's father, who was fearful and submissive by nature, wanted him to go to the *panchayati* to admit his crime and ask for pardon. When the son refused, he persuaded him at least to keep his mouth shut throughout, and made him take an oath on this. The *panchayati,* with Dewan at its head, got off to a very serious start. Gambhira did not say a word. The panel heard statement after statement about the meanness and vulgarity of a man who could beat women. Nobody referred to any act of stealing. Gambhira, unable to contain his fury any longer, began to speak. The real concern, he said, must be that the women were becoming accustomed to stealing. And yet, what was of far greater concern, he went on, was the fact that four able-bodied males in the family had turned themselves into invalids. Having got this off his chest, Gambhira walked out. The *panchayati* continued, and finally pronounced him guilty and imposed a fine.

Gambhira came from a rich peasant family. Unlike the untouchable labourers and other lower-caste peasants whom he was soon to lead in an uprising, hunger was not his problem. But the autocracy of the landlord and the arrogance of the upper castes was a problem for him. For he was a Teli, an oilman—a caste whom the upper castes of his village had categorized as *solken* (inferior); the Telis were excluded from upper-caste homes and food, and even from public wells. Many Rajputs, like those in the family whose women pilfered grain from his house, were poorer than the Telis, but faced no social exclusion.

Gambhira

In 1977, the year in which the landlords' armed men raised Darpa to shoot dead two people and burn alive three, events closely followed one another in Chhaundadano. In no other year had the peasant organization suffered such heavy losses; and in no other year had the landlords felt so insecure, so shaken. The police were there to stamp out extremism. How happy the landlords had been, when Gambhira was put behind bars under the Maintenance of Internal Security Act in the Emergency! After his release in April 1977 the movement had rekindled, through him and under the leadership of the Vinod Mishra group of the CPI-ML.

Gambhira had become a revolutionary through encounters with the propagandists of the Naxalite movement outside his village. He was young, embittered and uncompliant. His father insisted that he take a job. So, after doing his Intermediate degree from a college at Motihari, the district town, he trained as a motor mechanic. Then, in the early 1970s, when he was aged 24 or so, he went to Calcutta where he got work as a mechanic at a workshop. There he was said to have come into contact with some Naxalites. Under that first political influence, he left his job and returned to his village.

His father was extremely annoyed. He wished to hear nothing of his son's ideas; all he wanted was to see him settled in life. It was he who persuaded Gambhira to open a pharmaceutical shop in the village, and gave him 1,000 rupees as starting capital. The shop was run for a year or so, during which time Gambhira canvassed his ideas among the people with whom he came in contact. But the shop was wound up for lack of money, because, as we have seen, he had given away medicines free or on credit to people who were sick but had no money.

Very soon, some starting capital thrust into his pockets again by his angry father, Gambhira went to Muzaffarpur, the largest town in North Bihar, to run a roadside eating house. While doing this, Gambhira came into contact with some of the S.N. Singh group of the Naxalites, which had split from Charu Mazumdar in September 1970. It was then that he came to know, and began to work with Bhagat Singh, who belonged to a small Bhumihar landlord family living not very far from Chhaundadano, and who was also attached to the S.N. Singh group.

Returning to the village again, Gambhira with Bhagat and a few others formed a Kisan Sangh, Peasant Association. (His father died shortly after.) Accompanying them for a very short time was a Naxalbari-inspired city youth named Sanjay. (Sanjay, the Chhaundadano peasants remember, suddenly disappeared from the area and was last heard to have formed a 'revolutionary' group of his own in Delhi, then in Muzaffarpur. Where Sanjay was at present or who else was in his group or if he still had any group the peasants would never know.) The Sangh held small meetings in the villages, and formed its committees taking members from the peasants as well as the labourers. The Sangh promised to challenge the autocracy of the larger landlords, and this brought middle and rich peasants and even small landlords to its support, although such support was not always openly expressed.

From the richer sections, the Sangh received activists for a variety of reasons. Ramchandra Sah, from a small landlord family of Pipra, was no doubt interested in dismantling the landlord regime, but he also came into the movement because Gambhira was from his caste. From another village came a rich peasant, Birendra Prasad, who had seen the wealth of his family lost (and his father taken to jail, where he died) in an endless dispute with their kin. The major landlords of his village were divided into two camps of Ahirs and Rajputs along caste lines. If the Ahir landlords were patronizing Birendra's father, then the Rajput landlords would take the side of his kin. Birendra blamed the ruin of his family upon these landlords. But at the same time he joined the Sangh, the Rajput landlords were on his side in the dispute. And the Ahir landlords, probably thinking that Birendra, with the strength of an organization behind him, would surely take action to harass their rivals, also began to support the Sangh. One of the Rajputs, Tokhan Singh, became one of its prominent workers.

The Chanaus found themselves awkwardly placed over the Sangh. It was not that they enjoyed any privileges from the big Chanau landlords. They had to pay the same interest for loans from them, and had the same much-less-than-half share of the harvests as their sharecroppers. Even the middle and rich peasants among them were as politically dwarfed as those of other castes. But the community was small and closely bound—the ties reinforced many times over by local marriages—and it would have been difficult for any Chanau to break away. The Chanaus no doubt fought among themselves; they had their small quarrels as well as longstanding hostilities like those between the abbot and Binda Singh, in which they were compelled to take sides. Yet to emerge spontaneously in support of an organization whose express purpose was to take on such landlords as Binda Singh or the abbot or those of Tinkoni was just not acceptable.

The Sangh, due to its affiliation to a Naxalite organization, came to be known as the party among its supporters and members, and the objective of the party, translated from Maoist terminology into the local popular language, came to be understood as *Gharib raj*. Establishing the Regime of the Poor called for an assault on the institution of *panchayati* in the first place; the landlords were to be stopped from imposing fines as they saw fit. The Sangh campaign caught on quickly at the Dubahan village, in spite of the fact that both the peasants and the landlords belonged to the same Bhumihar caste. One day, a landlord ordered a peasant to pay a fine of 40 rupees. All the peasants gathered to oppose this, and although the fine was paid, the very fact of the people gathering to denounce the arbitrary imposition of fines, for the first time, must have worried the landlords. Thereafter no fine went unopposed in the village. The landlords, one day in October 1974, reacted by spraying the peasants' homes with bullets, killing the Sangh's main activist in the village and a boy of 18.

The offensive shocked the Sangh; but what was more, part of the blame for it was put upon Bhagat Singh. It was Bhagat who was in charge of Dubahan village on behalf of the organization. Some of the Sangh members even expressed a suspicion that Bhagat had 'collaborated' with the landlords in the planned offensive. The suspicion was based on the feeling, quite common among members, that Bhagat was not a man of firm political commitment. They had nicknamed him 'boss' because of his personal bearing; he would often impose his wishes, or act on impulse, and what was worse, he loved nothing more than sitting down with bottles of liquor by his side to eat hot and spicy lumps of meat from a goat especially slaughtered for him. His character was attributed by the members to his feudal background.

While Bhagat remained with the S.N. Singh group he uniquely attached himself to the Socialists. After the Dubahan incident, he in fact came forward to propose that, in order to avoid repression, the Kisan Sangh be dissolved and the work instead continued under the banner—'under the cover'—of the *Khetihar Mazdoor Kisan Sangathan,* the Farm Labourers' and Peasants' Organization, of the Socialists. Following the refusal of Gambhira and other Kisan Sangh activists Bhagat left the Sangh and joined the socialists' *Kisan Sangathan.* After that Gambhira and others thought the Kisan Sangh had been maligned because the landless labourers were absent from its title. So the Kisan Sangh changed its name to *Khetihar Mazdoor Kisan Sangh*, the Farm Labourers' and Peasants' Association.

After a 19-month period of dormancy during the Emergency, the *Khetihar Mazdoor Kisan Sangh* pulled itself together, and Darpa became the centre of struggle, and Binda Singh its main target. The labourers of Darpa began by ignoring the ex-*zamindar*; they resolved to have all their disputes settled among themselves. As it began, the abbot was very pleased; covertly he supported the labourers; he wanted to see his rival cut down to size. Binda Singh, proceeding in his usual way, imposed fines *in absentia*, but the 'guilty' would not put in an appearance. This angered him and he sent his men to the hamlet with a message of warning. He stopped making loans to the labourers; he ordered that goats or pigs found in his crop fields be held and slaughtered at once. And he let it be clearly known that only those who pledged undiminished loyalty to him would be accepted for work on his farms. This new rule would apply even during the harvesting, which needed very many hands.

The abbot who, except for his words of encouragement, had not been of much help to the labourers, allied himself with Binda Singh as the antagonisms between the latter and the labourers grew intense. When nothing that Binda Singh did persuaded the labourers to change their attitudes and behaviour, an exercise was planned to make the threat real. From behind the fence of the monastery one morning a hired squad started spattering bullets on Darpa. It was not a direct raid on the inhabitants: the bullets hit this tree or that wall at random, sometimes just whistling through the air; their purpose was to publicize the ultimatum. The fear-stricken labourers fled Darpa and did not return for three months. Meanwhile, the landlords sent demolition squads to the hamlet. Some of the earth houses were razed to the ground; trees were felled, and the labourers, possessions, their rusty buckets and small, worn-out grinding stones, were carted away.

This created an entirely new problem for the Sangh. The 400 men, women and children from Darpa needed shelter and food. Binda Singh, Zahur Dewan and the landlords of Tinkoni had already warned all the employers in the cluster of villages against taking on any of the Darpa labourers. (Starvation would perhaps dampen their inspired valour.) But the Sangh was able to tide over the crisis. It was decided to ask the Sangh members and sympathizers to bring grain contributions so that a food stock might be built to keep the labourers going. Gambhira himself went to the peasants to urge them to help, and the response was good.

There was fresh reaction from the landlords. Any Darpa labourers who were spotted going in ones or twos towards the Chhaundadano bazaar were detained and beaten up. In the midst of these incidents of repression, a landlord of Tinkoni was 'annihilated'. Immediately armed police came to camp at the Kabir monastery.

Within less than two weeks of their arrival the police were able to catch Gambhira. His movements had been closely watched for some days by loyal servants of the landlords. On the night of 2 July, when he was sleeping with six other Sangh activists at a peasant's house in Bathuahian village, the police surrounded the place around 2 a.m. They woke Gambhira and told him very politely that they had come to take him to the monastery where the abbot was awaiting, to put an end to the conflict at Darpa by a compromise. Gambhira did not believe this, but then probably recalled that the abbot had been sympathetic to the Darpa labourers for a while; also, with armed police encircling him, he had no choice. So he and his six comrades were escorted in the darkness out of Bathuahian.

They were passing through the groves that separated Bathuahian from Tinkoni, along the footpath through the trees, when not less than 100 figures, the landlords and their bullies, holding guns and clubs, noisily emerged from behind the trees from both sides. They stopped the seven captives and, surrounding them, started striking wildly at them, and at Gambhira in particular. The police stepped aside, though joining in occasionally with abuse and a few blows with their rifles. All the way to the monastery the assault went on. On the long porch of the monastery they were hung by their feet from the ceiling. In this position their bodies received blows from rifles, clubs and fists for over seven hours, well through the morning.

People flocked to the monastery in the morning. They were told that Gambhira and six others were under arrest. The captives were united in order to be driven to Chhaundadano police station in a tractor. Unable to stand, they had to be carried into the trailer. Guarding them were the police; a few of the bully-boys joined them. Gambhira was singled out for more beating on the way. He was again hung up by his feet at the police station and hit, until, finally, there was no breath in his body.

Over 10,000 people, 500 of them women, gathered together for Gambhira's funeral in the village. The place where the pyre was lit was fenced in with slim bamboo sticks to erect a memorial; it still stands there. In the months that followed, the Sangh single-mindedly undertook the task of punitive annihilation. Their leader was avenged by the death of each of the key men who had been of service to the police in his capture. Rajendra Singh, the nephew of Binda Singh, was killed; so was Brijbhar Rai, a bully-boy from Rathuahian village where Gambhira was caught; Zahur Dewan, the ex-*zamindar* of Gambhira's village, was pushed to the ground by a group and stabbed almost to death; Ramaji Mahato, the abbot's retainer had his body slit open.

Chhaundadano

Very soon the landlords left the arena, and the police had to deal with the revolutionaries. No longer were *panchayatis* held or fines imposed. Ill treatment of the labourers' women stopped. The landlords no longer swore without thinking; they became cautious, and frightened. They no longer moved about freely. In short, though they had made no surrender, they retreated a pace; and the police filled the vacuum. The feudal authority was broken; but state power was not so vulnerable. The police were strengthened in the Chhaundadano area; they went on adding names to their list of suspects; they went on raiding houses to seize 'wanted' men. They even picked up people at random. A young peasant, Hauhar Pandit, who faced no charges, was held and beaten senseless. Many of the Sangh members were thrown into prison; others went into hiding in the neighbouring districts of Nepal, the international border being just one-and-a-half miles to the north.

Faced with police terror, the Sangh decided to move a step further. Possibly the change of tactic was due to the lingering influence of the ideas of Johar, the general secretary of the Charuist group from July 1974. Johar wanted the armed action to be directed towards the 'mobile enemy', which, in practice, meant the police forces driving into the villages or patrolling the rural areas. His argument was that it would be unwise to allow the police forces to encircle what were in effect the 'guerrilla bases'; they must be ambushed on the way, and forced to retreat.

Chhaundadano was no guerrilla base but, amid an incessant assault by the police, the idea of going on the counter-offensive had a strong appeal. On the night of 21 September (still in 1977) a group of Sangh men ambushed a party of policemen walking back to the monastery camp from Chhaundadano police station. The attackers charged them with farm implements, such as choppers, on the dirt road through the populous village of Pipra. A couple of the police were gashed about their bodies and their colleagues stepped back and began to fire. The ambush had to flee. And the harassed police, leaving the dirt road, took a detour along the zig-zag ridges of the rice fields towards the monastery, but just outside the Pipra village they were stopped again, this time by a large mob. It was, however, without weapons to meet the police fire. The police cleared a path with a volley of bullets; three people dropped dead; several were wounded.

This was the second time in about two weeks that the Sangh had suffered serious losses. The first was when five people were killed at Darpa, within hours of the death of the abbot's retainer. Questions began to be asked, within the Sangh; the organization's forces were becoming scattered. A crippling mood of retreat had set in. In fact a number of activists and sympathizers, particularly from upper sections among the peasants, withdrew from the movement.

At a stage when the vigour of the uprising seemed to have been squandered, the state approached Chhaundadano in its other guise. As district magistrate of East Champaran, from 1978 to 1980, an officer, Beck Julius, was posted into Chhaundadano which was seen as an area of special concern. He let people make much of the fact that he was a tribal and not a high-caste Hindu, and hence could be trusted to be simple, honest and sympathetic towards the communities, oppressed as was his own. In public, he never restrained himself from expressing sympathy with the underdog; he had a silver tongue. Not long after his arrival, he visited the villages of Chhaundadano, taking the poor by surprise; he went from house to house, speaking in support of their 'just struggle' against landlord oppression. People crowded round the visiting officer in their hamlets, and he told them he admired Gambhira Sah for his courage and determination: 'I wish every one of you to have the same kind of courage to fight injustice'.

He promised to be of personal help to the peasants and labourers of Chhaundadano. As a token of his love he sent five chickens to each house in Darpa. He gave instructions to his office in Motihari, the East Champaran district town, to let anyone from Chhaundadano see him without delay. And he did have some success. A number of peasants came forward to take petty construction projects on a contract from the government; some others quickly obtained licences to open ration shops under the public distribution system. A branch of the rural bank was inaugurated at Chhaundadano town, promising easy credit to the poor.

The reforms of Beck Julius caused as much damage to the movement as had police repression. Both reform and repression were different sides of the same coin. They threw the organization into a state of confusion. People in jail or in hiding, one here one there, the third somewhere else; people either passive, or running to join Beck Julius's schemes;   people disheartened by Gambhira's death, people waiting for a new leader to appear. The confusion was worse than the dormancy had been during the 19 months of the Emergency.

By the early 1980s the Vinod Mishra group had moved away from Charuism, and renounced the ideas of Johar. Efforts were now to be concentrated upon drawing different sections of people into the movement. The IPF was formed. And in accordance with this transformation, the organization at Chhaundadano —now under the banner of the Kisan Sabha, Peasants' Association, an all-India body—set itself the task of mass struggle and mass mobilization, on such immediate demands as a minimum wage for day labourers and secured tenancy for sharecroppers. Annihilation was abandoned as a key to the concept, though it still was to be permitted when necessary; in one such exceptional case in the early 1980s a debauched rich peasant of Tinkoni was killed in his bedroom for seducing the wife of a poor peasant in the village. The Kisan Sabha was one of the main constituents of the IPF; its progress and expansion meant the progress and expansion of the IPF; and the IPF's progress meant the Mishra group's advance.

In the period when the change of tactics came from above, the organization wanted to use all the scope there was for democracy to function. But in 1978, the year Beck Julius, the district magistrate, set out to shower petty benefits upon Chhaundadano, things seemed to have gone too far. That year elections to the village councils were held all over Bihar. The Sangh decided to take part in the elections, but could not be sure of victory anywhere. And in Chhaundadano, if the Sangh was to expand it needed to win in at least one village. So there was a move at Tinkoni. The Chanau landlords, who had always held the village council in Tinkoni in their firm grip, were also not very sure of a straight victory, due to the presence of the Sangh. There was an agreement between the two sides: the landlords would have their man as the *mukhiya*, the chief executive of the village council, while the Sangh's man would be the *sarpanch*, the head of the village council tribunal. After this adjustment the results of the elections were a foregone conclusion at Tinkoni.

It was difficult to say who gained more from the arrangement, but in the following months it became clear the landlords had. No more did they extort fines from the lower classes, or gun them down, but they still had the cunning to out-manoeuvre them. The Sangh's *sarpanch* was a middle peasant. In the months following the elections, he was turned into a non-person at the village council. The *mukhiya* became all-powerful; he was a Chanau backed by the Chanau landlords. The *sarpanch*, too inexperienced in the power game, failed to prevent the landlords from enjoying the benefits of the government schemes through their *mukhiya*. He could hardly stop them, for instance, from changing the list of the villagers receiving government old-age pensions, so that the names of the untouchable labourers were replaced by those of peasants from the *mukhiya*'s caste. In listing these names, the landlords were making an effort to keep up caste solidarity.

It was Tinkoni, and not Darpa, which became the focus of the Kisan Sabha's economic struggles in the 1980s. At Darpa, the abbot, probably thinking he had done too much harm, had grown afraid after the murder of Gambhira Sah and had fled, never to return. No one looked after his hundred-odd acres, though one or two minor disciples live at the monastery. The land, in small plots, had been leased out to sharecroppers, most of them poorer Chanau peasants of Sukhala-hia. A few of the Darpa labourers claimed they had paid the abbot for them and had even tilled plots for a year or two, but the same plots had been given to Chanau sharecroppers, and the money paid by the labourers had been lost. In 1982 the Kisan Sabha led another lot of sharecroppers, not Chanaus but lower castes, to seize as much as 120 acres belonging to a Tinkoni landlord, Harindra Singh, who offered no resistance. Since then the sharecroppers have been sowing and reaping crops twice a year, and give no part of the harvest to the landlord.

There was then a wage strike at Tinkoni which dragged on for a year. The labourers had received 2.75 kilos of paddy or maize at the end of each day for a long time. It was the standard daily wage in the area; even Binda Singh paid this rate. The Tinkoni labourers, pressing for a rise for the first time, wanted four kils of paddy or maize, and also breakfast. The wage for harvesting was one out of every eight stacks of grain as work progressed; they now wanted one in six. The employers refused, and the labourers were told to look for work elsewhere.

The Tinkoni employers could not get labourers from other villages on account of the solidarity of the workers, but the fields had to be worked; and the landlords would plough and sow themselves. So the claws of feudal authority, wounded but far from dead, began to dig in. The poor and middle peasants of Tinkoni, who were not within the Kisan Sabha, were vulnerable. The landlords asked them to work their fields; they cajoled, they threatened, they said they would ban them from having plots for sharecropping, they would fling them out of the village. Frightened, the peasants pleaded to be spared; they said they had their own small plots; who was going to work them? But the landlords replied: 'The women and young boys in your families will cultivate them'. And the peasants would not have to worry about what their women and children would have to eat; meals would be sent to them from the landlords' homes. And on top of this, the peasants would get four kilos of paddy as their daily wage, the rate the landlords had refused the labourers.

So the landlords' work did not suffer and the Kisan Sabha met to decide that the Darpa labourers should strike in solidarity, to exert pressure upon other substantial landlords like Binda Singh. This strike continued for eight days, at the end of which the major landlords got together to agree to a compromise; the daily wage in the area would go up to four kilos as demanded, but there would be no breakfast. The harvesting wage would be one in seven stacks.

While such struggles were conducted on immediate issues an opportunity offered itself to the Sabha to make a dent in the Chanau caste solidarity. It flowed from the rivalry between two Chanau landlords. Harindra Singh, whose 120 acres the Sabha had captured, and Ramchandra Singh, the *mukhiya* of the village council. Harindra had encouraged about 30 sharecroppers who were tilling ten acres belonging to Ramachandra to claim the land, in accordance with share-cropping law. Ramachandra reacted by ordering his retainers to open fire at the sharecroppers who had gathered on the land; no one was killed, but the sharecroppers would not leave, and the conflict with Ramchandra escalated. Then suddenly, Harindra pulled out, probably fearing revenge. Left in the lurch, the sharecroppers turned to the Kisan Sabha for support. The Sabha decided to support them, but on condition that the sharecroppers would never return to Harindra to seek his patronage. With the occupancy claims lying with the sharecropping board, the Sabha wanted the sharecroppers to remain firm in their legal battle against Ramchandra, all the more because 15 of the 30 sharecroppers were Chanaus—and Ramchandra was a Chanau.

Internal stresses

Ironically, even as the Sabha appeared to be broadening its support it was faced with declining membership. The process of decline had set in at the height of police repression, and it had not ended with the turn in policies. Among the prominent members who left was Birendra Prasad, the first convener of East Champaran District Kisan Sabha. He had been the convener of the 'district' unit (which was, in practice, made up of members from Chhaundadano) from 1981 to 1982. Like many others, he was wanted by the police and his name figured on the list of accused in the case of the murder of Brijbhar Rai, one of those suspected of having aided police in capturing Gambhira. The police had, after Brijbhar's murder, established a camp at Bathuahian. Birendra fled to Nepal, without consulting or informing any member of the Sabha. In his absence the Sabha members got together to hold a demonstration against the excesses of the Bathuahian camp police.

For some time the landless labourers in the Sabha had felt ill at ease with others who, like Birendra, came from the families of rich peasants or petty landlords. During the course of struggle, certain leading activists had emerged from among the landless labourers.

Ganesh Ram, now the president of the district committee of the Sabha, was one of them; he was an untouchable from Darpa, aged about 40 and semi-educated. When Birendra was chosen as district committee convener, Ganesh was already a member of the Bihar State Committee of the Sabha. Somehow Babban Tewari, the then convener of the Bihar State Committee, had become close to Ganesh. How much was due to personal relationship, and how much to the Vinod Mishra group's greater reliance (as Mao taught) upon the landless labourers was difficult to say.

Babban had Ganesh in mind for the convener's post when he arrived at Chhaundadano for the 1981 meeting scheduled to constitute the district committee. But in a private session with Ganesh before the meeting the latter declined to accept it and was believed to have told him that the post should go to Birendra; perhaps he thought a peasant as convener could incline the peasants towards the Sabha. In the meeting, which took place in Birendra's large house at Bathuahian, several members suggested Ganesh's name (unaware of the earlier discussions) but Babban, sometimes angrily, waved them silent, and declared Birendra's name accepted when it was proposed by Ganesh. In the reconstitution of the district committee in 1982, Birendra was not accepted even as a member by Babban. (In 1983, Babban himself was thrown out of the Sabha. He then began to build up a peasant organization of his own, inviting Birendra to join it!)

While Birendra was being accused of inactivity and capitulation to the police —'He was so desperate to get his name off the list of the accused in the Brijbhar murder case, he even gave a bribe of a thousand rupees to a police agent in my presence,' a Sabha leader said—Birendra surprised his opponents with charges that the Kisan Sabha did not enjoy democratic freedom, that 'the Party' (the Mishra group) actually took the decisions and imposed them upon the Sabha. The Sabha was controlled by the party; the IPF was controlled by the party. And, Birendra went on, the party's Central Committee would pay no attention to complaints from below. As an illustration, he cited the case of Roshan, the party propagandist. Roshan was staying at an untouchable labourer's place in Tinkoni; one morning, while the labourer had gone out to answer the call of nature, his wife's screams had drawn people from neighbouring huts. She alleged Roshan had tried to molest her while she was asleep.

The prestige of 'the party' was at stake. Many people in the Sabha did not believe the woman; they said that she was having an affair with another man in the village, and since Roshan had come to stay at her house, the lovers were unable to find a place to meet, and hence they had 'planned' the episode. It is not possible to know the truth. In any case, the allegation made it necessary for the Sabha to meet and discuss the matter. At the meeting, the woman tendered an apology, but the group led by Birendra in the Sabha did not believe the woman's 'retraction'; they claimed to have sent complaints about this to the Central Committee to which there had been no response.

Whether Birendra and a few others resigned or were expelled is now unimportant. The fact was, his group had left the Sabha. After some time this group joined another CPI-ML faction, led by Chandrapulla Reddy of Andhra Pradesh. While the Kisan Sabha continued its economic struggles in the area, the Birendra group also started various peasant agitations. During one the police opened fire, wounding Birendra in the leg. The Kisan Sabha continued to be the larger organization but faced the danger of remaining confined to landless labourers.

Efforts were made by the Sabha to bring the peasants in via the struggles by sharecroppers and peasants for easy credit and quicker and more adequate supply of farming inputs. In the general elections in May-June 1985, the IPF nominated candidates in East Champaran district. Ganesh Ram ran for election, but lost.

12. The Santhals' Struggle

Shiboo Soren

On that midsummer afternoon of 1979, the dusty second-hand jeep rattled along the Godda road, faster than one would expect. Shiboo Soren was at the wheel, then, as now, the most popular leader of the Santhals, in the dress he seemed very fond of wearing, a long, light-hued homespun *koorta* and white cotton pyjamas. Occasionally, when the traffic ahead was lighter, Shiboo took his hand off the wheel to gently comb the wet streaks of his long saintly beard with his fingers. He was whiling away the boredom of the drive by telling hilarious stories, all taken from real life, and his political experience, which was then a decade long. He had countless anecdotes about officials, politicians, money-lenders, fixers—every sort of person he had either worked with or against since he became an activist. Everybody in the jeep joined in the laughter, but the narrator, looking ahead through the windscreen, did not laugh—except very occasionally, when he laughed full-throatedly like a child, like the real tribal he was.

He told a tale about a moneylender, an extremely cruel man with a thick oiled moustache: one day the tribals of the village decided to squash him. A mob advanced on his house and the moneylender came out and saw them, and turned to run away across the fields; running like a hare, the knot of his *dhoti* got loose after a few yards, and he almost dropped it but ran on. The mob behind began to enjoy the chase. Shiboo also remembered an encounter with an official of the Santhal Parganas district. He had asked why so few Santhals were recruited for the Bihar state police forces, to be posted in the district. 'You know,' said the officer, 'the police recruitment rules are very strict about a man's physical requirements—his height, chest measurement, running distance. In this district, the Santhals do not fit requirements: they have a height of only four feet something.' Shiboo knew that was absurd, but fighting down an impulse to say so he coolly flung the ball back: 'But then, in this district, even the thieves are no taller than four feet something. You appoint five-feet somethings in the Bihar plains, where the thieves are also five-feet somethings, don't you?'

No one was spared Shiboo's humour, not even the men described as his 'right hands'. 'This Suraj Mandal, the glutton!' he would begin, 'he is so fond of chicken. Whenever he sees, at someone's house or on the road while driving, fowls scratching about on the grass his mouth starts to water. He will stop and stare greedily at them as if he would like to swallow the poor creatures live right away!'

Suraj Mandal responded to the gibing with a smile broadening into a laugh: he must have grown used to his leader's sense of humour. Almost every moment of the last three years he had been with Shiboo, like a shadow. They travelled about together: they addressed public meetings together. People advanced various theories about this relationship. The most common was that Suraj ('Have you seen him? Have you noticed his shady, tough face and his deep-set devilish little eyes?') had for some years been the leader of a gang of wagon breakers on the Eastern Indian Railway; and he clung to Shiboo's company only to wipe his record clean. Others said he was 'planted' in Shiboo's tribal movement by Indira Gandhi's Congress Party in order to wreck it from within. Yet another theory was that Shiboo, his life constantly in peril because of the campaigns he had led, needed to have a 'minder' for his protection, a Suraj, by his side.

There seemed to be elements of truth in all this. The man believed to have brought them together was a Youth Congress leader, Gyan Ranjan, who had known Shiboo and his family for some time. Shiboo addressed Gyan as *bhayya*, elder brother; and Gyan, unmindful of the presence of others, would behave patronizingly towards him: 'I have made Shiboo whatever he is today', Gyan used to say, to anybody who cared to listen. The Santhal leader said nothing to refute this, yet watching him for a few days and listening to what he said, you had the feeling that he knew how to go about things and saw himself as no one's puppet.

Shiboo seemed to get quite a few advantages from Suraj's companionship. True, he wanted to have someone at his side for his personal security. But the Santhal leader perhaps also wanted to show through this companionship that his organization was not restricted only to Santhal tribesmen. In Santhal Parganas district, all the tribes taken together, the Santhals the largest among them, made up only 35 per cent of the population. Suraj came from the lowest sub-caste of the intermediate caste of the Mandals, many of whom had migrated from Bengal over the past century or earlier, many as village traders and moneylenders. Moreover Shiboo came from another district, Hazaribagh, in northern Chotanagpur; although there was a large population of his tribe locally, he would have felt the need to have local people to support him, and Suraj would be of help here.

The jeep sped along the highway. Suddenly Shiboo put his foot on the brake. A man driving a car in the opposite direction had waved him to stop. Both got out and walked up to the grass verge. Gyan and Suraj didn't move. The man getting out of the shiny light-coloured Fiat was perhaps in his mid-thirties; he wore a trouser suit and polished shoes, brushed his hair back with his fingers and lit a king-size cigarette as he began to talk to Shiboo who stared idly at the ground. Suraj recognized him as a businessman of Dumka, the district town of Santhal Parganas. Nothing of their conversation could be heard from the jeep.

The businessman spoke gravely, forgetting about the cigarette between the fingers of his right hand. It was impossible to read Shiboo's feelings from his face, characteristically; in any encounter with an *important* man from the plains his face became inscrutable. He spoke only a few words and a few more, as his hand waved to say goodbye to the businessman. As Shiboo walked across the road to his jeep, the businessman stared briefly, with apparent annoyance, at the back of the Santhal leader and, stubbing out his half-smoked cigarette under his shoe, moved hurriedly towards his car. Shiboo turned the ignition key and the jeep moved forward. Gyan didn't ask about the businessman. Much later, in October 1982, C.S. Munda, a leader of the Munda tribe who had just resigned as the secretary of the Ranchi district committee of the Communist Party of India, was asked in a newspaper interview: 'What do you think of Shiboo Soren's flirtation with the Congress(I)?' To which he replied: 'I was once in his [Shiboo's] car and saw him filling up the fuel tank at Gyan Ranjan's place [in Ranchi]. I expressed my resentment [about the impropriety of his taking so much petrol without any payment from a Youth Congress leader who didn't have a clean record]. He [Shiboo] laughed and said that there was nothing wrong in fleecing people [the plainsmen] who had fleeced us [so long]! So that is his attitude'.

Shiboo was not clever when he began; he had learned such things later. In 1969, when he was about 26 years old, his cause had been private. A major money-lender, Bistu Sah, had organized the secret murder of Shiboo's father. By extracting a very high interest, Sah had tightened his grip over no fewer than 30 villages in the Hazaribagh district, one even in adjoining West Bengal. Against outstanding loans, the moneylender seized pieces of land, small fishponds, cattle, household goods and jewellery from a very large number of people. Shiboo's father also occasionally borrowed from him, but used to pay back regularly, and spoke fearlessly against Sah's excesses and cheatings.

The family was not on the whole poor. Shiboo's father was a teacher at a lower primary school, but was also an efficient poultry farmer breeding chickens and ducks at his home in Narsinghdih village in the Hazaribagh district. He had a social conscience and would always work for a cause. He took part in the freedom movement, but did not devote his life to it; he attended the sessions of the All-India Congress Committee held in 1940 in Ramgarh, in his district. When the Congressmen of his district campaigned to have the Raja of Ramgarh stripped of his *zamindari* shortly after Independence, Shiboo's father joined them. He became influenced by the ideals of Vinoba Bhave, and once, when Bhave was campaigning for Bhoodan in the Gaya district, he travelled down to meet the Bhoodan saint, taking Shiboo, then aged 13 or 14, with him.

Because of these activities—and because he was more than an educated Santhal, a teacher—the old man enjoyed a social position; people of his village and the neighbourhood looked to him when in distress. The news of his murder shocked them; that night he was walking four miles to the railway station, accompanied by a servant carrying bags of rice and beaten rice for Shiboo and his elder brother who were living in Gola, studying at the high school. Under cover of darkness he was killed by men employed by Sah, who was annoyed at his frequent interventions.

There was also the episode at the house of Shiboo's mother's sister. Her family had run up debts it could not pay back. The moneylender took her to court, and through the magistrate secured an order for the attachment of her house and goods for the recovery of the outstanding debts. With his men, Sah arrived at her house, armed with the order to evict her; she resisted; the moneylender slapped her as he dragged her outdoors. Shiboo's father was outraged at the disgrace inflicted on his sister-in-law. Hurriedly he summoned the villagers for a meeting. The meeting was held at the site where at the old man's initiative, a small temple was being built. People expressed indignation against the moneylender, who had also been asked to be present. But Sah flatly denied the charges; he said on oath that he had not touched the woman, let alone hit her. No judgement could be made, but the moneylender was publicly humiliated.

After Shiboo's father's death, the family felt lost. No one was then earning, though there was some land to cultivate. The poultry farm dwindled. Shiboo's mother could not stop grieving; her sense of justice was so outraged that she found it impossible to think the world a fit place to live in unless Bistu Sah reaped as he had sown. She would say: 'I have five sons. They will bring justice.'

The family fell on hard times. Shiboo had to give up school and go in search of a living. He went first to one or two forest contractors in the district, but they were *dikus* (*diku*, outsider, alien, non-tribal, man from the plains, exploiter) and had no work for him. A friend of his father's then took him to Moorie, near Bokaro steel city, and used his influence with people in the aluminium factory to get the Santhal boy a daily wage job there. But at the factory working hours ever lengthened and he was paid no more than a rupee a day. Shiboo came back home to work in the family's fields, embittered.

Every day in the village, and at home, he heard many stories of Bistu Sah's cruelties. When he visited or passed by the government offices, the police station or the courts in the town, he felt more and more that these places were the strongholds of the moneylenders. Knots of them could always be seen chatting or moving about. Increasingly, Shiboo felt that there was no individual or institution to which the impoverished could appeal, to get the *mahajans* (moneylenders) punished for their crimes.

His faith in the system's justice was much shaken by his own encounters with it. A year or two after Shiboo returned home to work in his fields, someone chanced to hand him a bound copy of the Bihar government's circulars on the law of land restoration to the tribals. He and others went through it and found to their surprise many provisions which, if faithfully implemented, could force the *mahajans* to give the land back to most of the people. Carrying the book with him, Shiboo went to Hazaribagh town to see the deputy commissioner. He saw a door-keeper standing outside the deputy commissioner's office, and asked to be let in. The door-keeper briefly looked the young, lean tribal up and down and shook his head. All entreaties failed to move him and Shiboo came back without an audience with the officer. To him, the door-keeper's lack of sympathy was just one more proof of even the poorer *dikus* looking upon the tribals with contempt.

It left no option, but a campaign. Shiboo, together with some other tribal youths, began to organize people against the moneylenders. They set up a committee called *Adivasi Sudhar Samiti*, the Society for Tribal Reform. As the organization's name suggested, the thinking behind it was that if the tribals were to fight the *mahajans* and other *dikus* they must first reform themselves. The tribals were too incapacitated as a community to do this, and the Samiti told them one serious reason for this was addiction to alcohol. Home brew had always been a part of tribal culture, but the *dikus* had made it into a business. Thanks to the *mahajans*, the Samiti went on, the tribals continued to lose their land and that meant a diminishing amount of rice from the fields. Less rice, then, could be set apart for making the *handia* (their pot beer brewed by leaving boiled rice to ferment under water in a pot for several days). The *mahua* fruit was also used, but very few tribals owned a *mahua* tree, which meant that liquor could usually be got only from the small *diku* brewer in the village. It was either the brewer himself or the *mahajan* who lent the tribals money to buy alcohol who finally took over the addict's land. They were losing land for the sake of liquor, and were not able to fight against it due to the effects of drink. At meetings of the Samiti, the tribals were told, 'A community of drunks cannot take care of itself. It becomes incapable of thinking.' The effect of propaganda was very slow, but the group attracted a number of youths, mostly school drop-outs, all wanting to restore the Santhals' self-respect. After it had gained some following, the Samiti took to direct action. The drunks were beaten harshly, wherever they were caught—in the liquor shops, on the way there, or in the village. Gradually, in two or three years, the focus was shifted to the land usurped by the *mahajans* and the tribals would march in their thousands, accompanied by the poor non-tribals, to the fields and there cut ripe paddy as a way to reclaim their lost plots. The police were soon in action, and a large number of the harvesters were thrown into prison, including Shiboo.

This was ten years earlier, and happened around Narsinghdih village. On the afternoon we have described, the leader was driving his jeep to Pakaria village where a public meeting was due that afternoon. The Santhal peasants of Pakaria had wanted Shiboo to see what the moneylenders and the policemen, together, had done to them. Houses had been looted and burned down. Women had been raped. From one village all the families had run away after the arson and looting, and were living under trees some distance away.

Not only in Pakaria were such things happening. In Santhal Parganas district, during the first four months of 1979, at least a dozen peasants, tribals and non-tribals had been shot dead, beheaded or stoned to death. The *mahajans* showed their upper hand in the refusal to honour agreements with the peasants, all of which were, of course, oral. Even in the few rare cases where the courts had ordered restoration of land to the debtors on the ground that the moneylenders had taken the harvests for a number of years, and had thereby been paid their money, the *mahajans* prevented the peasants from reoccupation—unopposed, of course, by the administration and the district police.

As the jeep left the metalled road to turn off on the village track, instantly raising clouds of dust, one of the two Santhal boys sitting in the rear, who had said nothing during the journey, suddenly leaned forward, and pointing to the left, at a set of brick houses 100 yards away, spoke to Shiboo: 'That's where they live. Now they are taking lessons in club craft from the RSS'. (RSS: *Rashtriya Swayamsewak Sangh*, the National Volunteer Association, a militant Hindu organization aiming to make India truly Hindu; training its volunteers in club craft and use of other weapons for the defence of the Motherland.) Shiboo threw a quick glance in the direction indicated, but said nothing. Down the road people seemed to be waiting anxiously, men and women, sometimes a whole family. There was a commotion in the crowd as the jeep was sighted. Several of the men wore nothing above the waist and had no shoes on their feet. A few, scattered in ones and twos, looked clean, wearing coarse cotton *koortas* and leather slippers; they appeared to be the Santhals who had been lucky enough to get education and a job in a government office or at the village school; they stood empty-handed, some of the others carried bows and arrows. Some of the women had brought the family's evening meal with them. At Shiboo's public meeting an hour later, the crowd was estimated at 40,000.

To the Santhals, Shiboo was the 'Guruji', and not just because he had shoulder-length hair and a flowing beard, though these, no doubt, helped his guruish ambience. The Santhals regarded him with innocent devotion. In times of heightened social tragedy, they looked for God's command to come through the holy man. Revolt, it seemed, was beyond the ordinary Santhal's imagination; it could be revived only through a mediator. Legends about Shiboo, and his power to perform miracles, were passed from village to village, legends that gave them courage and energy. According to one legend, Guruji was once surrounded by the moneylenders bent on killing him. But Guruji kicked his motorcycle into action and rode off like the wind, tearing through the gang. They chased him to the foot of the hills; Guruji rode up the hill, and with his motorcycle leapt from the top over the valley to the top of the hill opposite. The moneylenders were stupefied.

Once, when some Santhals were asked why they had followed Shiboo's command, they told the story of how Guruji had met Indira Gandhi in Delhi. They started talking, but in the middle of the conversation, Indira Gandhi went out of the room for a few minutes to attend to some other work. Meanwhile, Guruji looked in the bookcase and found a law book, hidden between other books, and read it through. He then came back and revealed that the land had always belonged to the Santhals, never to the *mahajans*. That, he said, was written in the law book!

Shiboo sat on a wooden chair outside the house of a well-to-do Santhal, while Suraj sat a few yards away on a string bed: Gyan Ranjan also sat at a distance. Some people stood on either side of Shiboo, but the view of the village land which he faced was kept clear. Men and women were milling into the lane from the dirt road, and were formed into a queue for a *darshan*, a close, worshipful audience, of Guruji; everyone greeted him with the traditional Santhal salutation. 'Johar!' Many of them gave an offering of money: rupee notes, one rupee, five rupees, ten rupees. 'Johar, Guruji,' the man or the woman would say, and would bow down and gently place the money held between his or her joined palms on the back of Shiboo's right hand which rested on his thigh. Shiboo, with grace, put the note into the pocket of his long *koorta*.

At the public meeting, Shiboo made a rousing speech, speaking of the moneylenders, the police and the politicians with virulence. For the enemies of the tribals he used words and phrases like 'dog', 'swine', 'son of a swine'. 'We shall crush them, knock them cold,' he shouted. 'From here, from this rostrum, I warn that if it does not stop we'll strip off their skins in the market place.' To tolerate what 'they' were doing was out of the question. The police were even destroying statues of Siddhu and Kanoo, heroes of the 1855 Santhal revolt against the Raj, and banning the meetings of *baisis*, the tribal councils. 'Can this be anything but a conspiracy to obliterate the Santhal culture?' It was to protect the culture and economic freedom of the *adivasis*, the original inhabitants, Shiboo said, that a great battle was on for their self-government, for a separate Jharkhand state. Sacrifices had to be made to achieve that.

'A Marxist experiment'

From his native area in Hazaribagh district, Shiboo had first moved to the coal-mining district of Dhanbad. As a young Santhal militant, he was brought there by a group of Marxist trade unionists in the early 1970s. The coal mines had been a frightening place ever since digging began in the colonial days. Low-caste men from the village of Bihar, Uttar Pradesh and Madhya Pradesh, in batches, were lured there and locked in, in camps around the mines. Low paid, overworked and restricted from moving about freely, they could not escape because the private mine owners employed a large number of roughnecks as security guards who were often from the poorer families of upper castes of one particular region, the Bhojpur-speaking districts of South Bihar and Eastern Uttar Pradesh.

The coal mines were nationalized in phases in the early 1970s. Before that, since the mid-1960s, a militant organization of miners, the Bihar Colliery Kamgar Union, had functioned. It had come into being through the efforts of some Marxist trade unionists, notably A.K. Roy. Roy was a technical officer at the Government of India's fertilizer factory at Sindri, a town near Dhanbad, who had joined a workers' strike in 1966, had been arrested and put in jail. He had the halo of sacrifice about him, someone who had given up an officer's job and handsome salary for the cause. In the years following he became a cult figure with his spartan life style and his daring.

Also in the mid-1960s, the Soviet-aided steel plant at Bokaro, near Dhanbad, was under construction. Large numbers of peasants were displaced through acquisition of their lands, and the contract labourers needed to be organized. Many of the peasants were Mahatos, a community of immigrants from the Magahi-speaking districts of south-central Bihar, settled over a century or more in the tribal region. Some of the Mahatos approached Binod Bihari Mahato, a lawyer of their caste at Dhanbad who was with Roy in the CPI-M. From a poor family, he had privately studied law while working and was now a practising lawyer. His fight in the courts up to the Supreme Court in Delhi, had resulted in the displaced people of Bokaro receiving unexpectedly higher amounts of compensation than the steel plant's original offer. The beneficiaries gladly gave Binod a handsome commission.

There had been confrontation between the Kamgar Union, affiliated to the CPI-M's trade union, the Centre for Indian Trade Unions (CITU), and the toughs who were sheltered by the Congress's Indian National Trade Union Congress (INTUC) before nationalization; it became very acute at the time of nationalization. The mine owners' toughs (the 'settler mercenaries' as Roy called them, to distinguish them from the original and the Mahato inhabitants of the tribal region) found it a most opportune time to fabricate new employee registers, entering thousands of new names. The private mine owners had hardly any employee registers, so the toughs had little difficulty in making, in league with other operators, fake registers with the names of relatives and co-villagers in place of the tribal and lower-caste workers with a genuine record of service. When the government took over the coal mines, the new names could 'legitimately' claim 'continuing service' while the tribals and the lower castes, the real workers, found themselves out of work. The Kamgar Union described it as *kali bahali* or black recruitment and tried to fight it. But in vain.

Some INTUC top men had also made money out of the 'black recruitment'. Thousands of new men from the region where the toughs came from were throwing out thousands of tribals and lower castes by force and fraud, but they had to get the Kamgar Union off the scene if matters were to proceed smoothly. They began to put it about that Roy was a Bengali who had only Bengalis as close comrades; that he hated the Biharis and wanted to see them all out of Dhanbad. Some of the propaganda gained too much currency, proving too embarrassing for Roy, too explosive, a phrase said to be from one of his speeches (which Roy said he never used). He was quoted as calling upon the coalminers to throw those with *lota* (drinking water jugs), *jhonta* (long hair) and *sonta* (a club)—marks of the trading Marwaris, the Sikhs and the upper-caste toughs respectively—out of Dhanbad. As a result Bihari chauvinism became dangerous for Roy, and so serious that he found moving about in the coal-mine area almost impossible; he was barred even from Sindri, his initial point of activity and his electoral constituency which, elected in 1967, he represented in the Bihar state assembly, until 1977.

It was to survive in the politics of Dhanbad, surcharged with Bihari chauvinism, that the Kamgar Union desperately looked for support. It decided that it could come from the local peasants, the tribals and naturalized immigrants like the Mahatos—communities which the Roy group called 'nationalities'—who lived in the villages around the coal mines. These peasants were oppressed by the moneylenders and land thieves: many had relatives working in the collieries where they were treated with contempt. Bihari chauvinism could be held at bay, Roy thought, by 'an alliance of the oppressed classes and the oppressed nationalities'.

This idea took shape with the formation of two community organizations. One was called the *Shivaji Samaj*, the Shivaji League (after the Maratha hero who braved the Mughals) and its leadership was given to Binod Bihari Mahato;

this Samaj was to work among the Mahatos. The *Sonat Santhal Sudhar Samaj*, the League for the Reform of Golden Santhal Society, was to be the other one; Sourendra Soren, a Santhal clerk at the Coal Board office, was made its general secretary. Both the leagues were to begin with a campaign for self-reform: to end liquor addiction, polygamy, child marriage, illiteracy; the thinking behind this, as in the case of Shiboo's Samiti, was that communities which had sunk into defeatism should be awakened to regain their optimism and virility.

The new campaign, when it got going, ranged from mass education to direct action. In the drive to stop drinking, the women showed a great deal of enthusiasm. They would bring complaints to the Shivaji Samaj activists about their husbands squandering all their earnings on drink. Both men and women brought information about, and worked against, child marriage and polygamy. In one of the widely-remembered actions to check polygamy:

The activists of the Shivaji Samaj lay in wait on the bank of the small Jamuni stream, with clubs and iron rods. Binod Bihari Mahato was there leading them. They all were there following a complaint that a Mahato, after leaving his first wife, was going to marry a girl of Jitpur village, on this side of the stream. The bridegroom's party was to come from Nawadi village, a few miles on the other side. As the men of the party arrived, and, folding up their clothes above their knees, began to wade through the stream, the Samaj activists jumped, shouting, into the water. And there, in the water, the groom and his men were severely thrashed. Sodden and mauled they ran back. For the deprived bride of the evening the Samaj later found another boy.

But while Shivaji Samaj was involved in such activities, the *Sonat Santhal Sudhar Samaj* would not get going. Sourendra Soren, the general secretary, turned out to be inept; and, being a Coal Board employee, not inclined to do anything that might risk his job. It was while looking for an active Santhal that Roy, Binod and the members of the Santhal Samaj heard of Shiboo. Some members of the Samaj went to Hazaribagh to see Shiboo, who agreed to replace Sourendra. He came to Dhanbad. In the first few months in his new area of activity, he went round the miners' quarters; he met Santhals in groups. 'The first thing that struck me about the Santhal miners,' Shiboo remembered, 'was that they didn't keep their bows and arrows with them. I told them bows and arrows were an inseparable part of our culture. We must have them in every Santhal's room.'

Shortly thereafter the direction and thrust of the campaign changed. On 4 February 1973, the Shivaji Samaj and the Santhal Samaj dissolved and merged into a single organization, *Jharkhand Mukti Morcha*, the Jharkhand Liberation Front. On that day about 20,000 people came to the meeting ground in Dhanbad: workers attached to the Kamgar Union, waving red flags, and peasants from the villages. The slogans were: *'Mahato Manjhi Bhai Bhai'* (The Mahatos and the Santhals are brothers): *'Lad ke lenge Jharkhand'* (We'll get Jharkhand by fighting). From the dais on which Roy, Binod and Shiboo sat, flowed charged words about the 'outsiders' who sucked the blood of the original inhabitants of Jharkhand; about the *pachhiarias* (men from the west, meaning the men from the plains districts in southern Bihar and western Uttar Pradesh) throwing genuine workers out of a job; about the *diku* moneylenders holding the original inhabitants in thraldom. The speeches were emotional, unbridled, couched in the language of the ordinary man.

The *Jharkhand Mukti Morcha* adopted a green flag. The red flag—of the Kamgar Union—was to stand for Revolution; the green flag for the peasant's prosperity. From then on would start what was described as a 'Marxist experiment'—unique in Bihar—to build a true worker-peasant alliance. Roy was its theorist and scientist. From him came the theory that the tribal-inhabited areas in Bihar were an 'internal colony'. According to him, Jharkhand was an 'internal colony' of the 'developed regions' of India. In a colony, he said, exploiters and exploited belonged to two different societies; they passed through different social processes and maintained a clear, practical distance from each other. Oppression in a colony was therefore ruthless and barbaric. In India 'internal colonies' such as Jharkhand had come to exist due mainly to two historical reasons. One was the caste system. This had kept the country divided for thousands of years into two societies—one (upper castes) who did no physical labour, and another (low castes) who were condemned to it. Because of this division the oppression of the low castes was ruthless and barbaric; they were not considered as part of the society to which the exploiters belonged.

The second historical reason, Roy said, was that India had developed as two types of societies; the river valley (feudal) societies and the forest (tribal) societies. Until recently, the two societies had not clashed or come in contact with each other. The vast population living in the forests had remained undisturbed while the river valley societies had extended as seaport (capitalist) societies towards the end of the eighteenth century. It was from the river valley and seaport societies that the leadership of the nationalist movement had come; and the same societies continued to dominate even now through Congress and other parties. Today the forest societies were the victims of their exploitation; they were heading towards ruin. India was thus divided between 'developed regions' and 'undeveloped regions', and the nature of exploitation of the latter by the former was 'colonial'. And just as India had been the largest colony of the British, so was Jharkhand the largest of Free India's 'internal colonies'. That was why, Roy concluded, the movement for the 'liberation' of Jharkhand was a challenge of all-India significance.[1]

Obviously, Roy's theory was not rooted in the Marxism in which he believed. One suspected it was an attempt to make a concept out of the everyday experience of the coal miner and the tribal peasant of Dhanbad, or Chotanagpur; an attempt to represent in ideas what the *dikus*, the 'settler-mercenaries', the outsiders, had been doing to the underdogs of native origin. It was also an attempt to provide an ideology for the aspirations of the tribal peasant for a separate Jharkhand state, for an autonomous region free of the outsiders. In practice, the coming of the *Jharkhand Mukti Morcha* on to the stage introduced something—an element of militancy—which had been absent from such earlier campaigns as Jaipal Singh's to achieve Jharkhand. Now the peasant was asked to seize back his land from the moneylenders. The slogans that caught on were:

'Why should the trader keep land?' 'Why should the officer, the lawyer, the doctor, keep land?' 'Why should land be in the hands of those who do not plough?' 'Chase away the moneylenders!' 'Restore the land to its original inhabitants!' 'The tiller shall harvest the paddy!' 'Indira Gandhi's socialism is a farce!'

From November of the same year, 1973, as the days of paddy harvesting approached, there started what the opponents of the Morcha described as 'land riots'. In large numbers peasants—the Santhals, the Mahatos, as well as the lower castes such as the Kumhars, Kamars, Rajwars, Tudis, Ghatwars—raided the paddy on the land that had slipped into the possession of the moneylenders. It showed how subdued but intense were their feelings when this harvesting quickly caught on in three districts (the Blocks of Tundi, Govindpur, Nirsa, Beliapur, Katras, Topchanchi, Baghmara, Chas and Chandankyari in Dhanbad district; Gola, Ramgarh, Mandu, Petarwar, Jaridih and Bermo in Hazaribagh district; and Bagodar, Nawadih, Gomia, Gande and Bengabad in Giridih district).

At every village the tactic followed was the same. Men and women came out of their villages in hundreds; there was no secrecy involved, the approach was straightforward, as was characteristic of the tribals. They paraded to the crop-fields striking their drums and blowing their ancient clarion, the *turhi*. The men would stand guard, forming a ring round the fields, bows and arrows in hand, while the women cut the paddy with sickles. The harvest was stacked and carried away in head loads.

Resistance was bound to come. In many places the moneylenders called in the police and several peasants were arrested. There were also direct encounters. The moneylenders at Guniato village in Hazaribagh district fired upon the harvesters; they were answered with a storm of arrows. The fight went on for a long time, until the moneylenders ran out of ammunition. Arrows were still zipping in; two of them killed the moneylender and his nephew. There were similar battles in other villages (at Maniadih and Charak in Dhanbad district, Pirtand in Giridih, and sometime later, at Cherudih in Santhal Parganas, where Shiboo had a narrow escape).

After a complaint by a moneylender, a police sub-inspector went to a tribal village at Topchanchi, near Dhanbad, to make arrests, but was himself taken prisoner. The village was set in wooded hills and a police search for the officer began, but he was not found. The authorities then approached Binod Bihari Mohato, the Morcha president, with a request that he accompany the search party; they thought if the president was there those who knew where the missing officer was would come forward with the information. Binod knew what had happened to the sub-inspector, and where; but to the authorities he showed a puzzled face; he calmly presented to the authorities the argument that the Morcha movement was anti-moneylender and not anti-police and so there was no reason why 'our men' would abduct the officer. Still, 'for your satisfaction', he agreed to drive around with the search party, to go to this village and that, even to that particular village. He stood as the police began asking the tribals who had gathered if they knew where the missing officer was. While they carried on their fruitless interrogation, Binod told them he would be back in a minute. He went away with some of the tribals, and looking back to be sure there was nobody else around, said: 'What did you do with the body?' 'It's hidden in that ditch.' 'Fools! After we leave you burn it. Tonight.'[2]

The Tandi model

After the harvest riots, and the murder of the police officer, the authorities, while letting the police do their job of keeping the rioters down, set about restoring the peasants' faith in legal procedure. It was thought that their loss of faith in the laws of land restoration had caused the rebellion. A number of camp courts were set up in the rural areas in which magistrates were to hear the peasants' cases as well as the moneylenders' and give judgement on the spot. The Morcha did not boycott the courts; it sent the peasants to present their cases. And there were a number of judgements that upheld the claims of the peasants and restored their plots to them.

In Tundi Block of Dhanbad district, a large area, spanning a cluster of villages, was released from the grip of the moneylenders. And here, the Santhal peasants began to build a unique model. (And here, Shiboo became the 'Guruji' and built an ashram.) The aim of the model was to re-create the ancient tribal co-operative. In this, each family was entitled to a piece of land but there was co-operation in labour; during sowing or harvesting each family borrowed labour from other families and gave them its labour in return. No outside labour was required, and they produced as much as they needed. That was the society they had always wished to return to: the Santhal utopia where the *dikus* had no place at all.

They ploughed for the paddy of 1974 collectively, pooling such resources as bullocks and wooden ploughs. And to keep the *dikus* out they decided to stack all the harvest at home: not a single grain would go to the traders. They also resolved that none of them would go to the law courts to settle a dispute with a co-villager; there would be village courts, the councils of elders, to hear and judge such disputes.

To keep the creditors away in time of food shortages, a *gola*, grain house, was set up to which all the families had to contribute. Every year, each family had to give twice the quantity of paddy it would require to seed its plot of land the next season; and then kilos of paddy as their subscription to the Morcha. Each family with children between 4 and 15 years of age had to give, in addition, ten kilos to run a night school. At the school, which was named *akil akhada* (or the brain's wrestling ground) the children would come to learn the three Rs.

But the Tundi model collapsed in less than a year, because the Morcha itself ran into serious trouble. Binod, the president, had already been under detention since April 1974; Roy was more often in prison than out; and important cadres like Sadanand Jha had been killed or imprisoned. The Morcha activists were on the run long before Indira Gandhi imposed the Emergency in June 1975. Shiboo was feeling personally insecure. 'I was being branded at that time as anti-national, as a saboteur who did not believe in parliamentary democracy or the rule of law. With that excuse they could have sent me to the gallows or the police could just have shot me, as they were doing to the Naxalites in fake encounters,' Shiboo recalled.

The police indeed arrested Shiboo, but he was freed, within a few days of custody, as soon as he publicly announced his support for the Emergency and Indira Gandhi's famous Twenty-Point Economic Programme. Binod came out of detention only two weeks before the Emergency was imposed and the police arrested him again. He, too, bought his freedom by supporting the Emergency and the Twenty-Point Programme. Both Morcha leaders' statements were broadcast over the radio. For the 19 months of Emergency, Binod shut himself in with his family, Shiboo began to go round in the jeeps of the Congress Party, and fell into the company of Suraj Mandal and Gyan Ranjan. The Tundi co-operative gave up its motto of self-sufficiency to receive truckloads of farm implements, and grain from private industry as well as the government as 'donations'. From a model of human relationships, the tribals had to switch to a model of farm prosperity.

There was a new scenario for the peasants, following the relaxation of the Emergency and elections of the Parliament in March 1977. Roy was still in prison when he filed his nomination for Dhanbad constituency, with the backing of the new united national opposition party, the Janata. Binod announced his candidature from Giridih, and approached the Kamgar Union and Roy supporters in the Morcha to campaign for him as well. But they refused, saying that if they worked for him, a 'traitor' during the Emergency, the Janata would withdraw its support for Roy. Roy won and Binod lost.

Three months later, elections to the Bihar state Assembly were held, and from Tundi constituency Shiboo filed his nomination as an Independent candidate. (In March 1975, an observer who travelled around Tundi with Shiboo had written: 'Shiboo has no regard for political parties: "I don't want to have anything to do with politics", was a repeated remark made by Shiboo in the course of our conversation.') Roy and Binod gave him no support during his electioneering. On the contrary, Binod, coming to dislike Shiboo, had set up a notable Morcha activist, Shakti Mahato, as a candidate against him in Tundi. The peasants who were to vote were extremely disappointed. Both Shiboo and Shakti obtained a very poor vote.

The Congress was removed from power, both in New Delhi and in Patna. Everything had been undone. The leaders of the Morcha were not on speaking terms; the Tundi co-operative had disappeared. There were no more camp courts held by the magistrates for quicker justice; without riots, the government did not need to show its efficiency in the implementation of its laws. The peasants were no longer seizing land; the Morcha, which had actually never acquired any organizational structure, was no longer functioning, even as a mob.

Shiboo saw no other way but to go back to Binod, to Roy and the Kamgar Union. He worked tirelessly in the election of K.S. Chatterjee, a Kamgar Union leader, at Nirsa constituency of Dhanbad district where the Assembly poll had been put off due to the death of a candidate. Shiboo then went with Roy and

Binod to Gomia in Hazaribagh district where the explosives factory was experiencing a long workers' strike. In spite of all this the mutual distrust remained. Though the leaders did not formally separate, Shiboo changed his work area from Dhanbad to Santhal Parganas. That was in 1978, and in a year of activity in certain parts of Santhal Parganas there was a wave of harvesting again. The peasants faced retaliation by the moneylenders, the police behind them, at Pakaria—where Shiboo drove with Suraj and Gyan to address a large public meeting—and other villages.

The outcome

Today, the *Jharkhand Mukti Morcha* has turned from a peasant movement into an electoral party. Shiboo was elected as a Member of Parliament from Dumka, the district town of Santhal Parganas, in January 1980; three months later, eleven of the Morcha candidates became members of the state Assembly, among them Binod and Suraj. The Morcha, till then, remained as divided as ever but, strangely, none of those leading the factions within it had thought of breaking away. There was a 'Shiboo group' and a 'Binod group' in the organization, and the division may be reflected in the alignments within the small Morcha unit in the Assembly. There was also a 'Roy group' which usually agreed with the Binod group. No opportunity was missed by one group to rail against the other, yet they stayed together.

But serious blows were in the offing. In January 1983, the Morcha held its first conference, at Dhanbad. The largest number of delegates came from Santhal Parganas, where Shiboo was devoting much of his time. It shocked the Binod group and the Roy group when Shiboo's men prohibited red flags at the conference; only one flag, the Morcha's green flag, was allowed. This became the rule after the conference and at no meetings of the Morcha could a single red flag be seen. The symbol of a 'Marxist experiment' with a worker-peasant alliance was dropped by Shiboo.

At the conference, the Review Report that Shiboo read out as the general secretary brought a greater shock. In a clever move, the Report had been held back from circulation before he went up to the dais to read it. In it there were attempts to discredit the Marxist group—the Marxist Coordination Committee of Roy—that had founded the Morcha. The Report said that the Morcha had not been able to develop any organization in its ten-year existence; it 'lacked a clear, concrete programme to build up a disciplined, collective leadership. . . . The alternative tried at Tundi failed to grow, and subsequently the leadership became arbitrary. Chaos instead of discipline increased. There were propagated as many types of views as leaders.' As though to give the report a look of impartiality there were self-critical references made by Shiboo, for example: one of the causes of the failure of the organization was the 'infiltration into the Morcha by the ruling party [the Congress]'. But the target of the Report was unmistakable:

While the Marxist Co-ordination Committee helped in the advance of the

Morcha movement it also blocked the Morcha from developing an organization. There are hundreds of cadres and leaders in Dhanbad and Giridih districts who show loyalty to both the organizations [the Morcha as well as the Marxist Co-ordination Committee] while in actuality they are loyal to none. . . . Expressing faith in Marxism it [the Marxist Co-ordination Committee] in real practice believes in total anarchy. . . in the last ten years the Co-ordination has not held any conference of its own.

Many of our friends might be curious why we are bringing in these references. As a matter of fact, it is necessary to do so, for many of us shall now have to decide about their loyalty. We cannot go about with a *dual loyalty*.

The supporters of Roy (the phrase 'total anarchy' was directed at him) and Binod were stung. Binod in his presidential address defended the Morcha's relationship with the Kamgar Union and the Marxist Co-ordination Committee. Without their support, how could the Morcha have proved to be so effective in a district like Dhanbad where the tribals formed only one-third of the population? The conference did not formalize the split. Binod was re-elected as president, and Shiboo its general secretary.

For Shiboo, the epithet in the Marxist camp was a 'sell-out'. It was used to signify his involvement with Indira Gandhi's Congress which began with the Emergency in 1975 and continued, except for the three years, 1977-79, when she was out of power. Roy and Binod, and the Kamgar Union and the Marxist Co-ordination Committee had remained anti-Congress throughout; they represented the coal miners who were oppressed by people sheltered by the Congress's trade union, INTUC. With confrontation at base level, the Marxists could only be the instrument of anti-Congressism in Dhanbad. Shiboo was hated by them for having practically gone over to Congress.

Towards the end of 1979, Shiboo resumed his ties, after word reached him that he might get a Congress (I) ticket for Dumka for the parliamentary elections in January 1980. The intermediary was believed to be Gyan Ranjan. But the ticket was made conditional: he could get it only if he could persuade K.S. Chatterjee, the Marxist Co-ordination Committee member of the state assembly from Nirsa, to defect and stand on a Congress (I) ticket too, against Roy in Dhanbad. One evening, Shiboo, accompanied by Gyan and a top Congress (I) state leader, the late Kedar Pande, went to Chatterjee in Nirsa. Gyan showed Chatterjee a couple of letters saying that appointments for Chatterjee with Indira Gandhi and Sanjay Gandhi were fixed for the first day between 1 and 3 p.m. at Ranchi, and that an aircraft was waiting at the Dhanbad airfield to fly them all to Ranchi. Chatterjee said it was ridiculous to expect him to go over to Congress, let alone get a ticket from it to stand against Roy. He respected Roy, he said: he would never desert him. The visitors went away. Shiboo did not get a Congress (I) ticket.

But Shiboo was desperate to run and strangely, the Marxist Co-ordination Committee came to his help; Roy forgave Shiboo his vacillations. The Committee gave him a nomination and allotted him, for his campaign, a couple of jeeps, a fund of Rs 25,000 and a hundred cadres, most of them colliery workers who had their homes in the Dumka region. He won by a small margin. Again, at the state assembly elections three months later, Shiboo announced a Morcha alliance with the Congress (I). Binod made a press statement to refute it, and eventually there was no alliance, but eleven of the Morcha were elected independently.

And again, Shiboo distanced himself from the Marxists within the Morcha. In the following months he derived some advantage, when some district leaders of the Communist Party of India left to join the Morcha. It was these ex-CPI leaders who now helped him to articulate his opposition to the Marxists: it was they who helped him write his Review Report for the 1983 conference. Shiboo then formed a Jharkhand Colliery Mazdoor Union as a parallel organization to the Kamgar Union. He became its president and Suraj its general secretary. 'The sympathies of the coal miners and other workers of Dhanbad for a separate Jharkhand state are a sham,' Shiboo now declared.

This was a serious allegation. In making it he wanted to emphasize that the Marxist Co-ordination Committee was interested only symbolically in the demand for a separate Jharkhand, and intended to make 'tactical use' of the *Jharkhand Mukti Morcha* for its own growth and expansion. The Committee had been restricted to the coal miners; it wanted to spread into the villages, to draw in the Santhals and other peasants, through the medium of the Morcha. There was, no doubt, some truth in the allegation. That the Committee aimed to set up a worker-peasant alliance through the Morcha was clear, but to say that it was not really interested in getting a separate state was going too far.

There were reasons why Shiboo did not like Marxists. His first experience with them was bitter. When he was leading the campaign against liquor, some CPI men in certain areas opposed it, on the grounds, he remembered, of materialism! He did not like the way the Marxists approached problems, always speaking in terms of theories and books. 'What's the use of loading a tribal's head with books?' he would say at public meetings. 'The tribals have nothing to learn from Marx or Lenin. . . . If there is a fire in a village, shall we look up in a book by Marx for instructions to extinguish the fire, or shall we run to fetch water?' He also said, 'We tribals are communists by birth. When we go hunting we share the game. Even our dog gets an equal share.'

Shiboo was uneducated and never made an effort to educate himself. He didn't read books. He was very intelligent, but not always able to think beyond rudiments. He had that rare gift of communicating directly with the common man, but felt ill at ease in the presence of Roy and Binod and others in the Morcha who spoke far more systematically and wisely at meetings. It might have been that they treated him in a patronizing or sometimes overriding way, and that Shiboo could see his personality becoming eclipsed. So he asserted his independence, but the reason why that took him to Congress was different. In that, he seemed to have been guided by his own sense of insecurity. He had made many enemies, and was afraid of the police. In 1983, as a member of Parliament, he had sought protection from the speaker, as he suspected the police and other elements in Santhal Parganas of planning to murder him.

The Santhals in the villages now saw less and less of Shiboo. There was no paddy harvesting after 1979. 'The Morcha is not calling for seizure of land, because it invariably brings more repression; poor people get arrested and killed,' Shiboo now said. This was hardly an excuse; it was passivity reminiscent of the fatalism of the pre-Morcha days. But it was perhaps the negative side of a charismatic type of movement. The Santhals wanted *dikus* out; they wanted to be led by a holy messenger; and having found Guruji they would not leave him, even if he worked no miracles. Even if he stopped asking them to throw the *mahajan* off Santhal land.

Today, the Morcha is formally split. Binod formed his own *Jharkhand Mukti Morcha* (Marxist); he has three members in the state Assembly, including himself, after new elections; he keeps the alliance with Roy's Kamgar Union. Shiboo's *Jharkhand Mukti Morcha* is almost four times larger in the assembly. Obviously, Shiboo's Morcha has turned away from struggle; the aim seems to be to get Jharkhand not by fighting, but by passing a bill in the legislature. At the time when Shiboo was a member of Parliament, a tribal leader said in a newspaper interview: 'The deviation [of the Morcha movement] to parliamentary politics has been a mistake. Shiboo Soren, who was my classmate [at school] told me that he thought it would be more effective working from within Parliament until mustering enough strength to get a resolution passed by the House granting statehood to Jharkhand. Pipe dreams!'

Divorced from Marxists and theories and struggle, Shiboo now concentrates on 'development'. Posturing as non-doctrinaire, a venerated Santhal rebel has ended as a run-of-the-mill developer. His 'only wish' now is to see full development of the tribal areas—new rail lines, irrigation, roads, better education. 'Previously I used to think that nothing can change until we get a separate Jharkhand. But now I am convinced that development is possible only in association with the *shashak varg*, the government. Once people make progress, once they are properly fed and educated, they will themselves start fighting to achieve Jharkhand,' Shiboo said. And as Shiboo worked for development, his *Jharkhand Mukti Morcha* became practically a sectarian organization, appealing mainly to the Santhals.

13. Life after Death for the Hill People

We go up the hill to meet Mohan

Pleasantly, the summer sun was still behind clouds when the morning passenger train from Sahebganj dropped the four of us at the small single-shed station. On the left, the station overlooked the Ganga which flowed east, before turning into West Bengal. To the right could be seen—across the railway lines, past the green wild trees, the growing rice paddy—rising gently and invitingly, the hill by the name of Chengdo Gadwa, our destination. At Chengdo Gadwa, 2,500 feet high, also green, a hill range stretched like a long wavy chain to the far right, presently cloud veiled. The left flank of Chengdo Gadwa towering over the railway lines and on, towards the river, had its feet rammed into the edge of the Ganga where the waves played splashy games with those huge feet. We went into one of the shops near the platform to have tea, and also stowed away biscuits, uncooked rice, spices, potatoes, and packs of cigarettes into one of our bags.

We—that is, two journalists, a social worker and Shivlal Manji, leader of the hill-dwelling community of Paharias—crossed the railway track, and started to climb Chengdo Gadwa. It was cool. The stony pathway which snaked up the thicketed slopes was just wide enough, except in some wider places where we stopped for breath, to take one person at a time, so when we met a man or woman with a headload of wood or other things going in the opposite direction we had to stop and find a gap in the bushy side lines. From where we were the Ganga looked narrower and, down below, the few Santhals hunched over their rice fields looked as small as children. We also noticed that the thicket cover of the Chengdo Gadwa gradient was not as dense as it seemed when seen from the station.

After about an hour we reached the inhabited top, and entered the village of Kaldi-bhita Targachhi: Shivlal Manji left us to the hospitality of 35-year-old Mohan Paharia who it seemed local hill-dwellers consulted about everything. Mohan, short, average build and curly haired, showed us into a tile-roofed hall filled with women and Gandhian spinning wheels. Shivlal hastily gave his instructions to Mohan in Hindi (and not, we noted, in the local hill speech). Shivlal was short of time; he had to walk back, catch a train, and get to the Morse communications office of the Sahebganj railway station, where he worked among Bengalis and Bihari Hindus. The Bengalis were, he told us on the way, Marxists constantly thrusting their theories at him and constantly failing to make those 'big theories' fit into 'my minibrain'. The Bihari Hindus, ever fearful that others' gods might overcome their gods (they brought a Christian convert back

to Hinduism by purifying his body by spraying it with Ganga water), preoccupied with preserving the forms which compounded the ritualistic myths, nevertheless had, Shivlal felt, certain good things to offer the isolated Paharias, such
as the centres for education or health run by the Hindu councils and associations,
as well as centres where boys were trained to use knives and clubs.

A young hill-woman brought the tea that Mohan Paharai had ordered for his
guests from the plains—from big cities, he said, evoking a laugh, like Patna!—
adding that to us Chengdo Gadwa would seem a narrow, dull little world. The
office-bound Shivlal had been made to ring for his cup of tea. And at least in
seeing a guest as God disguised as a visitor, and so detaining Him no matter
what urgent matters cried for His presence elsewhere, the Paharias seemed to
be at one with the Hindus. But the similarity did not end with the reverentially
yet despotically served tea. In further imitations, the hill dwellers had adopted
the worship of the God Shiva; today every village on the hill had a stone phallus
of his. Yet it was not a complete Hindu influence; the Paharias had adopted the
habits and styles of all those communities which they perceived as being higher
and better than themselves. Taking imitation too far they had, for instance, got
accustomed to beef-eating (actually 'pressured' to do so by the Muslim moneylenders, Shivlal told us). And from the Santhals came the women's dress now
much sought after by young Paharia women like this charming, sharp-nosed girl
who, after wordlessly setting five steaming China cups on the seat of an
unoccupied wooden chair, was standing a few yards away, face turned away,
but ears open for the noise of our sips to die away, for the emptied cups to be
removed, for her woman's responsibility to be over.

This woman of eighteen was alleged to be crazy about the 'Santhal fashion',
and had to put up with much comment about it because it threatened to alter the
taste in clothes of all the young women of Chengdo Gadwa. My eyes caught
Mohan watching her severely as we sipped out tea, from her turned head to her
ankles: she was in her fashionable dress of four pieces: a long skirt over a longer
petticoat and a blouse, as well as a *dupatta* called a *panchi* thrown over one
shoulder, its end hitched at the waist. Shivlal soon excused himself and after he
was gone, after we too had finished our tea, then, as a pair of bangled hands,
guided by lowered eyes, reached out for the empty cups, Mohan gave a sidelong
glance at the owner of the hands and said to her, in sneering tones. 'You are all
right now? Ann?' Since our host had spoken in Hindi we took the remark as an
invitation to questions.

Who is she?

'My wife.'

The woman, seventeen years younger than her husband, collected the cups
in silence and walked away.

'My third,' Mohan volunteered flatly. Noticing our widened eyes, however,
he immediately became alarmed.

'But why are you writing all this down? The *gormint* has laws against more
than one marriage, hasn't it? Are you going to report me and see me put behind
bars or what?'

Even toothache can be fatal

And then Mohan explained. Geeta, the third wife, and his second wife were both sisters of his first wife. He had never wanted to marry more than one woman: his eldest wife, said Mohan, was a veritable Lakshmi, a goddess, and still his most beloved. But after both his parents-in-law had died his wife's sisters, more vulnerable as orphans since they were women, had no one to turn to. Except to him. So from their hut in a nearby cluster, the two sisters had one day arrived at the largest of all the huts on Chengdo Gadwa and cried and cried, and then proposed they should become his wives. Mohan was moved by their plight, but did not immediately agree. He needed the approval of a council of elders and, above all, permission from his Lakshmi-wife. Only after this did he allow himself to become a polygamist.

In Shivlal's room in Sahebganj, Heeralal Pranat, a seventy-year-old freedom fighter now doing social work among the hill-men, had mentioned the case of Mahesh Singh, the Paharia *Sarpanch* of Marikuti village, who was one-handed and at sixty years old had no fewer than four wives. 'He had married them because none of the women had a male relative in their families,' Pranat said sympathetically.

But these were rare examples. Polygamy did not lurk behind every door on the hill, and behind whichever door it was, it certainly did not crouch there like a crime. It was out in the open, known to all, and approved of: for the hill society had nothing else to offer its destitute women, had no other ways of livelihood to suggest. 'If the Paharias are to survive and reproduce,' Mohan said, and it almost sounded like one of his convictions, 'the only solution at present seems to be polygamy.' But this was a personal view. And if the question of morality no longer entered into any discussion of it, the question of practicality did. For where, after all, were there men rich enough to become polygamists? Poverty was the reason why women elected to make other women's husbands theirs also and poverty was the reason why almost all the men would turn them away.

Life was extremely hard, often impossible, on the hill. Every morning you had to descend the winding path to go to the towns to sell, if nothing else, your labour. To make more money, the children were asked to come along. Each person walked down carrying 15 to 25 or more kilos (children carried less) of timber logs or firewood or baskets of jungle produce on head or shoulders. They even went 25 miles to the west to Sahebganj if a train was available. And on the way home they purchased whatever rice the day's rupees allowed, and when the family returned in the evening they quickly cooked the rice in their pots, ate and immediately went to bed, exhausted. So by day Chengdo Gadwa looked uninhabited and desolate, the doors of the straw and wood huts covered with stripped bamboo nets. One seldom saw a man; one saw a few women too tired from yesterday's work or unable to acquire a bundle of wood, and small knots of children playing in the lanes. After dusk, even these children and women were shut in with the weary rice earners and there were no signs of human life on the hill. Only the village dogs barked, and from the surrounding jungles came a cacophony of animal and bird noises.

Mortality is appalling. In 1891, the Paharias in Bihar numbered 136,497; today, nearly a century later, instead of normally increasing in population, they are much fewer.* So many in one sub-tribe died each year that it was now almost extinguished. The subject of mortality among Paharias had, in the last 20 years or so, featured in nearly all the newspapers of Bihar, but was never seen in the plains as a fit subject for public outcry.

Hill men were said to be dying of *Kala-azar*, malaria, tuberculosis, dysentery or just continuous high fever; disease from which no one normally dies today. It was happening in Kaldi-bhita Targachhi too. Bodies worn out and no longer able to carry quarter-quintals down the hill, lay immobile in huts where the measures of rice boiling in the pots diminished like the family income. Money-lenders, reluctant to invest in tomorrow's corpses, never came forward to help.

Shortly after arrival in the village we were shown in one hut three young women who, haggard, hair matted, eyes bulging in drained faces, arms like sticks, unable to work, were surviving on crumbs. For the last three days Mohan had been giving them food. But how long could he or anyone continue to do this?

That afternoon, Mohan led us away through the hilltop bushes to another village on Chengdo Gadwa, past a stream, which flowed into tiny ridged paddy fields, a stream that sounded almost like a three-year-old's irrepressible chuckles of laughter. There, in the village by the name of Sarsa Pahar, the first sight to meet our eyes was a man reclining on a string bed outside the door of his hut, his back turned to us. A woman, presumably his wife, sat on the edge of the bed, leaning over, and gently stroking his overgrown hair.

We had no choice but to invade the cool day's boon of privacy. At once the woman rose to her feet but the man made no movement. The eyes that quickly surveyed us and then dropped back to the immobile body were no longer the innocent eyes of a hill woman, but the hard, vacant eyes of a middle-aged woman four days after the death, in an accident, of all her three adult sons. As we retreated to the other side of the lane Mohan gathered from the woman necessary information through businesslike questions in Malto, the hill speech, and reported back to us. Her husband, Mesa Manjhi, aged about 30, had been in his sick-bed for two weeks, ill with toothache. With *toothache!*—we gasped. Yes, reported Mohan coolly, it was a very severe toothache, unmitigated by any jungle medicine treatment: he had a cavity and was unable to leave his charpoy to work and earn money, could only spend his days and nights convulsed in pain. That meant that his wife could do nothing but sit 24 hours a day by his bedside. The family was just the two of them: there was a male cousin who had been looking after them, but one day he went down the hill and never came back. She sent no one to seek him out, and neither could the people of Sarsa Pahar have made it their concern: for a man or woman to vanish was hardly news.

The starving couple had recently picked up a twelve-year-old girl (whose

---

* Population: *1872*, 86,335; *1891*, 136,497; *1901*, 88,114; *1911*, 101,287; *1921*, 95,572; *1931*, 97,328; *1941*, 106,322; *1951*, 101,094; *1961*, 101,094; *1971*, 107,683.[1]

entire family had died from unspecified illnesses one by one) from another hut. She carried wood loads down the hill for them, as much as a child could carry, and returned before dark with 400-500 grams of uncooked rice, to keep the pot boiling. The day was not far away when this child herself would be confined to a cot, never to get out of it again. Was toothache a *disease*? Why the hell did Mesa not go down and see a doctor at the Block dispensary or any damn doctor? The answer led us further into the dynamics of life on the hill: Mesa could not move by himself, and so two, at least two, pairs of shoulders were needed to convey his sickbed down to the doctor: and upon Sarsa Pahar or Chengdo Gadwa, there were no pairs of shoulders offering such a service without the payment of compensation for the loss of daily earnings, which was put at five rupees. If Mesa was going to die of toothache, the tribe could do absolutely nothing, for as a community it was a shambles. Other pots could not go off the boil just because one had gone cold.

The high rocks against the pleasant cool sky; the paddy fields; the green slopes and the delightful view from above of the narrowed-down great Ganga and the huddled trees and, between them, a single-shed railway station looking like a toy in the distance; the beauty of the hill women; and the narrow snaking stream given to laughing like a child; all the poet's phantasmagoria concealed beneath its picturesqueness was endless, mind-shattering horror. Chengdo Gadwa was where orphaned women begged for shelter through unlawful marriage, where men and women were permanently lost and never inquired about; where death was possible from toothache; where rice in boiling pots ever dwindled; and where, before three guests from big cities like Patna were invited, they were apologetically advised to buy their rice and potatoes and spices in case they planned to spend a night on the hill.

Borrowing money

Green was not so green. In Kaldi-bhita Targachhi (*kaldi*, banana; *bhita*, plantation; *targachhi*, palm trees), banana plantations were now no more, only a name. As we had already noticed during our upward journey, the thicket over the slopes had its hollows. Once upon a time, the Paharias lived happily, blissfully even. Whatever their position in the past they certainly could not have been as stressed, as precarious of existence as their descendants are today.

To be a hill-dweller in the past was to be a free man. Practising what is termed in our times shifting cultivation, he would select, well ahead of the coming of the rains, a patch of topsoil on the hill and clear it of standing trees and shrubs and leave leafy twigs and shrubs together with animal dung to sun-dry or be set on fire, to rot and eventually turn into the best fertilizer the primitive peoples had ever known. Ploughs were a piece of technology that belonged to the *civilized* plainsmen. The hill-dweller required just a digging stick with which to make appropriately spaced holes into which he inserted his seeds deep enough not to be washed away when the rainwater ran, irrigating his patch.

With others of his family and his clan, the hill-dweller in those times had all the territory around to himself. In two or three years, when there was depletion of fertility in the topsoil of one patch, he, leaving that patch for 10, 15, 20 years to allow Nature to reafforest it for his return, moved to another patch of the hill or the next hill and so on. It was the nature of their agriculture that the resources would one day be exhausted. They never felt inclined to come down and settle in the valleys. (When in the 1830s the English divided the jungle land of Daman-i-Koh, the present Santhal Parganas, and invited the Paharias to come down from the hills and cultivate the area, they declined, after which the Santhals were brought in.) The upper territory was bound to be restricted. In the course of time there were fewer unoccupied hills for the dweller to cultivate, so that he now had to return to his former plots in a much shorter time, before the plants or shrubbery had time to regrow and to reinvigorate the soil, or, when cut and dried, to yield the requisite fertilizer.

The situation was now desperate. There was no room to manoeuvre. The inhabitants of Chengdo Gadwa were confined in Chengdo Gadwa. Shifting cultivation now meant only a shift from one plot to another plot, within the accepted outlines of your hill. Methods were the same however: *jogudi*, the digging stick (the hill peasant's plough) was still there (though animal-driven ploughs were sometimes adopted) and so was the mulch-fertilizer. But now each cultivated plot was given only one year lying fallow. In Kaldi-bhita Targachhi, they grew their maize and *bajra* and *barabati* beans the same old way, changing plots annually. Among the 35 or so families there, one found three or four steady ones, like Mohan's who also owned portions of hill terraces for rice paddy. Rainfall provided water for their paddy, or a narrow stream diverted by the rock-and-earth embankment. The diversion was where the irrigation technology of the hill had reached, and gone no further.

Hence for all their tragic situation, first they were themselves to blame. Their obstinate hill-oriented, primitive way of life could lead only to extinction. But let us ask a couple of questions. One, were the plains a garden of Eden? and two, of what use—now—was it to the hill-dweller to be told 'You didn't take the right decision centuries ago, or even as late as the 1830s'? In the last few decades (academically, it could be said to be too late) some of them had said goodbye to the barren hills and gone in seach of unclaimed fragments of cultivable land below, rarely to find any. Among the three Paharia sub-tribes almost half of one tribe and about one-fifth of another were now down in the plains, many without so much as a small fraction of an acre. One tribe had, as we have seen, almost died out.

The Saurias, in one of whose villages, Kaldi-bhita Targachhi, we were that day, were all still living there, and mostly owned minute fractions of an acre which offered, provided the rains came, fractions of a quintal of maize, *bajra* and beans every alternate year. Mohan was among the rarest of the rare in having three acres of paddy land, and five acres of rotating plots, in addition to twelve acres of bamboo plantations and trees (not including some more that was to come under his name from his dead father-in-law). It was from families like Mohan's that poor or landless folk got work and wages. One reason was that the skill of sowing fields with a digging stick was known only to hill men. The

Santhals and lower-caste labourers were summoned from below at the times of paddy sowing, weeding, and harvesting of other crops. Again, from such families the poor also took rotating plots on a lease for which we were told they paid two or three rupees per acre per year, a comment in itself upon the estimated productivity of a hill plot.

Low productivity was one reason why the moneylender living down the slope had never begun to usurp pieces of land on the hill. Against outstanding loans he accepted only assets that he could sell in the country bazaar. He would come up the hill and demand whatever was hidden underground or in the ceiling fastenings of the straw hut and, if nothing was available (which was almost always the case) would untie animals, usually goats, from their stakes outside and drag them down the hill.

Now that the hill was occupied by tomorrow's corpses the moneylender had not stopped coming but he lent only to those sufficiently rich to have a cow or goats or sheep, or have not just good land but also the luck to have had rain and flourishing crops. In recent years, though, petty loans had come through a rural bank of the government to some of the able Kaldi-bhita Targachhi householders. Secondly, there had been an episode without precedent. Nizamuddin, a nightmare of a moneylender from the plains below, had long terrified the dwellers of Chengdo Gadwa. He came to the village one day in his usual style. He walked back with a pair of goats from a hut where everyone was out except a tiny girl, who cried and cried . Mohan fumed with anger and wrote out and despatched a lengthy complaint from the village to the officer in charge of the Taljhari police station below. Unlike his predecessors, the officer ordered the moneylender's presence and clubbed him, with quite an audience watching agape, from outside the police station. With that epoch-making news the hills and the valleys buzzed for a long time.

The Nizamuddins were quieter now, but waiting to burst in again. After all, the Taljhari's chief policeman would some day be replaced by one of his more normal colleagues. And even rural banks were banks, money-minded institutions unwilling to throw more than a pittance into the gutter merely to earn a beggar's gratitude, without repayment. A.K. Chakravorthy, a bank manager whom we met on our way back at his office at Maharajpur, the country town down the other side of Chengdo Gadwa, consulted his outsize tabulated records. About 80 per cent of the advances had gone to the tribals, the Paharias and the Santhals: the Paharias had borrowed mostly for agricultural and allied activities, also to buy cattle, for which the government provided them a 50 per cent subsidy—and the moneylenders, said Chakravorthy, eyes now away from the records, had undoubtedly received a 'great setback'. Then, we asked about his main figures. 'No,' replied the manager in flat tones. 'Repayment is not satisfactory.' Won't that help the moneylenders back on their feet? 'Yes: financing by us will have stopped.' Chakravorthy, his voice still flat-toned, answered. 'It's up to the borrowers.'

In a corner of the Kaldi-bhita Targachhi's tile-roofed hall, where we sat late in the afternoon interviewing people, we heard a voice above the others. '*Gormant* has removed the *mahajans* (moneylenders).' Chujo Pradhan, aged

55, was giving his judgement. He too, like the bank manager, had all the figures—but was quoting from memory. Yet as his interview progressed the old hill-man cancelled his own launching observation. Under the government-subsidized cattle distribution scheme, 90 per cent of households in the village had each been given five goats. And the goats, he said, were all scrawny; most soon died. So that the question which arose was not only *how* but also *why* should they repay the Rural Bank? As for the cash loans for agriculture, said the old hill-man, they ranged from Rs. 100 to 900 and the bank had rules that you must start repaying the next year—and if you have any idea of the productivity of hill maize, that is a foolish rule. But no matter how convincingly these pleas were made, the bank manager entertained just one obsession and had recently grabbed hold of the old man as he was heading for the Maharajpur bazaar and had spoken to him, in a tone very different from that of our data-sheeted interview: 'You people: aren't you going to pay? *Theck hai, theck hai*, you will see. I am going to get you all thrown into jail.'

Some domestic difficulties

The government schemes were dying like the people. Some distance from our hall a well had been half-dug, and abandoned. Money came for *antyodaya*, with men to superintend from far-away Sahebganj. After three days of excavation the villagers' instinctive knowledge had been confirmed: the site was not suitable for wells. And the Sahebganj venturers went back, paying wages to the diggers but nothing to the men who had transported five bags of cement on their backs up the twisting pathway to Chengdo Gadwa, which took one hour if you walked empty-handed.

Even our hall smelled of sickness. Here, a *khadi charkha kendra*, spinning wheel centre, was being run by the same venturers of *antyodaya*. The idea was to teach Paharia women the skill of spinning, giving them each two rupees a day as an incentive. There were 25 spinning wheels, set in rows and filling much of the hall floor, one woman behind each, drawing out the thread and turning it: among the women were Mohan's three wives, the youngest of whom, Geeta, had on our arrival in the morning gone out of the hall to return with hot china cups of tea. But as we were received by Mohan into the hall, not only Geeta's but almost all the spinning wheels had frozen. And should you city-dwellers think we were facing the usual stare of the villagers, you would not have been fair, to those women. They had not received a rupee of their incentive money for more than 15 days, and had taken us as superior officers here at last to pay the debts. Two rupees a day was a pittance, sufficient only to buy 500 grams of rice, but these women had elected to squat all day at the *khadi* wheel, for in this they say was one way of escape from the slowly-killing job of gathering, bundling and bearing 20 kilos of headloads down the hill. And in promising this escape the *antyodaya* venturers had set their spirits ablaze.

Even the instructor, a Sharmaji, whom the venturers had posted to the centre at a salary of 400 rupees a month, had stayed only for a few days and left with his baggage to rejoin his family in Sahebganj from where—so the hill people, only too familiar with fugitive teachers, believed—he never stopped drawing his salary. It was in the instructor's room that we were lodged overnight.

It was not a small room, but it looked so, cluttered after the instructor's departure with all sorts of broken objects and piles of cotton and pieces of wood and, amidst them, string beds. The instructor had left behind a couple of aluminium cooking pots in his hasty flight. After dark—the women already gone and the hall was left only with the rows of spinning wheels—we sat down to cook our meal and took out our packets of rice and spices and potatoes, and it was then that we, all male cooks, remembered that we had bought no cooking oil or salt.

We went to Mohan's door for salt and oil. He had left us an hour ago and we were told by a child in the lane that he was resting his back and calling us inside. We stepped in, crossing, not without effort, the one-foot-high door sill. Why was it built so high? And why were there no fewer than three doors in one room? Mohan explained: 'I recently felled a tiger with a single arrow. Here, a few yards away from these huts. Every house here, you have seen, has two doors: we have three. Because you never know when a jungle animal is at your door. I'm here at this moment, resting on my bed, and (Mohan pointed a finger upwards) the next moment: I'm *upar, saaf.* I'm away beyond the stars for ever. So the other door is for you to escape—if you can. And the door sill is high enough to keep away big slithering snakes.'

Mohan talked to us, still lying on his bed, stroking the back of his little daughter, now sleepy. Big, criss-cross pieces of wood flamed in the hearth in one corner. Mohan's single but large room, which was all that made up his house, looked crowded. A wood pillar propping the ceiling at the centre: full, unpicked corn strung like streamers, by a cord stretching under the ceiling; heaps of wood and bundles of all sizes rested against walls, or hung from sticks in the wall: against one wall, a large striped bamboo pot to store rice: cloth mats on the floor and four string beds. At night Mohan's two boy servants slept on the mats and on one bed the children, including a son of eight, while one bed each was given to the three wives, so that, when everybody had eaten and the children had gone to sleep, and the lantern had been blown out, the choice about where to sleep must be imagined to be Mohan's. During the half-hour that we talked before we were sent off with our essential ingredients, we were introduced to his first and second wives: the third charpoy lay unoccupied. '*Teesri wali*, my third one, is in a tantrum today,' said Mohan. 'My other ones have children to care for—you can see that—and then there is this spinning business which keeps them away nearly the whole day. So they told Geeta to share the household work: she is young and has no children yet and therefore, my elder wives said, she could at least fetch water every morning from the stream and do the washing-up if not cook. On hearing this, she stamped her foot and rushed out of the room.'

We returned to our room to settle down to the cooking. Unskilled male fingers cut each potato into four and washed the rice, without picking out and blowing away the pieces of husk and particles of stone: and put the rice into an unknown quantity of water to boil in order that it might be fit to eat. But the instructor's pot won't boil; it began to hiss, but after that no sound came. The instructor (at least in the case of our rice) was not to blame; our trouble lay in the fire: male chauvinist fingers from the plains had an additional problem on the hill—they knew nothing about how to build a fire with wood. Flames flared when we soaked a piece in kerosene (used after consultation with Mohan and his eldest wife) but the kerosene having burnt there was only smoke and we would soon have no kerosene left. We choked the oven with small pieces of wood. We blew all the air out of our lungs only to evoke coughs and streaming eyes.

And then we heard footsteps and *dupatta*-wrapped giggles outside the stripped-bamboo gate of our hall: there was Geeta with two other young women. Geeta and one woman came in and sat down by our smoky oven and Geeta drew out all the blackened wood and put it back piece by piece in a criss-cross pile, to leave room for the air, and then, taking the small hollow bamboo tube looking like a flute without holes, brought by her second friend, she breathed through it and we could, to our shame, see the flames starting to catch.

To be a woman was to be skilled in these things. So (now that their rice was bubbling the failed cooks asked) why didn't Geeta minister to the needs of her family? She instantly became agitated. 'Who told you that? Mohan? Go and ask anyone. Ask these women. Who does all the work in that house? Go and ask those women in that house too.' It seemed as though in shaking hands you had unknowingly squeezed a sore finger whose owner cried out in pain. 'But it's not the chores that I mind. I lost my temper today—yes. But why? If your husband goes to town and spends three or four days there while you wait and wait at home, what can you do? He goes to the cinema with other girls, buys them sweets. And here I am, in this single piece of *panchi*: and if I am caught in pouring rain or take a bath I have no clothes to change into.'

Mohan looked in before we went to bed after Geeta had left and we had eaten our meal. We tackled him about his waywardness and his eighteen-year-old wife's lack of clothes. He was incensed. 'Go and ask anyone,' he cried. 'Does any other woman at Chengdo Gadwa have so many clothes and cosmetics as Geeta has? I have given her all that: I have bought her *lungi*, blouses, brassiere, *panchi*, all in terycot, polyester, while other women dress in cotton or rags: she has *bindi, kajal*, a pair of sandals. Ask anybody: is there a man on this hill as rich as Mohan Paharia? My forefathers were *pradhans* British-recognized village chiefs: they left for us two large iron pots full of silver coins hidden under the floor of our house—the same house you were sitting in an hour ago—but one evening in 1972 the dacoits who live in the Ganga's riverine patches, those Muslims and Swalas, surprised us with a raid, blindfolded me and tied up my wife; they let off crackers—Diwali crackers—and when they heard them the rest of the population, as though electrified, ran into the jungle: you know how famous Paharias are for their cowardice. Had they used their arrows, the looters would have been overcome. Anyway, the silver coins were gone. And I just put it out of my mind. Wasn't I still rich? In this village, where's a man who doesn't owe me money? Shall I show you my books? Not less than 2,000 rupees are outstanding, and I don't pester anyone, for I know what they have to give.'

Mohan went on: 'Another thing, this going out with other women that she accuses me of. I went to the cinema in Sahebganj once with girls and boys from this village. The girls of my village are like sisters to me. Geeta goes too far; she does not understand many things. I have land, plantations, things people of this hill can never dream of having. I have credibility. If Mohan Paharia sends a signed chit down to the bazaar every moneylender will without the slightest hesitation give you 100 rupees. I have grain in my house. I have two servants. Never, never, has anyone in my family carried loads of wood downhill: have my wives ever known how heavy a bundle of fifteen or sixteen kilos is? We don't carry wood: we sell it. If anyone is still not contented how can I help?'

How the Paharias regained courage

The Saurias, unlike the Mals and Kumarbhags, who had migrated to the plains, had among them families like Mohan's, who had collections of private trees—*ryoti*, tenant, or jungles, as they were called. Not only trees—and of course the clay plots for cultivation—but also portions of the rocky expanse of the hill was owned by the Saurias. The rocks had attracted birds of prey from the capitalist world: they had pillaged them for lorry loads of stones, leaving large brown scars amidst the green slopes. Because the hill owner was not much given to thinking, the Marwaris, Sindhis and Biharis found their dreams of wealth come true. The process began by dispatching a 'fixer' to the owner of the coveted hill portion to persuade him to come along to see a man with bags of money waiting to serve him as much delicious food and toddy and spirits as he could consume. After the meal and drinks in the town, the 'fixer' followed this up by saying that the *babu* with the money bags would always help his family in need and also immediately pay Rs 100 or Rs 150 in cash once he agreed to the grant of a five-year lease before the magistrate. After these promises a rehearsal of the court scene was arranged in which the lawyer would ask the *pahar malik*. the hill portion owner, a set of questions before the magistrate: Are you *x* Paharia? Do you agree to give your land to *y babu* for five years? *Dharam-karam se bolta hai*, do you speak on oath? Have you received Rs. 20,000 from *y babu* for the lease? Have you received the amount in cash? All the dialogue that was allotted the *pahar malik* in this scene was saying 'yes' five times. Once the magistrate put his seal to the lease documents, complete with blue thumb-impressions, the only question was when to pay the Paharia the Rs 100 or Rs 150 promised, the amount of Rs 20,000 of course remaining only on paper.

And although these new hill *maliks* had for decades been scarring and discolouring the slopes—adding to the monumental work of the forest contractors—there had been no outcry from the environmental watchdogs. It was the Paharias—the Saurias, Mals, Kumarbhags—whom the forest officials almost invariably accused of being anti-ecological. The Paharias tilled the soil above and were stripping the hills, scarring them: the Paharias cut away government trees and sold them in peices: it was they who made impossible any progress of the Forest Department's ecological plans. So wherever they were, within

Sahebganj or the other districts forming the old Santhal Parganas, the Paharias saw their men frequently held in custody for these crimes. They were tortured and put in prison; piece of skin were ripped off their backs. In one case a bicycle was ridden up and down a Paharia's chest. Even a glimpse of a forest man could fill a Paharia with horror. To end this horror was one of the chief aims that the Paharia *Samaj* (Community) *Utthan*(Uplift) *Samiti* (Committee), formed on 11 November 1971, had set for itself. But it was a weak organization.

Then, on 4 August 1980, in Kathikund, the forest men dragged a Paharia, Ramu Dehri, down from his hill, beat him and clubbed him: they lay him on the ground, on his back, and placed a big rock upon his chest, together with a huge log of wood. Blood poured out of Ramu's mouth and his body was swiftly carried out of sight. It took ten days for about 300 Paharias to assemble in order to go to the Kathikund Forest range office to express their indignation. On reaching the metalled road, they excitedly waved down trucks and buses, and packed themselves in and on them, the men with axes, swords, lances and clubs. They asked the drivers to take them to the Forest Range office where, outside the building, they first saw a forest official's motorcycle and instantly set to work. The tyres were ripped and somebody looked into its fuel tank but there was no petrol inside for setting the vehicle on fire (the official having, probably on learning of the approaching mob, hurriedly emptied it). After this discovery a queue rapidly formed beside the vehicle and several jets of urine filler the tank until it over-flowed. Thereafter one official, a forester, was grabbed: he was lifted in the air and thrown to the ground: he was raised and dropped again; he went up once more and was again consigned to the force of gravity: it was, we were told, like a washerman beating his cloth upon the stones.

The police arrived but arrested no one, probably to avoid provocation. The hill men demanded Ramu's body but registered no case. For several days following, they set themselves just one task: hacking down the trees that lined the roads. Tree after tree was prostrated: although the forest officials passing in their jeeps saw all this, they thought it better not to stop their vehicles. The sight of hundreds of weapons, the desolation at the roadside, the stink of urine in the fuel tank and the air-to-ground beating became a nightmare to haunt the forest officials.

The torturing ceased after that, Shivlal said, speaking in his railway quarters home. He was present, he said, at the Kathikund Forest range office during that raid and was the one who prevented the hacking down of three officials caught in the building. The Paharia *Samaj Utthan Samiti* was involved in the raid. And Shivlal was respected.

Rarely among the Paharia, Shivlal was educated up to matric level, a year at college and then a 'good' railway job, a rarity that was made still more conspicuous by a father, now dead, who had been a *pradhan* and yet a fighter in the *Tirandaz Sena*, the Bow-shooters Militia, that some Santhals had raised around Dumka during the Quit India movement of 1942. His father was also a Congressman and known to Bihar's provincial leaders of the Congress. When the Utthan Samiti was founded Shivlalal became its general secretary, and has since continued in that office, without so much as a distant challenge to his leadership. The hatred, long in operation, of the forest officials, the police, the moneylenders, the Santhal bullies, plainsmen in general, was primarily what formed the sentiments of the people of the hills. And Shivlal, almost alone, was working to shape these sentiments into an ideology.

The ideology had its foundation in history. The Paharias, it was emphasized, had a 3,000-year history, with a distinct identity, their own kings, their own systems of social organization, their own languages, an independent way of life. They had once been the masters of the *aranyanchal*, the jungle region: to remind people of that, the Utthan Samiti, instead of giving administratively recognized names of places in Sahebganj or around, spoke of *aranyanchal*, when speaking of its working area: Paharia Samaj Utthan Samiti. Aranyanchal—that was how it was identified. There were two great sources of pride with which this ideology was seeking to fill Paharias in order for them to hold their heads high. The first flowed from the fact that they had kingdoms of their own, from a monarchic glory. And the second from the fact of their being the original inhabitants, the first diggers of the soil in the region. And to these two glories a third was also added: the martial glory, the glory, according to Shivlal, of going down fighting in the hill wars with British troops, armed with modern weapons.

Should you find a mythology in all these glories it hardly matters; truth or myth, once a community takes them and holds them to their heart, no power on earth can erase them. Shivlal believed in the glories, he spoke about them, he was writing and publishing about them.[2] The ideas were bound to stream downwards from Shivlal and, sooner or later, all the Paharias would be speaking of their past; already, second-rank leaders like Mohan were saying that they had discovered that the Paharias had been living around Sahebganj since 302 BC. But Shivlal could not be blamed. Is there any community which is not proud to be the original inhabitants of a certain part of the earth, and is proud of its monarchic or imperial glory? These two most powerful sentiments had, in various periods, moved other communities in other parts of India; even the Biharis, when seeking separation from Bengal at the turn of this century, spoke of the Indian empire of the ancient 'Bihari Emperor' Ashoka.

But Shivlal, in formulating his original ideology of past glories, also added some ideas of the present. Since the ideology was not yet written down it could draw on theories circulating in Sahebganj. There was no dearth of peddlars in the town who pressed their doctrines on the Paharia leader, especially since he or the Utthan Samiti had no attachment yet to any political party. If devotees of one author thrust a book into his hand, one from another set of devotees gladly loaned him a collection from his shelves, while sometimes Shivlal bought books himself from the bookstalls in the town. Reading thus at random, Shivlal's own thoughts became eclectic. Barring Marxism, against which he had developed an unexplained resistance, Shivlal had been impressed by thoughts from Jayaprakash Narayan, Ram Manohar Lohia, Gandhi, and Guru Golwalkar, among others. He held Narayan and Golwalkar in particular, exponents of two seldom-meeting ideologies, as his two gurus.

Narayan's idea of no-party democracy had a great appeal for him; but on a wall in his sitting-room hung a picture of Deendayal Upadhyaya, a leader, long dead, of Jana Sangh, now renamed the Bhartiya Janata Party, a Hindu right-wing party; and Shivlal, as he explained his own ideology to us at great length, unmistakably betrayed a leaning towards Hinduism and Hindu organizations. Hinduism, he said, was like a gigantic and very old tree; Islam, among the religions, was the 'younger'. So the moral question according to him was: should we cut down the Big Old Tree? The Paharias, said to be a small yet 3,000-year-old civilization, looked like attaching themselves to another old and great civilization and, while never allowing themselves to become indistinguishable from it, drawing political strength from this relationship.

Already it seemed that the Paharias had yielded to the greater civilization. Shivlal was not alone in hanging a dead Hindu leader's picture on his wall and had liked reading Guru Golwalkar's *A Bunch of Thoughts*. The Mals, Shivlal's sub-tribe of the Paharias, were cow-worshippers: they had dead cows buried. The Saurias, Mohan's sub-tribe ate beef (allegedly under the evil influence of the moneylenders from the youngest religion) but Mohan had recently started an anti-beef campaign amongst his people. He moved about with a cane, trying to spot Saurias at the stalls of the bazaar in Sahebganj, held on Thursdays and Sundays, where the Muslims 'openly' sold cooked beef. But even beef eating did not drive the Saurias away from the greater civilization; they were, after all, worshippers of the Shiva phallus; and like the Mals, they observed the festivals of *Holi* and *Dussehra*, though instead of colours, which were costly to buy, they used water and mud and cowdung, and during *Dussehra* new outfits were not necessarily made.

Yet what meaning did this community pride in past glories and the slow adoption of Hindu customs hold for the ordinary distressed Paharia? There, on the hills, they were dying in hundreds, in thousands. They were dying even of toothache: they were vanishing off the hills. How could a community which was no longer a community but a long line for burial entertain those lofty concerns that Shivlal set for it? But Shivlal had given long thought to this. Yes, he said, today, existence was the Paharias' only concern. He had to be in this world before he could think of restoring communal glories. Great idea had to wait to do him proud. And that thinking was underlined even by the design of the flag that the Utthan Samiti had adopted.

The flag was a black-green-blue tricolour, symbolizing the Samiti's intended line of community progress. The black at the base represented the Paharias' ignorance, illiteracy, poverty, death, their present condition, which was almost a hell. Then the Paharias would struggle and come up to *dharti*, the Earth, the land of green. Finally, they would ascend to the blue which stood for the heaven spoken of in the Hindu *dharma-grantha*, the scriptures. It was a great vision, a vision that could materialize only if the hill men could get together and fight. And, though the Samiti, even after 15 or so years, was a very loose organization, stray struggles were taking place. The mob raid on the Kathikund Forest office, the beating of the official and the defiant axeing of the highway trees was just one. A group of looters at Mohan's village, where once dacoits had walked away with his two potfuls of silver, had, while going down the slopes with their booty, faced a spray of arrows coming from behind the night-darkened bushes. Also, the moneylenders had changed some of their tactics.

And in turning into reality the vision of the Paharias fighting their way to the top, Shivlal thought of the Hindu connection in a concrete, practical way. He believed in God, and (though despising all its rituals and hypocrisies) still found Hinduism better than other religions; but his religion was not the reason why he showed himself to be closer to such organizations as the *Vishwa Hindu Parishad* (the world Hindu Council) of the *Rashtirya Swayamsewak Sangh* (the National Volunteers' Association). The reason was that these organizations helped the Paharias fulfil a purpose: some things they offered fitted the Paharias' needs. The aim was to make the Paharias brave again, and the Hindu organizations imparted training in martial arts, with clubs and knives and physical culture. Already, batches of Paharia boys were training. 'If you want to know the secrets of your enemy's prowess,' Shivlal said, 'you must coil yourself up inside his belly.'

Today the Paharias were relearning martial arts, and learning these anew from their enemies, the plainsmen. Who were their enemies? Who was not? People from all the communities of the plains looked down upon them as no more than a small, fast-disappearing crowd of foolish, diseased, timid and emaciated people—easy to rob, incapable of offering resistance. In the town they were powerless; the buyers fixed the rates for their wood and hill produce. In the markets, and in the streets, incidents of beating for rare episodes of boldness had taken place, and fear had eaten deeper into the soul. And it was not that people of other communities were bold only in the town, when the hill man was far from home, alone, and where he had to come every day; his oppressors would no less bravely come as far as his hill, or his home, if they wanted to.

Then they arrived at the hill, usually in numbers. They could be from among the Yadavas, or the Musahars and other Hindu peasants, or the Santhals or any community; and they came with various purposes. They could bring their herds of cattle for a great feed on the hill slopes, or like Santhals, could come with axes to cut away Paharia trees. The wanton grazing destroyed the little plants that would have grown into trees, and the Paharias' maize and beans. This was a major reason why the hill men stopped cultivating *sabai* grass, the raw material for ropes and paper (to resume which the Utthan Samiti was pressing the government to open police stations at the hills). The frequent hacking down of the private trees by the Santhals from below threatened to leave their owners almost without a living.

Poor themselves, fighting their own battle against immigrant squeezers, demanding their separate Jharkhand (which like *aranyanchal* meant Land of Jungles), the Santhals were seen and spoken of by the Paharias as bullies. Because they cut down their trees, picked their vegetables and fruits, burned down their huts and sometimes assaulted them with their tree-cutting tools, Shivlal had a list of major Santhal attacks; he dated the first to 1979. That was the attack on a hill village called Budhadih, when all the 34 Paharia families ran off into the jungle and the Santhals set their houses on fire. The scene of the second event, the following year, was none other than Haripur, Shivlal's native village where 20 Paharia houses were similarly razed. In a later incident, in 1981, two of the Paharias who failed to escape were caught and one of them was hacked to death during a still bigger raid upon two villages, Dhamni and Kadak-Dhamni. Stray raids continued.

Poor oppressing the poor: the division at the ground level made political unity of Santhals with Paharias impossible. There was no support given by the Paharias to the movement for a separate Jharkhand, neither was the demand actively opposed. But Santhal leaders like Shiboo Soren had never bothered to go to the hill men; had not so much as spoken to Shivlal or any other leader of the Utthan Samiti. Shivlal once approached Shiboo with complaints about the Santhal raids, and Shiboo, expressing surprise, said he knew nothing about them. 'If one tribe tyrannizes over another tribe, how can they fight others?' Shiboo said, assuring Shivlal that he would see that such attacks were stopped. But nothing actually came out of it, except a two-sentence reference to Paharias by Shiboo at a public meeting.

It was a divide that suited the government. Ever opposed to the Jharkhand movement, the government, through upper-caste district officers infinitely hostile to tribals generally, set out to accentuate the divide by paying closer attention to the Paharias—much to the Paharias' bewilderment—and by repressing the Santhals who, in the old Santhal Parganas district, which included Sahebganj, provided the main support to the Jharkhand movement. Police were let off the leash, several Santhals were driven into jail, moneylenders became active again, Shiboo Soren made himself scarce, avoiding appearing in public for fear of the police catching and killing him. The diehard officers boasted of bringing the Santhals to heel. But the Paharias were beginning to like these officers. Shivlal fondly remembered especially one deputy commissioner, U.D. Choubey (whom the Santhals despised the most) who had taken so much care of the Paharias as to order the employment of almost all, about 85, of the matriculates from the hill community, as village level workers, office assistants, irrigation employees. He told the Paharia to wake him even after midnight if they needed him for any emergency. Shivlal said he himself had once got Choubey's audience in the middle of the night; he also remembered how on another occasion Choubey, on his way to a Paharia village, had a breakdown of his jeep; he got out quickly and continued on foot. The Santhals called Choubey a bully and badmash-in-office. Shivlal said repeatedly: 'He was a saviour to us.'

Grievance was heaped upon grievance to keep the two tribes apart. If the illiterate wood-selling Paharia had strong feelings against the tree-hacking Santhals, the educated ones resented being denied a reserved job, for all the jobs reserved for the Scheduled Tribes in Santhal Parganas went only to the more numerous Santhals. Choubey tried, said Shivlal, to set these things right. And there was nothing wrong in that: 'If there is food, should the man of the house [Shivlal meant the Santhals] eat it all or share it with his wife and children [the Paharias]?' Employment and education were stepping stones to the Utthan Samiti. *Shiksha*, education, brought *gyan*, knowledge; and *gyan* brought *sahas*, courage, made you understand your rights, become conscious and proud.

And in Kaldi-bhita Targachhi, on the second morning of our stay, Mohan, voicing the same views, had also given a clue to what was vaguely implied in Shivlal's mention of 1979 as the year of the beginning of the Santhal raids. The raids, said Mohan, accompanied the rise of the *Jharkhand Mukti Morcha* led by Shiboo Soren in the district. 'If we tried to stop the Santhals,' Mohan said, 'they would say they were there under the *hukum*, orders, of Shiboo Soren.' Other threats followed the mention of this *hukum* such as, 'We can put you all in one fist and squeeze you', and for all the Paharia knew, the intimidators might well be in the town, or just below the hill, waiting for him to pass on his way to the bazaar. Yet with courage built up by Utthan Samiti, and led by Mohan, the hill men of Kaldi-bhita Targachhi had once taken the risk of facing the tree-choppers, had snatched their axes and chased them down the slopes and challenged them to come again the next morning. Acceptance of the challenge was shouted back, but never actually followed; instead, the tree-choppers let it be spread about that they were waiting down below to chop Mohan Paharia into pieces at the first opportunity.

Mohan said he gave his enemies in this hill-valley war plenty of opportunity. But although he was not as much afraid for his life as was Shivlal (who returned straight home from his office and whose children had instructions to turn evening callers away if they did not recognize them) Mohan was not indiscreet. The next day, as Mohan moved about Maharajpur town with us he was quiet and wary but not apprehensive; we surveyed a stone pit, talked briefly to some workers, walked into the Rural Bank for the interview with the manager, came out, had tea at a stall in the bazaar and a chat with some men whom Mohan knew and lastly, before squeezing ourselves into the train back to Sahebganj, sat for half an hour with the principal and teachers of the state government's Middle School, Maharajpur.

The school was closed for the day. In a chair on the school verandah sat the principal engrossed, when we arrived, in a copy of *Manohar Kahaniyan*, a devastatingly popular shock-horror Hindi monthly which he placed, still open, cover down, on the table beside him. The principal, an upper-caste man from the plains, spoke highly of the tribal boys in general, though he sounded insincere. He said the tribal boys had 'all the intelligence' but they suffered from a poor home environment, also lack of money, and incentives at school; the government should be 'liberal' in granting funds to attract them to schools.

In his own small way Mohan was contributing to the growth of education among the Paharias. He had taken several boys from Chengdo Gadwa, some girls too, from their homes and had them admitted to the middle school that we visited. Sometimes he himself provided them with a few rupees or coins as an incentive. How he wished the *boodhus* (half wits) to get *buddhiman* (wise enough)! How much he personally bore the burden of the hill population! How much every Sauria looked to him! And here, abruptly, Mohan raised the subject of Geeta. His young third wife, he admitted, was no sister of his eldest wife, but his second wife was. Yes, Geeta was poor and forlorn, he helped her; who else could she have looked to? She had been married before, to a Sauria of Mandro, the next hill. She soon turned against the marriage, saying she disliked her husband's physical appearance; he was a dwarf and his face was pock-marked.

It was in keeping with the 'tradition' of her family. When Geeta's father had taken a new wife her mother had gone off with someone else. When she arrived at Mohan's door, Geeta was not looking for shelter; she just wanted food because she had eaten nothing for four days. It was after she had eaten she suggested marriage and then insisted upon it; she told Mohan that she could wash up and do other things in his house. (Here even Mohan skipped the part of the story that should have dealt with his own intention to set up a new string bed in his single room.) But now she often disturbed his peace of mind. She was going to town, moving about alone, talking to the vendors at the bazaar, asking them for betel and other things, free of charge. That was a very bad habit, was it not? Mohan said he warned her that if she did not stop tramping the streets like that she would meet the fate of a Santhal woman who behaved similarly: she had been stripped in the town and her breasts chopped off. (Or, as we feared, Geeta could be a target for the woman-abductors and brothel-keepers, if what Mohan was saying was true.)

A well-heeled man, Mohan hated vagabonds. He hated the poor if they became thieves or beggars. That was why he did not think highly of the Mals, Shivlal's sub-tribe of Paharias. Many of the Mals, now in the plains, possessed no land at all and had fallen into the habit of stealing maize and vegetables grown by other people. Mohan's next remark gave further in sight into the complexity of the hill problem: the men of the hill, all Paharias to the outside world, were deeply divided along sub-tribal lines. The Saurias, the Mals, the Kumarbhags, each of them had a dialect of their own, barely understood or rarely learned by the other (and that was why Shivlal, on our arrival in Kaldi-bhita Targachhi, had given his instructions to Mohan in neither his Mal nor Mohan's Sauria speech, but in Hindi, which both understood). There was no intermarriage between the three sub-tribes; they lived in their separate sub-tribal settlements.

There were, too, doubts about each other's intentions. In the Utthan Samiti the status of Shivlal as leader was not as solid or unblemished as it would seem from outside. At Kaldi-bhita Targachhi, the Saurias, although they had not yet said so, had a feeling that Shivlal leaned much more towards the Mals, and such feelings were encouraged by trivial-sounding events; one such event occurred recently when, after the end a Paharia rally at Sahebganj, the Saurias were told to go home, but the Mals were asked to stay for a meal. And moving about with us in Maharajpur, Mohan, too, voiced his suspicion to Shivlal. 'Does Shivlal Manjhi say he got too many Paharia boys a job? Then, tell me how come all of them were Mals? Nobody, no-body today works for the welfare but members of Shivlal's own caste or tribe.'

Conclusion

Yet for all the despair, internal strains among the Paharias stayed internal, not merely in the sense of being hidden to outside eyes; they *were* internal, which meant that the sub-tribes were united to face dangers from outside, and to present unity and identity while fighting a common enemy. And if the slogan for

Jharkhand could bring the Santhals together, the idea of *aranyanchal*—still an idea, not accompanied yet by agitation—could become powerful enough to forge this identity without much effort, a 3,000-year-old history would then be talked about in the village lanes up and down the hill. A community of ex-kings would awaken to its pride. The Hindu leaders would blame each other for not completely Hinduizing the whole community, and the leftists wonder, once again, if there would ever be solidarity of the exploited peoples of India.

Unintentionally, efforts were being made to prevent it. Choubey, the deputy commissioner, on behalf of the state, made an effort by absorbing the community's educated men into government. There were efforts made by the political parties to offer Shivlal an election ticket, which Shivlal had refused, saying he was 'too small' to think of embarking on a political career—at the moment. He told us what he had not told them: 'I might go into politics after retirement from service'. But for all his candour, Shivlal was, we suspected, hiding one thing even from us. He and *aranyanchal* would enter politics together, perhaps within a decade.

From a community organization, the Utthan Samiti, like the *Jharkhand Mukti Morcha*, would then possibly be turned into a political party which would contest seats for the assembly on a plea of establishing a Paharia voice in the legislature—seats it would probably lose. Subdued money-lenders and stone-pit owners, men doing business with wood from the hills, and the tribal-despising urban middle class would commit themselves to the Samiti's destruction. And then, as Mohan, aspiring to be a politician himself, confirmed, there were the Santhals who would never vote for a Paharia. To us in Maharajpur, Mohan first said, 'Had I passed my matric, I would have liked to have run for membership of the State Assembly.' But as he went on, he said to impress us, 'Didn't you see how everybody in the bazaar (at Maharajpur) looks to me as the leader of Paharias?' Leader of Paharias only; Mohan, in his boast, forecast his chances. We threw out a casual suggestion that he might try his luck first at a lower level, say, for the post of *mukhiya*. Mohan thought for a while before he replied: 'In the *panchayat*, the village council, the Santhals and the others living below have 1,000 votes. On the hills, there are only 700'.

14. Some Conclusions

An attempt has been made in these pages to describe how the lower classes in India's countryside have been trying to change their living conditions. The focus, obviously, has been not upon the whole of the countryside, but on certain selected spots in the agriculturally backward Bihar state in which these classes have revolted. The question of the possibility of a revolution or great rebellion through the whole of India demands serious debate (especially in view of the poverty and the cruelty that the rural poor are subjected to) which falls outside the scope of this book. Yet it is hoped that the accounts of the struggles in the preceding chapters may give some idea of how revolt breaks out, takes shape and suffers its vicissitudes in the countryside.

As must already be obvious, for a revolt to begin even at a small level, in a village, several factors must coincide. The number of such factors can be infinite, varying widely from place to place, sometimes unimaginable. And the interrelation of these factors, the accurate pinpointing of the causes leading to the coincidence of these factors, might prove to be impossible. It might be relevant to note here that studies of agrarian movements in other parts of the country have also borne out the complexities involved in arriving at a neat explanation of a movement's origin. At what point the people in a particular part of the countryside will suddenly rise to resist age-old oppression is unpredictable. There cannot be anything like *fundamental laws* of the origin of revolt.

Of course, exploitation and cruelties produce what, in common parlance, is termed the 'accumulated anger' that causes a revolt to break out. Oppression, in other words, every day, little by little, digs its own grave. But how can oppression create conditions for its own liquidation unless an awareness of itself is created in the minds of the oppressed? For what, after all, is meant by 'accumulated anger' but accumulated consciousness of oppression? How can consciousness originate in a victim of oppression in a given area without the aid of an external ideology, that is, a greater, higher consciousness? Assuming that the ideology reaches him only at the point of origin of the revolt, it becomes difficult to account for his consciousness *before* the revolt begins—the consciousness that is said to accumulate. The ideology gives him direction, courage, tools to analyse his situation, awareness. Yet not all the knowledge he possesses about the conditions of his existence can be credited to the ideology; some awareness of these conditions has predated its arrival for, in the absence of such an awareness, the ideology would not have developed in the first place.

That there exists some awareness of injustice before the coming of the ideology—that is, before the whole population of, say, a village rises in revolt—is an observation supported by the existence of 'social bandits'. By its very nature, the fight led by social bandits is neither political, nor informed and disciplined by an ideology;[1] evidence from several parts of India's countryside where such bandits operate points to the same view. Yet, as Hobsbawm notes, there could at least be some men (becoming bandits) 'who, when faced with some act of injustice or persecution do not yield meekly to force or social superiority, but take the path of resistance and outlawry'.[2] Hobsbawm cites the instance of Pancho Villa. Considering such cases, the conclusion is not only that awareness of oppression predates the outbreak of revolt (Hobsbawm's book opens with a significant quote from an anonymous 'old brigand': 'We are sad, it is true, but that is because we have always been persecuted') but also that individual rebellion is possible before the mass revolt.

Indeed, we may present innumerable instances from the rural part of Bihar state alone where men from the subordinate classes, a labourer or a poor peasant, have *individually* reacted very strongly to the conditions of existence imposed by the landlords. All such men, however, do not necessarily take to the path of banditry. It might be that an individual labourer or peasant resists injustice simply because he happens to be powerfully built, young and plucky, in other words, proud of his physical strength. This pride and confidence may, for example, one day drive this man to challenge his master's retainers to a fight: but not all individual rebels display such dare-devilry. Many who found conditions intolerable would run away to live in a town or another village. Emigration is escape, not rebellion; yet it is a step ahead from the point of acceptance of one's fate, and a sure sign of awareness of oppression.

Apart from cases of individual rebellion or escape, we would argue, there is evidence both from villages observed in this book and from other rural areas, which would suggest the existence of a wider awareness. In our narratives there are several occasions when the oppressed labourers and peasants look back upon the past with horror and anger. You do not need to be equipped with an ideology to *discover* your persecution. If you are a farm labourer in a village in Bihar and are kept hungry it is true that you may not blame the US agribusiness monopolies, for you are too ignorant to imagine them, but you certainly know why food is being denied you, and by whom. After long hours of work, a blow to the face (not to speak of torture), snatching the harvest from your homestead plot, restricting your freedom of movement (restrictions, so great at times that, as was seen in the chapter, 'The Abbey in Bodh Gaya', you could not visit close relatives in a nearby village), liberties taken with the women of your family, and innumerable other acts, need no external agency or extraordinarily perceptive powers to arouse an awareness of being persecuted. Does one need to be told how to recognize physical pain? Does one need intellectual help to see why one's family is denied freedom while the landlord's family is not? Comparison of living conditions within the village itself can educate the oppressed to be aware of injustice, and arouse indignation. Whether you immediately resist a particular act of injustice or not is immaterial for our point here, we are only trying to suggest that a much wider (suppressed or expressed) awareness of injustice is already there at the beginning of a revolt.

The next question is: how does revolt begin? A limited awareness of injustice among the downtrodden does not make a rebellion. From our studies of the seven agrarian organizations it appears that there have to be several other forces at work. First the oppressed must become convinced that, unlike in the past, they now possess adequate strength and support to challenge their oppressors. In the oppressed population of a village, this conviction is found to grow with the promise of support from outside. This can come in various forms, and may not necessarily be concrete.

Law, for example: indisputably, the laws of agrarian reform have not been implemented. Yet it is seldom noticed that the official self-congratulatory propaganda about these laws unwittingly yielded one positive result: it raised the expectations of the lower classes of the countryside; it provoked them. A situation was created in which they felt that the government was speaking for them, and in a situation in which the government itself—in their eyes the supreme power—stood for ending the injustice against them their fear and hesitation had no place. Clutching at the laws, they had moved forward in many villages. By doing so they had usually reaped fierce repression and disappointment. Yet, in Bihar of post-independence days, there were brief periods when the government appeared to be doing much more than merely making the legislation, and shouting about it. These brief periods—the ending of the Permanent Settlement in the mid-1950s, installation of non-Congress state ministries composed, among others, of socialists and communists in the late 1960s, the establishment of camp courts in the villages for quick disposal of agrarian reform cases in the first half of the 1970s, and the imposition of the State of Emergency from June 1975 to March 1977—were times when the rural poor gained courage and initiative.

The government's extraordinary exercises to apply its own laws were short-lived and peripheral. Even today the government keeps on talking of 'special drives' to carry out agrarian reforms. There is a close relationship between these extraordinary exercises or special drives and the challenges thrown down by the lower classes of the countryside. These exercises are undertaken with an eye to restraining public outcry, looming or already in operation; they thus produce a cause and effect relationship with the upsurge in the countryside.

Laws, and the government's exercises seemingly to enforce them, however, could not, by themselves, prepare the oppressed for a break with the past: for mobilization they had to be combined with other thoughts and sentiments. Our studies of the seven agrarian organizations help us to identify some of the other factors that powered the movements.

One of them was perceiving the landlord as an *alien*. In Korahia, the CPI-led village, the landlords were seen as outsiders because they were non-resident. The landlords of CPI-M's Jhakia were not considered to be the original, and hence legitimate, inhabitants; they were emigrants whose ancestral roots were dubious. In the Chhaundadano of the CPI-ML the Chanaus were also emigrants, and it was as such that the tribals regard the moneylenders and landlords from the plains of Bengal and Bihar. In Bodh Gaya, the monks and the farm managers had no local roots; they came from other parts of southern Bihar or Uttar

Pradesh. Similarly, those whom the Paharias were beginning to fight they also saw as aliens. A gulf was created between the non-native landlords and the native population which was to remain unbridged—perhaps unbridgeable. They were culturally divided; their customs, marriage laws, and sometimes even the language or dialect they spoke, often differed.

Lack of cultural harmony alone, however, would not have been sufficient grounds for conflict to flourish. This situation became explosive because it was combined with the fact that, in all cases, the aliens were also rich and prosperous—*they* were prospering at the cost of us. In the villages we observed, the oppressed had numerous stories of particular settlers who were poor when they arrived but eventually became rich. 'They arrived here with a *lota* (water jug)', the tribals would say of the Marwari traders, 'and now they are involved in everything.' The monks of the Bodh Gaya monastery were similarly regarded: 'None of them brought anything from home, but they ended up with buildings, and land and good food each day'. Therefore, the landlord, a prospering alien, was presented as the common enemy of various classes, peasants as well as labourers.

But these factors would not have led to rebellion without the intervention of individuals—local leaders—who were usually non-peasants. Some students of peasant movements tend to take the view that the peasant makes his own rebellion; this is a romantic view and underrates the role of the leaders.

Who were the local leaders in the organizations we studied? In the first place, they belonged neither to the families who ruled as autocrats nor to those who were landless and extremely oppressed; they, in fact, had no single, neat class origin. In Korahia, the leader was from a former petty landlord family with sufficient land; so, despite the fact that the family was one of the intermediate caste of Yadavas who do not shun labour in the fields, they had no need to work their fields. The leader in Jhakia belonged to an upper-caste family, declining in wealth but still with adequate landholding; neither he nor other members of his family worked in their own fields. In Chhaundadano, the leader was from a rich peasant family of the intermediate caste of Telis. The landholdings of the family of the leader of *Jharkhand Mukti Morcha* were not large but they had a non-agricultural income; the family stood midway between the exploiters and the peasants. The Paharias' leader was rich and semi-educated and did not have to work his land. The Jesuits and the Medical Mission Sisters belonged to the urban middle class, like the young men and women of the *Chhatra Yuva Sangharsh Vahini.*

There may be doubts whether these leaders could be described as charismatic, but it seems certain that their arrival on the scene aroused the oppressed peoples into revolt. The fact that the leaders were from families that the people at the bottom of the pyramid saw as *good, high* and *respectable* emboldened them; the oppressed felt their leaders had an authority that could match that of the exploiters.

We have to try to understand what drove these individuals, mostly non-peasants, in the sense that they did not work their fields, to fight the landlord-autocrats. That they belonged to the middle sections of the society (no more precise description is possible) hardly explains anything. Yet what could be observed was that by belonging to the middle section, unlike the people at the bottom, they were not resigned to fate. They were either moving up or down the social scale and reacting to these changes of status; they would constantly redefine their location in the village hierarchy. In the cases we studied they were mostly going down the scale. It was an acute awareness of decline that produced part of the ammunition for their rebellion. The leader of the Jhakia movement said in an interview:

> We are the oldest settlers in my village. Our first ancestors came probably seven or eight hundred years ago. My father was the *tehsildar*, the rent collector, to the Maharaja of Bettiah. We had huge stretch of land. Then at the turn of the century in came the Thakurs from somewhere outside. They were terribly crafty; they started buying up and taking other people's lands in mortgage. They were becoming rich. They manoeuvred to sow discord between the Bettiah Raj and my father, which led in 1922 to the distraining and auctioning of most of our land. It was the Thakurs again who did the bidding. We, the oldest family, were becoming poorer day by day and the emigrants, wealthier. This fact has had a great psychological impact upon me since childhood.

This was echoed from the leader of the *Jharkhand Mukti Morcha*:

> We were a happy family. But there was a big moneylender living close by who had taken over the land, the animals and goods of most of the people around. My father, who was a schoolteacher, had also borrowed from him but we had not lost everything to him. We had some land and my father had been a successful farmer, with cattle, chickens and ducks. But, in certain cases of atrocity by the moneylender, my father had gathered the people together and intervened. One night the moneylender's thugs murdered him. That was a great tragedy; our income fell sharply; I had to give up my school and roam about in search of a job, in vain. We had difficulty meeting basic needs. The moneylender was sitting at the top of everyone's head. . .

The leader of Korahia, as well as many of the activists of the *Chhatra Yuva Sangharsh Vahini*, also had this sense of decline. The leader in Chhaundadano could not be said to have been conscious of a sense of decline, but he was certainly conscious of his inferior caste status in relation to the landlords, however high his family income..

The pioneers thus usually came from families in social decline, But in any village there would be several such families and not all of them rose in revolt; rebels were not mass produced. It was not that were no ideologies to fertilize such a mass-production, nor was there a dearth of historical precedents; it was precisely these two factors—pre-existing ideologies and historical precedents— that shaped the minds of those who became the pioneers. The *Jharkhand Mukti Morcha* leaders could look back, inspired, upon the tribal rebellions; at Jhakia, the communist movements, including that of the Naxalites, showed the way;

Korahia was aware of struggles against the landlords in other parts of Madhubani district; by the time of Bodh Gaya the struggle of the landless had become almost an integral part of the ideologies of all shades of the left; and even the Catholics were influenced by the liberation theology flowing for almost two decades from Latin America.

There is no simple answer to the question of why ideology and a tradition of rebellion did not have a uniform impact upon these middle-status people. Perhaps some understanding might emerge from an assessment of how these factors influenced those whom we are calling 'pioneers'. Firstly, the pioneers had had some education. In most cases, apart from the Jesuits and the young men of the Vahini, they had not been able to reach degree level. Some dropped out of school, others left at higher levels. Their formal education had not been of much use in so far as pursuing a profession was concerned. Nevertheless, whatever they had learnt, from their books, from their teachers and from other educational experiences, put them above the illiterate majority of the village. They could not only read and write; they could draft a pamphlet or a petition, tackle officials with confidence and imbibe the literature from the organizations to which they belonged.

Secondly, most of them took a plunge into activism when they were in their teens or their early twenties. They resisted attempts to make them conform; they acted against their parents' wishes. Every father wanted his son to take his studies seriously and at the very least find a livelihood to help the family. The experiences of education, and of the towns where the schools or colleges were located, encouraged the young men instead to act independently.

They chose the peasant organization because they came in contact with individuals already subscribing to certain ideologies, and were politicized in that way. It may be suggested, therefore, that ideology alone cannot move people; an ideology varies in potential from one individual to another, and is not uniform in effect. Major politicization may follow; but it is not feasible at the outset.

Yet to be attracted to an ideology of rebellion it is necessary to be sensitized to injustice—as well as to a sense of decline. It was an awareness of injustice to themselves that drove them to the mass of the people; it was an awareness that they were not alone in suffering and, therefore, that the causes of suffering could be removed collectively. That led to the leaders' identification with others, even with the untouchables. We should note that here we are not taking into account the changes that took place in the relationship between the leaders and the oppressed at later stages of the movements. These changes probably resulted from a sense of retributive satiation among the leaders after the landlord-autocrats' retreat or due to new responsibilities after marriage, prospects of promotion, or tempting opportunities from other sources.

But at the outset the attitudes were certainly different; this romantic identification was in fact decisive. Without it, the leaders would have found no initial acceptance by the other sections. The very fact that the men and women at the bottom of the social ladder are the last to contemplate a revolt on their own points to the need for a strong, tenacious and, above all, sincere leadership; also they test the sincerity of the leaders at every step. There is adequate testimony to suggest that a long time passed before the oppressed came round to accepting the leaders' exhortations as credible. After listing broadly the ingredients that went into the making of a rebellion, we must evaluate its progress.

To us, the movements we have studied were bringing about changes of great significance. Primarily, they had a tendency to disrupt irreparably, if not altogether destroy, the old relationship between peasant and master. It would hardly be an exaggeration to say that the villagers we observed were witnessing their own battles for freedom—for peasant freedom from the local regimes of landlord autocracy. Shocked at first by the coming of Independence, and subsequently by the abolition of *zamindari*, these regimes had soon recovered; no doubt they lost their rights to collect rents and levies (as a result of which a section of the peasant population escaped from their grasp, obliged now to pay only a nominal rent to the state) but they still had large estates. In those estates, the masters exercised absolute authority. Families of unfree men worked these estates; but bondmen were not the only objects of tyranny. These could be the poor peasants who tilled pieces of the estates as sharecroppers; they could be peasants who borrowed money or grain from the master and returned the loans in the form of their plots of land or the harvests from them. In some areas, as in Bodh Gaya, even the peasants who were small but independent could be made to submit to the rules set by the local landlords; in Bodh Gaya for instance, they were forced to do a few days labour on the monastery's farms.

The bondage we saw in our villages was by no means atypical of much of rural Bihar, and perhaps the whole Indian countryside; the villages we studied were not just a few pockets or enclaves of bondage. Among all those kept down by the landlord regimes, the situation of the labourers was undoubtedly the most tragic. Work for them seemed never to cease; after long hours of work in the fields, tasks awaited them at the master's household. They could not wear new or clean clothes, or comb or oil their hair, or be seen wearing shoes. Under some regimes, no father could marry off his daughter or get a wife for his son unless the master put his seal on the arrangement; the father was not even free to send his daughter off to her husband's family.

There was no day off; no one was free to travel. Even visits to married daughters of close relatives living in nearby villages were prohibited. Guests had to wait until dark for their hosts to return home at the end of a long day's toil. To be a woman in a labourer's family was, in itself, to be as cursed. She was an easy victim. The masters, their sons or their overseers—in Bodh Gaya, even the saffron-clad monks—took full advantage of her vulnerability. Schools were closed to the labourers; a free vote could be only a secret ambition; a minor error brought certain trouble, and trouble meant all the forms of torture the retainers were capable of imagining and devising. Such was the regime of village autocracy.

The movements surged defiantly, and attacked and paralysed the regimes. The means they employed to strike varied, not only from movement to movement, but also within every movement (except that led by the Catholics which was uniformly non-violent). It seems significant that almost all the movements used physical force (sometimes firearms, but generally clubs or farming and hunting implements) to face those deployed to put down the revolt. Probably the stark realities of the situation sometimes left the labourers without choice. For within the village, and by distant observers, the results of the battle were evaluated only in terms of war. Victory, therefore, was all that mattered. There were major collisions of the two sides, major trials of strength in the course of almost every movement. They had all made rapid progress, once the labourers (and the peasants) had 'won' by forcing the retainers to run away from the 'battlefield', often with casualties. Such clashes took place even in the Bodh Gaya movement led by the Vahini, an organization committed to 'peaceful' struggle; the labourers' triumph over the landlords' men in one or two villages was a tremendous boost to the morale of any who were still hesitant.

Whatever the means, the common feature of the movements was the determined effort (sometimes short-lived) to end the tyranny of the landlord. In essence, every movement articulated and tried to fulfil the longing of the oppressed for freedom. The crumbling regimes of village autocracy seemed to be clearing the way for the emergence of a new kind of rural society, a society made up of free peasants and free labourers; labourers who no longer needed permission to comb or oil their hair or to travel.

But the organizations we studied did not aim only to break landlord power; the battle did not end there. Each organization, though it differed largely on how to bring it about, was working for revolution. Except for the two organizations connected with the Santhals and the Paharia, each of whose objective was to restore the golden age for its tribe, within a limited geographical area, the aim of all the movements was national revolution.

For revolution to succeed it was imperative that the agricultural labourers and the peasants should unite in a people's front. To lump together these two sections (let alone sub-sections) under a single category of 'peasantry' would be to deny reality, for their relations to land have not been the same. It is, therefore, useful to consider whether labourers-peasant unity has been achieved in the villages we observed.

Before we examine our villages it is instructive to remind ourselves of the relevant experiences of past movements. Let us begin with the Telangana revolutionary struggle in 1946–51. In Telangana, the labourers, the middle peasants, the rich peasants and even the landlords fought together against the princely ruler of Hyderabad. But no sooner did free India's Army march into Hyderabad than the united front dissolved. The labourers and poorer peasants found themselves deserted by the landlords, rich peasants and middle peasants; for these upper sections of rural society the revolution was over once the princely ruler was ousted.

Kanu Sanyal discusses the attitudes of the various classes in the 1967–68 Naxalbari uprising in these words: 'As regards distribution of land, our policy was to confiscate the land fully and distribute the same entirely. As a result, in many cases the rich peasants prevented this task from being carried out under various pleas. In many other cases, the top section of the middle peasants, being in the leadership in some cases, managed to divert the emphasis from confiscation of land to making raids on *jotedars'* (landlords')houses and thus deprived this work of its importance. In some cases again there developed acute contradictions between the poor peasants and the middle peasants in matters of distribution of land'.[3]

Not very different was the experience of the 'Land Liberation Movement' led by the CPI and the Socialists in 1969–70 in Bihar and other states, and aiming to seize land concealed by the landlords. In evaluating the agitation, a leader of the CPI observed that even the poorer sections of the peasantry were found to be reluctant to join the landless labourers during the agitation.[4]

Lack of labourer-peasant unity had also marked the Kisan Sabha movement of the 1930s and 1940s. Although the Sabha never tired of declaring that it wanted 'both the peasants and agricultural labourers to realize the great and growing need of their united front against all the powerful vested interests which have been crushing them both for ages past',[5] its overriding concern was always the issues of the peasants. Rahul Sankrityayan's writings, quoted in the chapter on the Kisab Sabha, need to be recalled here. He strongly disapproved of agricultural labourers organizing independently of the peasants (the tenants). He strongly denounced the formation of two farm labour organizations in Bihar, believing that they were fostered by the *zamindars* to weaken the peasants. He concluded: 'The rights of the peasants and agricultural labourers are, in the ultimate analysis, two sides of the same problem. The condition of the agricultural labourers is no doubt pitiable and a solution must be found. But we must bear it in mind that we cannot bring about all revolutions in one go.'[6]

In our villages, except for those under the Vahini and the Catholics, the peasants and labourers united in the struggle. The association became possible because they saw the landlord as their common enemy. The movements of the Vahini and the Catholics were confined to the agricultural labourers, partly because of the local situation and partly because both organizations gave priority to the mobilization of the 'people at the bottom'.

The united front in other villages, however, was proving to be not very stable. No sooner did the landlord bow out than the contrasts between the peasants and the labourers came to the fore. The peasants comprised most of the leaders while the labourers formed the bulk of the led. It was the labourers who, in the dangerous war with the landlord, were in the forefront, taking due risks and making the greatest sacrifices. They naturally attached great value to such sacrifices and felt disappointed, if not cheated, when the issues that concerned them attracted little enthusiasm, or often hostile reaction from their allies.

Yet the labourers could do nothing about it, since the organizations that led the resistance were the only such organizations in their villages. There were times no doubt when they—using the freedom they had achieved and now valued—vented their dissatisfaction or indignation at local committee meetings or in talks with the committee leaders. They were neither shouted down nor turned away, but often even would be manipulated so that they either lost their pleas or killed them by indifference. A labourer of Jhakia, the CPI-M's village, complained to the writer: 'The leaders of the Kisan Sabha, I tell you, are a useless lot. They pay no attention to the problems we take to them. Now the *maliks* (big employers in the village) are threatening to cut the wages that were raised during the movement. But the leaders seen unmoved'.

Sometimes the peasants and labourers would be locked in conflict. In Korahia, some members of the CPI organization made rival claims to a few plots of land. Such disputes were not limited to the village. They all—labourers, who had never had a piece of land of their own, sharecroppers, who had tilled this or that plot, and middle and rich peasants with the capacity to buy more land—hankered after the land 'evacuated' by the landlords. There was a no less intense scramble for pieces of the monastery land in Bodh Gaya. Hunger for land obviously was something afflicting not only the landless; it was everybody's problem.

Not only land but wages caused cracks in the united front. On the question of wages, the entire peasantry would close ranks. Any demand drove even the middle peasants into opposition, despite the fact that the middle peasants, relying largely on family labour, needed to hire barely more than a few hands at such peak periods as sowing and harvesting. Thus a handful of employers— the landlords and rich peasants of the village—almost always succeeded in disregarding pleas for an adequate daily wage. But in order to prevent the organization from disintegrating, the local leaders of the movements did sometimes intervene; they negotiated a compromise by which the wage level went up, though not to the point the labourers wanted, or needed.

In addition, caste was, of course, keeping the peasants and the labourers apart. The peasants (as well as the landlords) belonged to the higher, or the intermediate castes, while most of the wage-earning or slave population were of lower castes (untouchable or touchable) or the tribes. The peasant, therefore, distinguished himself from the labourer not only on the grounds that he was a peasant (that is, someone who had land of his own and therefore did not have to work for others) but also because of inherited tradition. If his position with respect to land gave him an identity, his position in the social hierarchy of his village gave him his pride. Such self-perception often kept the peasant from getting too close to or mixing with labourers: the very idea of having to sit by a labourer at a meeting was unacceptable. This jeopardized organizational beginnings, for a joint front was only a revolutionary fantasy if the peasants were not prepared even to come to a mixed gathering to discuss what needed to be done.

In the face of common oppression, however, peasant prejudices had slowly moderated. (It should be noted that we are discussing only the peasants who joined the movement: those who did not continued to be wilfully immune to such liberal ideas.) Even the participating peasants did not overcome their prejudices entirely. The taboo on commensality, for one, was still faithfully observed. If the labourers were invited by a peasant to a feast (as, for example, they were in the CPI-M's Jhakia village) they would be served separately from the peasants. In CPI's Korahia, even members of the party executive committee absented themselves from the dinner prepared for all in the hamlet of the Chamars, the leather workers. By these standards, the local leader appeared to be much more liberal, and in fact, it was that he appeared to transcend barriers of class and caste that initially established the labourer's trust in him as a leader.

Not that caste prejudices had been completely obliterated among the labourers, but they were melting away much faster than they were among the peasants. As we observed earlier there occurred an irreversible rupture of the interdependent relationship between agriculture and crafts in the village. As a result, the social division of labour which supported the caste divisions had changed; the ex-craftsmen were thrown into the ranks of the agricultural labourers. With the traditional agricultural labourers they were forming themselves into a class, and acquiring the appropriate consciousness of that class. In Korahia, the agricultural labourers in the movement came from several castes: different castes among the untouchables were the Mallahs (boatmen, fishermen), Badhais (woodworkers), Lohars (ironsmiths), Kumhars (clay workers), Yadavas (cowherds), Koeris (vegetable growers), Dhanuks (paddy reapers), Telis (oilmen) and Muslims (weavers, etc.). Originally the movement of *Jharkhand Mukti Morcha* was not limited to the Santhals, but included the Mahatos, Kumhars, Kamars, Rajwars, Tudies, Ghatwars and other castes too. Such solidarity marked not only the movements we studied, but also the struggles in other areas.

Thus, the agricultural labourers threatened to emerge as a separate class. Of course, in the larger part of Bihar countryside the autocratic regimes of the landlords continued. But in the villages where the regimes were shattered, like those we observed, the oppressed classes lived in relatively greater freedom. Nevertheless, observations suggested that, after the fall of the landlord regime, the agricultural labourers and the peasants were moving along two different lines. The organisations were finding it extremely difficult to unite the two lines; they realized that the polarization could not be stopped. Freed peasants, much like the tenants after the end of *zamindari*, aspired to become good farmers, wanting cheaper inputs and higher prices for produce from the soil, while the freed labourers now nurtured the ambition of becoming well-paid wage-earners, some of them, of course, also vying for a parcel of land.

Notes

PART ONE: Myth and Reality

Chapter 1: A Thriving Trade
1. Datta, K.K., *Freedom Movement in Bihar*, Vol.3, Patna, 1958, p. 360.

Chapter 2: The Decline of Caste Society
1. Other castes were kept out. The Kayasthas, for instance, were barred from military service because the British officers considered them to be low-caste *shudras*. In fact for a long time, through court cases and petitions to the government, the Kayasthas under the Raj had to make a stand to be accepted as no less than Khatriyas. Today, neither in Bihar nor elsewhere, is any demand heard from the Kayasthas for recognition as Khatriyas. Perhaps because, apart from the Brahmans and the Rajputs (Kshatriyas), the Kayasthas and the Bhumihars have now been socially accepted as upper castes. The Bhumihars had fought for their recognition as Brahmans.
2. Carroll, Luck, 'Colonial perceptions of Indian Society and the Emergence of Caste(s) Associations'. *Journal of Asian Studies*, Vol. XXXVII, No. 2, February 1978.
3. There were as many as 446, 225 *zamindars* in Bihar at the end of the Raj. The *Techno-economic Survey of Bihar*, Vol. 1, New Delhi 1959, p. 198 provided the following table listing *zamindars* according to their income (annual rent). (Quoted in Jha, Shashishekhar, *Political Elite in Bihar*, Bombay, 1972, p. 223.)

Income group (in '000 rupees)	Number of zamindars
5 or less	353,650
between 5 and 20	70,560
between 20 and 100	20,600
between 100 and 250	1,390
between 250 and 500	35
between 500 and 1000	7
above 1000	3
Total	446,245

PART TWO: Under the Raj

Chapter 3: The Rising of the Chiefs and Some Different Aims

1. Dutt, Girindranath, 'History of the Hutwa Raj', *Journal of Asiatic Society of Bengal*, Vol. LXXIII, Part I, No. 2, Calcutta, 1907, pp. 178-226.
2. Downs, Frederick S., Professor of Church History at the United Theological College, Bangalore, in his review of 'Crisis in Chotanagpur by Fidelis de Sa', *Indian Church History Review*, Vol. X, No. 1, June 1976.
3. Ibid.

Chapter 4: The Wrecking of the Countryside

1. Gopal, S., *Permanent Settlement in Bengal and Its Results,* London, 1949, p. 9.
2. Hunter, W.W., *Bengal Records*, Vol. I (1782-93), London, 1894, p. 78.
3. Cunningham, H.S., *British India and its Rulers*, London, 1882, p. 162.
4. Hunter, W.W., op.cit., p. 95.
5. *Royal Commission on Agriculture in India: Evidence taken in Bihar and Orissa*, Vol. XIII, London, 1928, p. 294.
6. Sinha, Ram Narain, *Bihar Tenantry (1783-1833)*, Bombay, 1968, p. 15.
7. Letter from A. Tufton, Magistrate and Judge of Bihar, to Secretary to Government, Revenue Department, 2 December 1800, cited in Sinha, Ram Narain, op.cit., p. 112.
8. *Royal Commission on Agriculture*, op.cit. (The questions and replies recorded at various points during the evidence-taking have been rearranged to make it easier to follow the problem.
9. Mukerjee, Radhakamal, *Land Problems in India*, London, 1933, pp. 39-54.

Chapter 5: Farewell to Bows and Arrows

1. Interview with N.E. Horo, president of the Jharkhand Party, 20 August 1978, in Ranchi.
2. Anonymous officer of Provincial Civil Service (retired), 'Chotonagpur as an enclave', *Hindustan Review*, Vol. LXVIII, No. 273, Patna, March 1936.
3. Ibid.
4. Sinha, Sri Krishna, 'The separation of Chotanagpur from Bihar', *Hindustan Review*, Vol. LXXI, No. 403–4, Patna, September/October 1938.
5. Sinha, Sachchidanand, in his footnote to ibid.
6. Sinha, Sri Krishna, op.cit.

Chapter 6: On the Move

1. The *Leader* (daily) in editorial 'Bihar Congress', reproduced in the *Indian Nation* (daily) Patna, 14 February 1937.
2. Sinha, Sachidanand, 'The financial plight of Bihar', *Hindustan Review*, Vol. LXVIII, No. 373, Patna, March 1936.
3. Results of the 1937 election to the Bihar Legislative Council:

Seats	Number of seats	Seats contested by Congress	Seats won won by Congress	Total seats won by Congress
General Urban	5	5	-	5
General Rural	73	72	2	68
Scheduled Caste	15	15	9	14
Mohammedan (Urban and Rural)	39	7	1	5
Women	4	3	1	3
Anglo-Indian	1	-	-	-
Europeans	2	-	-	-
Indian Christians	1	-	-	-
Commerce & Industry	4	-	-	-
Landholders	4	1	-	1
Labour	3	3	1	2
University	1	1	-	-
Total	152	107	14	98

The position of various political parties in the Assembly after the election was: Congress 98; Muslim Independent Party 15; Muslim United Party 6; Europeans 2; Constitutionalists 2; Anglo-Indians 1; Indian Christians 1; Loyalists 1; Independents 24.

4. Some scholars such as Fuchs, S., 'Messianic movements among the Santhals', in J. Troisi (ed.), *The Santhals: Readings in Tribal Life*, Vol. VIII, New Delhi, 1979, have termed these tribal campaigns for liberation 'messianic movements', a term which could be inadequate and misleading.

5. Datta, K.K., *Freedom Movement in Bihar*, Vol. 2, Patna, 1957, p. 235 (footnote) and p. 242.

6. Das, Arvind N., 'Peasants and peasants organizations', *Journal of Peasant Studies*, Vol. 9, Number 3, London, April 1982, made this observation on the basis of the annual official reports: Mansfield, P. T., Bihar and Orissa in 1930-31, Patna, 1932: Williams. R.A.E., Bihar and Orissa in 1931-32, Patna, 1933; Wilcock, J.S., Bihar and Orissa in 1933-34, Patna, 1935; Soloman, S., Bihar and Orissa in 1934-35, Patna, 1937; Narayan, K., Bihar and Orissa in 1935-36, Patna, 1938 and Wasi, S.M., Bihar in 1936-37, Patna, 1938.

7. Datta, K.K., op.cit., p. 315.

8. Ibid.

9. Hunter, W.W., *A Statistical Account of Bengal*, Vol. XI, *Districts of Patna and Saran*, London, 1877, pp. 123-4.

10. Gupta, Rakesh, *Bihar Peasantry and the Kisan Sabha (1936-47)*, New Delhi, 1982, p. 45.

11. Sankrityayan, Rahul, *Dimagi Chulami* (A collection of essays in Hindi), Allahabad, 1979, pp. 54-67.

PART THREE: Roads to Freedom

Chapter 7: The Jesus Path
1. Levai, Blaise (ed.), *Revolution in Missions*, Vellore (India), 1957.
2. Kappen, Sebastian, *Jesus and Freedom*, New York, 1977.
3. Fernandes, Walters, 'Public issues that demand answers', *Jivan*, Vol. VI, No. 4, New Delhi, April 1985.

Chapter 8: The Abbey in Bodh Gaya
1. Narayan, Jayaprakash, *Face to Face*, Varanasi, 1970.
2. Sachchidanand, S. (ed.), *Jayaprakash Narayan: Kranti, Samajik aur Sampoorna* (in Hindi), Patna, 1982.

Chapter 9: The Battle of the Sharecroppers
1. Chaudhary, Sukhbir, *Peasants' and Workers' Movement in India, 1905-1929*, New Delhi, 1971, pp. 138-9.
2. Datta, K.K., *Freedom Movement in Bihar*, Vol. 2, Patna, 1957, p. 407.
3. Ibid., p. 406.
4. Sinha, Indradeep, *Some Questions Concerning Marxism and the Peasantry*, New Delhi, 1982; and Bhartiya Khet Mazdoor Union, *Fifth National Conference, Reports and Resolutions,* New Delhi, 1981.

Chapter 10: How the Thakurs Were Contained
1. Namboodiripad, E.M.S., *Conflicts and Crisis: Political India*: 1974, Bombay, 1974, pp. 33-4.
2. Ibid., p. 35.

Chapter 11: A More Radical Line
1. Samanta, Amiya Kumar, 'The Terai Upsurge', *The Calcutta Historical Journal*, Vol.VI, No. 1, July-December, 1981.
2. CPI-ML, 'Programme adopted at the First Party Congress held in May 1970' in Sen, Samar, *et al.* (ed.), *Naxalbari and After; A Frontier Anthology*, Vol. II, Calcutta, 1978; 'The Second Declaration of the Revolutionaries of the CPI-M', in ibid.
3. Ibid.
4. Revolutionaries of the CPI-M, 'First Declaration, November 13, 1967" and 'Second Declaration, 14 May 1968', in Sen, Samar, *et al.* (ed.), op.cit.
5. Mazumdar, Charu, 'Carry forward the peasant struggle by fighting revisionism', in Sen, Samar, *et al.* (ed.), op.cit.
6. Samanta, Amiya Kumar, op.cit.
7. Sanyal, Kanu, 'More about Naxalbari', in Sen, Samar, *et al.* (ed.), op. cit.

8. Samanta, Amiya Kumar, op.cit.

9. Ibid.

10. Ibid.

11. Mazumdar, Charu, 'Carry forward the peasant struggle by fighting revisionism'; and 'To the comrades', published in Deshbrati, 1 August 1968 and Deshbrati, 17 October 1968, cited in the Naxalite Tactical line, in Sen, Samar, *et al.* (ed.), op.cit.

12. Ibid.

13. Mazumdar, Charu, 'Speech at the first congress of the CPI-ML' in Sen, Samar, *et al.* (ed.), op.cit.

14. CPI-ML, 'Political-organisational report', *Documents of the Third All-India Congress (December 26-30, 1982)*, Liberation Publications (place of publication not mentioned), 1983.

15. Datta. Subroto, 'One divides into two', in Sen, Samar, *et al.* (ed.), op. cit.

16. CPI-ML, 'Political-organizational report', op.cit.

17. CPI-ML, Political Report of the Third Congress. 1983.

18. Ibid.

Chapter 12: The Santhals' Struggle

1. Roy, A.K., *Lalkhand Ya Jharkhand* (in Hindi), Dhanbad, 1981.

2. Interview with Binod Bihari Mahato, Dhanbad, 13 August, 1983. Manjhi, Shivlal, 'Santhal *jati ka itihas* and Paharia *jati ka itihas*' (in Hindi), Ranchi, 1979.

Chapter 13: Life After Death for the Hill People

1. Manjhi, Shivlal, 'Paharia jati ka itihas' in *Vana Bandhi* (Hindi), Vol. 3, No. 5, New Delhi, May-June 1983; and 'Santhal jati ka ithihas' in *Vana Bandhu*, Vol. 2, No. 2, November-December 1982.

2. Ranjhi, Shivlal, 'Santhal *jati ka itihas* and Paharia *jati ka itihas*' (in Hindi), Ranchi, 1979.

Chapter 14: Some Conclusions

1. Hobsbawm, E.J., *Bandits*, Penguin, Harmondsworth, 1972.

2. Ibid., p. 35.

3. Sanyal, Kanu, *Report on the Peasant Movement in the Terai Region, September, 1968*, in Sen, Samar, *et al.* (ed.), op.cit.

4. Sinha, Indradeep, 'Land liberation movement in Bihar', *Mainstream*, New Delhi, 10 October 1970.

5. Gupta, Rakesh, *Bihar Peasantry and the Kisan Sabha* (1936-47) op.cit., p. 45.

6. Sankrityan, Rahul, *Dimagi Chulami* (in Hindi), Allahabad, 1979.

Zed Books Ltd

is a publisher whose international and Third World lists span:

- **Women's Studies**
- **Development**
- **Environment**
- **Current Affairs**
- **International Relations**
- **Children's Studies**
- **Labour Studies**
- **Cultural Studies**
- **Human Rights**
- **Indigenous Peoples**
- **Health**

We also specialize in Area Studies where we have extensive lists in African Studies, Asian Studies, Caribbean and Latin American Studies, Middle East Studies, and Pacific Studies.

For further information about books available from Zed Books, please write to: Catalogue Enquiries, Zed Books Ltd, 57 Caledonian Road, London N1 9BU. Our books are available from distributors in many countries (for full details, see our catalogues), including:

In the USA
Humanities Press International, Inc., 165 First Avenue,
Atlantic Highlands, New Jersey 07716.
Tel: (201) 872 1441;
Fax: (201) 872 0717.

In Canada
DEC, 229 College Street, Toronto, Ontario M5T 1R4.
Tel: (416) 971 7051.

In Australia
Wild and Woolley Ltd, 16 Darghan Street, Glebe, NSW 2037.

In India
Bibliomania, C-236 Defence Colony, New Delhi 110 024.

In Southern Africa
David Philip Publisher (Pty) Ltd, PO Box 408, Claremont 7735,
South Africa.